LLEWELLYN'S
2021
Magical Almanac

Featuring

Elizabeth Barrette, Danielle Blackwood,
Blake Octavian Blair, Walter J. Carey II,
Chic and S. Tabatha Cicero, Kerri Connor, Divina Cornick,
Monica Crosson, Melissa Cynova, Autumn Damiana,
Raven Digitalis, Ash W. Everell, Kate Freuler,
Sasha Graham, Raechel Henderson, James Kambos,
Tiffany Lazic, Daniel Moler, Thorn Mooney,
Mickie Mueller, Diana Rajchel, Suzanne Ress,
Jhenah Telyndru, Melissa Tipton, Charlynn Walls,
and Charlie Rainbow Wolf

Llewellyn's 2021
Magical Almanac

ISBN 978-0-7387-5483-3. Copyright © 2020 by Llewellyn Publications. All rights reserved. Printed in the United States. Llewellyn Publications is a registered trademark of Llewellyn Worldwide Ltd.

Editing and design by Lauryn Heineman
Cover illustration © Rebecca Solow
Calendar pages design by Llewellyn Art Department
Calendar pages illustrations © Fiona King

Interior illustrations: © Elisabeth Alba: pages 42, 46, 63, 66, 214, 217, 220, and 275 © Merayla Allwood: 92, 95, 209, 213, 265, and 269; © Kathleen Edwards: pages 18, 24, 76, 79, 193, 197, 248, and 253; © Wen Hsu: pages 1, 9, 12, 29, 32, 51, 91, 100, 104, 107, 173, 194, 203, 223, 224, 227, 230, 236, 250, 266, 272, and 279; © Mickie Mueller: pages 11, 15, 69, 72, 175, 178, 242, and 245; © Eugene Smith: pages 36, 39, 82, 87, 200, 204, 256, and 260; © Amber Zoellner: pages 4, 7, 52, 60, 182, 187, 235, and 239

All other art by Dover Publications and Llewellyn Art Department

Special thanks to Amber Wolfe for the use of daily color and incense correspondences. For more detailed information, please see *Personal Alchemy* by Amber Wolfe.

You can order Llewellyn annuals and books from *New Worlds*, Llewellyn's catalog. To request a free copy of the catalog, call 1-877-NEW-WRLD toll-free or visit www.llewellyn.com.

Astrological data compiled and programmed by Rique Pottenger. Based on the earlier work of Neil F. Michelsen.

The publisher and the author assume no liability for any injuries caused to the reader that may result from the reader's use of content contained in this publication and recommend common sense when contemplating the practices described in the work.

Llewellyn Worldwide Ltd.
2143 Wooddale Drive
Woodbury, MN 55125

Table of Contents

Earth Magic

Air Magic

2021 Almanac

Fire Magic

Water Magic

Coloring Magic

Earth Magic

Walking Spells: Making Magic on the Move

Melissa Tipton

For years, I associated casting spells with creating a stationary magic circle or setting up my altar. In a pinch, I would sometimes cast a spell on the go, but I didn't intentionally use this movement as part of the spell, which was odd, given how regular hikes in the woods are also an important part of my spiritual practice. Why not put the two together? In experimenting over the years with movement magic, I've discovered some potent practices for casting what I call "walking spells."

There are two phases to these spells, the first of which is optional if you're already clear on your spell's focus. Phase one is divination and phase two is spellcasting, and for both, there are endless ways to adapt and personalize these practices. Here, I'll outline the basic framework as well as provide fun ways to tweak and customize it.

Phase One: Divination

Perhaps you have a general idea of your reason for casting a spell, but you want to get *crystal* clear in order to boost the effectiveness of your magic. Or maybe you have many things that you want to work on, and you're not sure which would be most productive to focus on first. In either case, performing divination prior to spellwork paves the way for more successful magic. I also like to use this phase as a sort of check and balance. Am I casting a spell that is truly in accordance with my highest good? If not, does the spell simply need some refining, or would another aim entirely be a better use of my time and energy? These are all wonderful inquiries for this phase.

Before setting off on your divination walk, settle on a question to get you started, such as "What would be the most effective spell to cast right now?" You might also narrow it down a bit: for example, "What would be the most effective spell to cast right now regarding increasing my satisfaction at work?" Or perhaps you already know that you want to cast a spell for more harmony in your romantic relationship, so you might ask, "I want to cast a spell for more harmony in my relationship with Kyle. What is most important for me to know before moving forward?" Or you might consider this: "I want to cast a spell for more harmony in my relationship with Kyle. What do my highest guides and teachers think of this plan?"

Before setting out on your walk, take a few minutes to calm and center yourself by focusing on your breath and closing your eyes. Bring your question to mind and say it aloud with the following statement:

I ask for the presence and aid of my guides and teachers on this matter. Thank you!

And now, head out for your walk. It can be valuable to bring a notebook or voice recorder to capture any insights. Imagine that the world around you is conducting a dynamic conversation containing valuable insights to your question. By walking and engaging with your surroundings, you are listening to and participating in this conversation. Remain open and curious without getting too bogged down with trying to "figure it all out." Here are some of the many possible ways the world might respond to your inquiry:

• With a street sign or other lettering that captures your attention
• With an animal, insect, plant, and so on that catches your eye
• With a snippet of overheard conversation or a song lyric
• With a pattern in the clouds
• With an abundance of a particular color
• By triggering an emotion, memory, or interesting thought

If you feel insight flowing through in regard to your question and this, then, leads to a follow-up question, keep the conversation

going: ask the new question (perhaps mentally if you're in a public place) and continue to walk with curiosity. Repeat this process until you either feel clear in regard to your spell or you have an intuitive sense that you've gathered enough information and it's now time to process it. If the latter, take some time once you return home or contemplate as you walk the clues you have gathered. I find writing this material down to be an invaluable step, but talking it out to yourself or a partner can work wonders too.

Adaptations to Phase One

While there are countless ways to adapt this phase to suit your needs, here are two fun options. If you use tarot or oracle cards, prior to your walk, draw a card in regard to your chosen question. You can spend some time interpreting the card, if you like, and adding insights to your journal, but to incorporate the card into your walk, try this: imagine taking on the characteristics of the person, animal, plant, and so on depicted in the card. If you have privacy on your walk, you can explore adopting movements or gestures that you think this character might have, or simply play with viewing your surroundings through their perspective and see how this inspires you to notice different things.

For example, let's say you pulled the Hanged Man from the tarot. If something catches your eye on your walk, what might it look like upside down? If you were hanging upside down from a feature in your landscape, what new details might you be drawn to from this new vantage point? If an area feels interesting to you, imagine what it would be like to hang out there for an entire day and night—what might you see or experience that differs from your present reality? The point is not to come up with the "right" response to any of these prompts, but to shake up your normal way of perceiving the world, and therefore yourself, leading to insights that can alter the way you work your magic when you're ready to cast the spell.

The second option is especially useful if you feel overwhelmed by potential messages on your walk. Use your intuition to choose one sensory mode, such as sight, smell, or touch, to focus on, and make a note of only the things that capture your attention through that mode. For example, if you smell baking bread and recall a memory of your grandma, pay attention, but don't worry about also tracking everything you're seeing and hearing.

Once you have clarity on the specific focus of your spell, it's time to move on to phase two.

Phase Two: Spellcasting

For successful spellcasting, you need a goal, which is what you worked to clarify in phase one, and you need energy to power it. If your goal still feels a little loosey-goosey, now is the time to give it a final polish. For example, if your goal is to make more money at work, it's often more effective to either determine a specific amount—for example, an additional $500 per paycheck—or a particular outcome that you wish to use the extra cash for, such as a trip

Whether on a city street or a forest path, make your magic on the move with these effective techniques for walking spells.

to Bali or that meditation retreat you've been daydreaming about. I've found that my spells are more likely to work when I'm specific about the outcome but open in terms of how that outcome unfolds. Plus, with specific goals, I can clearly see when they work, because the target, such as an extra $500, is harder to overlook than a vague "more money" goal. This, in turn, is a confidence booster that your magic is working, which sets up a positive feedback loop for future spells.

Once you have your goal, it's time to build energy to direct toward this goal, and for this, you'll head out for a walk. Before you do, though, you're going to create an energetic filter aligned with your goal, because as you walk, you'll be drawing in energy from a variety of sources, and you want to ensure that they're not at cross-purposes with your spell. To create the filter, find a comfortable seat, close your eyes, and focus on your breath. Bring yourself into a more calm and present state, and then imagine an energetic bubble around you. Yes, you already have this in the form of your aura, but here, you're going to imagine an additional bubble enclosing the aura. If a particular color seems more suited to your goal, such as green or gold for money or pink for love, you can visualize the bubble in this color. When the image feels strong and clear, say to yourself three times:

This shield attracts only the energies most in harmony with my goal of _____ and blocks out all other energies.

Finish with "And so it is!"

Set out on your walk, and allow your focus to home in on the following as you begin, spending a few minutes on each one. First, notice the impact of your feet on the ground and the rhythm of your steps. Second, become aware of the movements in your body and the energy generated as you travel through space. Third, become aware of the energies around you, as if you're moving through a dazzling web of interconnected energy. At this point, you should be feeling more in tune with your body and your surroundings. Call up the image of the energy filter you created, and then see and feel how this filter is magnetically drawing relevant energy from near and far into your sphere. Allow this process to continue as you bring to mind your spell goal. Focus on this goal with intensity, imagining what it will look and feel like to enjoy the desired outcome as energy continues to stream into your bubble, building and awaiting release.

When it feels like you have drawn in as much energy as you need and it feels ready to "pop," focus with all your might on the desired outcome, and *release the energy!* You might do this by breaking into a run or jumping, exhaling forcefully, throwing your hands into the air, or powerfully imagining the energy rushing forth to carry out the spell's directive. (The latter is great when you're in a busy public place.) Give thanks for the fulfillment of your spell, then release the

energetic filter in any way you choose. I like to hold the intention that the bubble is dissolving while snapping my fingers three times. Continue walking, and allow any excess energy to stream out through your feet and into the earth, helping you return to a calm and grounded state.

Adaptations to Phase Two
As with phase one, there are many ways to adapt this walking practice; here are two ideas to get you started.

One, work intentionally with the spirits of your area by incorporating found stones, coins, feathers, or other magical partners into your spell (I always like to ask the spirit for permission first), drawing on their innate qualities to enhance your magic. For example, stones dropped into running water are great for releasing or banishing spells. After obtaining permission, hold the stone in your hand, letting it take all the energy you wish to release until you feel emptied of this weight. Then, drop the stone into flowing water and trust that these energies are being washed away, dissolved, and repurposed in new, more affirming ways into the larger cycle of being. Interestingly, I have noticed a correspondence between slow-moving water and rapidly rushing water in terms of how quickly or forcefully my energy shifts, so experiment with this in your own practice.

Two, as you walk, visualize and sense your movement creating a path within the larger web of energy composing and emanating from everything in and around you. See this path generating a current where energy is now able to flow with more ease and less effort, like a channel carved in stone by flowing water. Know that as you walk this path, you are forging a channel of ease and impetus for the energy of your spell, and when you release the energy, see it rushing through this channel, seeking and uniting with your desired outcome.

This is merely a taste of the boundless options for walking spells and other movement magic, so use your intuition and imagination and have fun with the possibilities!

Being a Practical Pagan
Blake Octavian Blair

You have trekked deep into the woods to a beautiful clearing, the perfect spot with its wildness and palpable spirit, to perform your ritual in the powerful liminal space of twilight. However, it's breezy—how will your candles stay lit? Twilight is slipping away, and it's becoming more rapidly dark than you anticipated. Can you see your ritual notes or book of shadows? It's time for ceremonial libations! The ritual cry of *Crap, who brought the corkscrew?!* rings into the night. Enter the practical Pagan.

When we are planning a ritual or magical soiree deep into nature, it is easy to fall into your romantic vision of the power, magic, and mystery of the experience you are planning. That is an important layer to consider, certainly. However, the reality of your experience may never allow the gaining of magical legs if you haven't gotten the practical logistics accounted for. Creating checklists and planning for less-than-desirable conditions and worst-case scenarios aren't the sexiest magical tasks, but they are necessary.

For outdoor rituals, I suggest creating a "Ritual Go Kit." For this kit, you'll want to gather a set of supplies you can keep in this container all the time as the base kit of essential supplies for the most common rituals of your tradition. For me, this would include a candle with a taller glass jar, a stick lighter, smudge and a fireproof smudging vessel, a rattle or bell, a drinking horn or a chalice, a corkscrew, a pouch of general offering materials, an altar cloth, and a couple of small, pocket-size flashlights. Also, it is a good idea to have a printed checklist of these items in the kit so that you can take a fast inventory. Items have a habit of migrating sometimes, and you'll want to know the kit is stocked properly. These are pretty basic items; however, let us have a show of hands of all who have been at a ritual where one of these essential items was forgotten? Okay, point made; you can put your hand down now.

I write this article not to point out the mistakes of other magical folk or groups; I'm sharing from my own experience of rituals I myself have been a part of (some that I ran, some I was just a participant) that could have gone just that little bit (or a lot) better if someone had remembered these elements. The good news is that can be you! You can be the savior of the day. You can be . . . the practical Pagan!

Sufficient, Safe Lighting

Let's start with lighting. I have been asked before to have a main role in a scripted ritual, have agreed to do so, and have been handed a script that was printed in 6.5 point font. Such small print is already a challenge for me to read in a ritual setting. To add to the situation, it was the end of twilight. Thank gods for my ability to ad-lib the general sentiment, because there was little chance of me being able to actually read the desired scripted lines. There are a couple of lessons to be learned here. First, no matter what the lighting, if you're printing scripts to be used, use a type size that can be easily read by most people. This is generally accepted to be around 12 point font at the small end.

The other lesson here is that if you're going to have a twilight or nighttime ritual for which people need to read something, make sure there is adequate lighting. I've seen this issue arise more than once. If the person who needs to read is not at the altar with sufficient candlelight, obviously the candles are not going to help. This is why I mentioned having small, pocket-size flashlights. They offer enough light to read the script but not enough to blind other people in the ritual. (You guessed it! I've been on the receiving end of that one too.) You can actually buy a red night-vision flashlight that allays much of these problems.

When lighting the candles and setting up other fire-related ritual work, time and time again, I've seen people forget to bring something to light a fire with. Luckily, because of this, I generally carry at minimum a pocket-size lighter with me, if not a full-length stick lighter. There is a bit of debate among magical ritualists over the appropriate item to make fire: must it be matches or is a lighter

okay? Well, I'm practical. I respect others' opinions on this, but I prefer a lighter for ease. I've also never seemed to get any complaints when I have a means for lighting fire and everyone else has forgotten! I also prefer the stick lighter for when I have to reach into deep candle containers, which shield the flames from wind. This both keeps the candles lit and adds a layer of fire safety.

Fighting Bugs

I've been summoned without forewarning to a ritual location that was so fraught with mosquitos that most of the rite was spent swatting in the air. Bug spray: this is another item in the practical Pagan's toolbox. Maybe you're not a fan of sketchy chemicals. Don't worry—I'm not either. There are several sprays on the market with less offensive ingredients, or you can make your own. Either way, bring it. It's hard to get into sacred space mode when you're in combat with flying bloodsuckers. On the same front, I've also seen citronella candle buckets as quarter candles. There is no shame in that! It may not cover the whole circle, but it will be a great help. Two birds with one stone . . . a score for the practical Pagan.

So now that we can sufficiently see, and we're not being attacked by biting insects, let's move along, shall we?

Libation Logistics

A good number of Pagan traditions include the ritual consumption of drink and the making of liquid libations. There are a couple of bases to cover on this particular topic. One, you need to be able to access the drink. Yes, I'm talking about opening the bottle itself. My mention in the opening to this article about the ritual cry for a cork screw comes from a true story. Corkscrews are a bit like the lighter. I find they are the top two forgotten necessary items.

Picture this on the screen of your mind: Twenty druids process deep into the wild, into a remote and snowy location. In twenty-five degree Fahrenheit weather and six inches of snow, we make a fifteen-minute hike to our desired location. We're Druids and we celebrate the seasons in nature, whatever the weather. We reach the location where we are going to perform the rite and form a circle, and a few group members begin assembling the simple altar atop a large stone sticking up out of the earth.

The central candle is lit, evergreen branches are placed, the drinking horn placed in its stand, and the bottle of mead is placed next to it. Ah yes, the mead . . . A wild discussion ensues about innovative ways to open the bottle. We discuss bumping the towel-wrapped bottom of the bottle on a rock to shoot the cork out, giving the bottleneck a swift swing with a sword, and everything in between. Thank gods, in the end, somebody off to the side produces a Swiss Army knife with a corkscrew they forgot they had!

The ironic part of this is I had earlier discussed with an elder in our group if I should bring a lighter and a corkscrew. They replied they were sure there would be plenty of both and it wasn't necessary. During this scene, I glanced

A LITTLE BIT
OF MAGIC

If you are serving libations to those who abstain from alcohol, it's a good idea to make sure the alcoholic and non-alcoholic drinking vessels are visually different and can be told apart.

over at them, and they looked at me with sly laughter. Ever since, no matter what, I always bring a corkscrew. I also have a hilarious story to tell!

The second practical matter is about the drinking vessel itself. Rather, the number of them. If one is having a ritual with up to twenty or so persons, a singular large communal vessel that is passed is likely sufficient. *Large* is a relative term, but you can use your own judgment for your needs. However, beyond that number of participants, it gets a little arduous in both time and logistics to keep full and pass a single vessel. It's best to go with pre-poured and distributed small paper cups (of recycled material if possible!). Some groups prefer this for public ritual in any regard. You decide what is right for you and your group. I do suggest that if you don't intimately know all participants, keep a second drinking vessel and a nonalcoholic libation on hand. There are those who abstain from alcohol for any number of reasons, and it's only hospitable to accommodate this need.

Location and Accessibility

Another common issue I find is the choice of a ritual site, so let's discuss some considerations when choosing a site and pitfalls to be avoided. First, parking. It simply does not work to have a parking lot that accommodates eight to ten cars if you're going to have twelve to twenty cars. Maybe your group is small and you don't have to worry about such things. However, if your group is blessed with growth, you may reach a point that even with carpooling you exceed the available parking at some sites. Also consider that your group will likely not be the only people using the site and utilizing parking there, thus further reducing available parking. This is important to think about. I realize that ritualists can become attached to certain ritual sites and pieces of land and you might not want to let go of a favorite ritual site of years prior. Not having sufficient parking and trying to "work it out" on the fly can cause undue stress and anxiety for your attendees. Problems are then beginning before the event does!

This is not how you want to start off the experience of your gathering. It is counterproductive to have a site that causes stress and logistical issues. The site may be beautiful and you may find the land magically and spiritually perfect. However, it is not perfect: it is not a conducive site. If it causes stress and logistical issues, but you personally or members of your group have an attachment to the site and the land, reserve that for your private rituals for which it is most conducive, and find a new and different site to build a connection to, relationship with, and memories at that is more conducive and a better fit for your growing group. You want the experience of your gathering to be as smooth as possible for your attendees to keep their focus and attention on the spiritual goals of why everyone is there.

The second consideration to keep in mind is the accessibility and safety of the site. If it is rocky, uneven, with dips, bumps, and slippery spots, it's probably not a good idea to have that be a group ritual site. Rituals generally entail circling, processing, ritualizing, and trying to otherwise focus. You don't need a site with hazards underfoot distracting you. I wouldn't try it in the daylight, let alone the dark with a large group. How can you ritualize when you're just trying your all to stay on your feet? I'm all for hiking to a ritual site, but make that hike somewhat reasonable and have the site be safe to traverse and without tripping hazards.

Try to pick a site accessible to your general attending demographic. If you have a regular attendee who has mobility issues, figure out a reasonable accommodation. Maybe that is offering to wheel them in a wheelchair to the site. Maybe that is simply offering to walk slowly with them and offer support. Maybe that means avoiding steep grades on a hike and opting for a site which has a flatter path to reach the destination. Happy mediums can be struck with forethought and insight. Again, pick a site that won't cause a distraction from worry about logistics so that the focus and mood of the event can be on the spiritual nature of the gathering.

Pre-ritual Prep

It is also good to have a brief pre-ritual huddle with anybody who has a speaking or action role in the ritual. This can help smooth out any kinks both physical action-wise or speaking-wise. Something particular to be aware of is pronunciation of names. If there are any particularly difficult names within the ritual of deities or

participants, make sure those who need to speak them know the proper pronunciation (especially if someone is using a magical name they haven't shared or used before).

Keep It Simple

On the topic of physical items and tools needed to perform a ritual, my personal preference is to keep it simple. I've attended elaborate rituals where people have hauled everything including the altar table across creation to build an elaborate display. I've also attended rites where the beauty was in the simplicity and the tools were laid directly upon the ground. The earth is sacred after all and is an appropriately sacred altar surface in itself.

In the shamanic circle I cocoordinated for two years, we always constructed an altar in the center of the circle upon a cloth laid on the floor. It consisted of a single candle, a few stones, a few feathers, our smudge vessel, and any objects brought by members that they wanted placed on the altar. Some meetings it was very sparse. Other meetings it was a bountiful milieu. However, it was always beautiful. Our Druid grove always celebrates outdoors, no matter the weather or the season. Our ritual sites vary from members' backyards to conservation land deep in the woods. Therefore, we tend not to go overly elaborate with the amount of supplies we bring. We generally stick to just the specialty items we need, such as a candle, a chalice or drinking horn, a corkscrew, smudge, and so on. If we want to decorate and further embellish the altar, we usually use found branches, leaves, stones, and other things from nature at the site. Also, we almost always fashion our altar upon the ground, a tree stump, or perhaps large rocks sticking out of the ground (something common in our beautiful New England landscape). If you'd like to spread a small altar cloth, this is another good item to place in your Ritual Go Kit.

· · · ☽ · · ·

I'm sure I've not covered nearly all the bases necessary to ensure you have the smoothest ritual possible every time. Things will still be forgotten, and some things will still be imperfect. However, hopefully these tips and experiences shared will help improve future rituals. We all make mistakes and find ways we can improve. The only fatal flaw is if we don't learn from them and do our best to do better next time. The goal isn't utter perfection but rather for things to go as smoothly as possible. It is my hope that sharing this article with you will help us all take steps forward to being more practical Pagans where it counts. Blessings of practicality be upon you!

Magickal Nail Polish: Combining Color and Crystal Magick

Kate Freuler

Crystal infusion has become a trend of late. It is the act of immersing a crystal in liquid so that the liquid takes on the healing and metaphysical vibrations of the crystal. The liquid is then consumed or used in some other way to manifest desired results.

Recently I stumbled across an ad for a water bottle that came with a crystal already embedded inside it, so you can drink crystal water whenever you please. While the product was very pretty, it was also very expensive, so I didn't buy it. It did, however, give me some ideas.

I started wondering what else I could infuse with crystals for use in my Craft but at a low cost. I really like the idea of everyday items being secretly magickal, and I like to handcraft these items myself whenever I can. One thing that came to mind was nail polish. Why not infuse it with crystals? From there I started thinking about all the beautiful colors and finishes that are available and realized that I could combine crystal magick and color magick in one. I then started brainstorming about all the uses of nail polish, which are certainly not limited to glamming up your fingers and toes. It can be used in place of any paint needed in rituals, spells, or amulets, and you can fine-tune its purpose according to what crystals you put inside of it.

Nail Polish Wasn't Always about Glamour

Nail polish was invented in China about five thousand years ago. It was crafted out of natural materials and dyes found in nature. Royalty were the first to wear nail polish in gold and silver colors to show their status. Only the upper class was permitted to adorn themselves with these hues, and if a common person were to do so, they could be punished by death. So while it seems nail polish was

worn for beauty, it also was a means of establishing rank within a society.

The ancient Egyptians also colored their nails and fingertips, typically with henna, for the same purpose. People of high status wore dark rich colors, while others were only permitted to wear lighter shades.

In the nineteenth century, scented oils were added to red pigment and applied to the nails for beauty purposes. This pigment was often made with flowers and berries.

Adorning the fingernails and toenails has been praticed for a long time. Even today you can sometimes tell a lot about a person depending on the color, decoration, and care given to their fingernails. For example, dangly fingernail charms glued to long talons clearly would indicate someone who doesn't work with their hands, whereas a craftsperson would have short nails out of necessity for their work. Some people like trim, neat nails while others like them to resemble sharpened claws. A lot of self-expression goes into nail art, and it certainly sends a message.

Choosing Your Polish

Before creating your crystal magick nail polish, there are a few factors to consider.

Most nail polish is very chemical laden but typically safe once dried. However, if you don't wish to put chemicals on your body, there is the option of making your own fingernail stain out of henna, which is explained later on in this article. There are also some less toxic brands of nail lacquer on the market now, although you may have to search a little to find them.

There are endless choices when choosing the shade and texture of your polish. Color is an important aspect of all kinds of magick, so there's a lot to think about here. For those who choose not to wear colorful polish, there's always the option of clear nail lacquer, which is almost invisible when dry. You can infuse this all-purpose varnish with crystals the same way you would colored choices.

Here are some general ideas for choosing a shade.

Green: Growth, money
Brown/Rust/Copper: Stability
Gold: Material gain, power
Yellow: Joy, warmth
Orange: Success, passion, change
Red: Sexual attraction
Black: Protection
Blue: Communication
Purple: Psychic ability
Silver: Magickal power
Pink: Love, friendship
Grey: Shadow work, banishing

Aside from color, nail polish also comes with sparkles, marbling, texture, iridescence, and other enhancements. Take this into account when selecting the shade. To me, an iridescent shade that seems to change colors indicates casting an illusion or glamour, whereas sparkles and glitter signify mysticism. A dark, glossy shade reminds me of a night sky, whereas bright matte colors have a loud, attention-getting vibe. This is personal, of course—what matters most is how you feel when you look at the color.

Making Your Own Natural Nail Color

If you're feeling really industrious or don't enjoy the chemical components of commercial nail polish, you can make your own with henna. Add crystals to this just as you would storebought polish. Keep in mind, this approach creates a stain or tint on your fingernails and will not be removable like paint. Henna will not fade over time on your nails the way it does on your skin, so it's a bit of a commitment, as you will have to grow it out naturally. Before you begin, be sure that your fingernails don't have any lacquer, dirt, or oil on them.

You will need:
1 tablespoon powdered red henna
Water
Small paintbrush
Bowl
Your chosen crystal chips

Put the henna powder in the bowl. Carefully add the water a drop at a time, mixing with a spoon, until it reaches the consistency of a smooth, thick paste. It should not be drippy or sloppy, but thick.

Place your crystals into the bowl, visualizing your intent.

Using the tiny paint brush, carefully paint your fingers and toes with a thick layer of henna. Allow the henna to sit for at least one hour and then wipe off the excess. This will give your nails a light orange tint. If you prefer darker, earthier tones, you can apply it several times.

Choosing Your Crystals

Before deciding which crystals to include in your polish, remember that they must be small enough to fit inside the tiny bottle. When it comes to crystals, size really doesn't matter: little chips are diverse, leaving so much room for creativity.

Storebought crystal chips, often called crushed crystals, are available at jewelry supply stores and craft shops, typically for use in making mosaics and jewelry. I've also seen them in pretty miniature jars from metaphysical stores. You'll notice that these tiny storebought crystal chips don't appear to be crushed but rather tumbled.

If you have a crystal at home already that you'd like to add a piece of to your polish, you can crush it yourself, as long as you're willing to part with it. All you need is a small bag made of very hefty material (such as leather), a piece of cloth, and a hammer. Wrap your crystal in the piece of cloth to keep the pieces altogether. Place the crystal inside the bag. Place the bag on a hard surface, such as a rock outdoors or on a cement floor, then use the hammer to smash the crystal. You will be able to feel a crunch when it breaks. Many crystals will smash quite easily, but they are a few that can be quite solid and require some force. Remove the cloth and carefully unfold it to gather your crystal pieces. Put them in a jar for safekeeping. This technique will produce various sizes of shards and sometimes powder. Select a piece that's small enough to fit in the little opening of a bottle of polish and you're ready to go.

Crystal Meanings

Here is a brief list of common crystals and their associations. You may wish to use the recipes I provide later or make up your own personalized combo with what you have on hand.

Rose Quartz: Love, friendship, self-love, gentleness
Clear Quartz: Amplifying power, purification, spirituality
Selenite: Moon power, intuition
Amazonite: Creativity, turning thoughts into form
Amethyst: Sobriety, pride, self-control
Peridot: Dispelling envy
Snowflake Obsidian: Working through trauma, confronting emotions
Sodalite: Communication, sending messages
Citrine: Warmth, joy
Lapis Lazuli: Spiritual wisdom
Tiger's Eye: Courage, truth, integrity

Carnelian: Passion, success, pursuing dreams
Turquoise: Absorbing and transforming negative energy
Agate: Protection, practicality
Unakite: Connecting to elemental earth spirits and animals

Cleansing Your Crystals

You may have heard of "cleansing" and "charging" your crystals. This is a way of clearing any accumulated and unwanted energy from the crystals to purify them, leaving them in their most energetically powerful state. For example, turquoise is believed to absorb negative energy and needs to be cleaned, so to speak, now and then. There are several ways of doing this. When you clear old energy out of your gems, it allows them to vibrate with their own power in its purist form. Prior to creating your magickal nail polish, be sure to cleanse your crystals in one of the following ways:

- Place them outdoors or in a window during the night of the Full Moon so they can bask in its light.
- Put them in bright sunlight for a few hours.
- Put them in water, and then let them dry (only do this with crystals that will not be damaged by water).
- Pass them through incense smoke.

Recipes

The most obvious thing to do with nail polish is paint your nails, and all the following recipes will work fine for that. Along with each recipe, there are also examples of other creative ways to use your magickal nail polish.

Protection Polish

Black tourmaline
Black onyx
Black nail polish
3 tablespoons dried rosemary

After you've put your crystals in the bottle of polish, place it within a circle of rosemary leaves. Leave it there overnight to absorb the protective energy of the herb. Wear this nail polish when you are in situations where you feel a need for extra protection for any reason. Alternative uses:

- Paint the top part of your house key—not the part that goes in the lock—to guard against break-ins.
- Secretly paint a dab underneath the door handle of your car or somewhere in the trunk.
- Paint a protection sigil on a rock and use it as a doorstop or porch decoration.
- Paint a symbol on the soles of your shoes to bring protection wherever you wander.

Solar Polish
Piece of black construction paper
Carnelian
Citrine
Orange or yellow sparkly nail polish

The color black literally attracts the heat of the Sun. Place the black paper in direct sunlight, where it will become hot. Add your crystals to the bottle, and then place the closed nail polish container on the black paper and leave it for several hours to soak up the rays. Wear this nail polish when you want to shine bright and create growth and warmth in all you touch. Alternative uses:

- Paint a Sun symbol on a piece of wood and place it in your garden to attract the Sun's blessings to your plants.
- Paint the image of a Sun on a piece of paper and hang it in a place that needs to be cheered up.
- Paint designs on the pots of your indoor plants to encourage healthy and hearty growth.

Witch's Path Polish
Quartz
Lapis lazuli
Silver nail polish

Paper and pencil
Symbolic items for the four elements

On the night of a Full Moon, add the crystals to the nail polish. Draw a pentacle on the paper and place the bottle in its center. Also place something in the appropriate directions for the elements (for example, a stone in the north, a bowl of water in the west, a candle in the south, and a feather in the east). Leave it overnight. Wear this nail polish when you have important spells to cast or when you are working on learning your Craft. Alternative uses:

- Paint a pentacle on the bottoms of your shoes to make your path in the Craft appear clearly.
- Paint a pentacle on a slip of paper and place it inside important books.
- Use it to decorate homemade wands or other tools.
- Paint sigils or pictures on workbooks used in your Craft.

Royalty Polish

One of my favorite colors of nail polish is shiny gold. When I wear it, I feel like a queen whose toes and fingers are tipped with gold.

Tiger's eye
Lapis lazuli
Shiny gold nail polish

Add the crystals to the bottle, and then place it in a spot where you keep jewelry or other symbols of status (costume jewelry is fine). When you wear this color on your fingers and toes, imagine it is made with real gold. As you paint your nails, picture yourself as royalty of your own life. This polish is excellent to wear when you need a reminder that you are valid, important, and powerful. Alternative uses:

- Paint a stick or bone and carry it as an amulet.
- Paint a picture of a crown on a small piece of paper and carry it with you.

Lunar Polish

White or soft silver nail polish
Selenite
Moonstone
Quartz

Add the crystals to the polish, then place it under the Full Moon, outdoors if possible, and leave it overnight to soak up the Moon rays. Apply when you need extra Moon energy, such as when you need to cast a spell but the Moon phase doesn't match your intention or when you are learning about Moon mysteries. Alternative uses:

- Find a smooth, round stone and paint it. Place it on your altar to signify the Moon.
- Use it for painting lunar or goddess imagery.

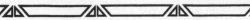

Prosperity Nail Polish
Green or gold nail polish
Pyrite
Emerald
Coins

During the waxing Moon, place the bottle in the center of a circle of coins and leave it for three days. Wear this polish while working to attract more money. Alternative uses:

- Paint one of the coins and carry it with you to attract prosperity.
- Use it to paint a dollar sign on a sticker and place this where you work to attract money.

Gentle Energy Polish
Neutral or light pink nail polish
Rose quartz
Moonstone
Fresh flower petals

Place the bottle inside a circle of flower petals, and leave it there until the petals start to wither. This polish is worn when you need to take a gentle, nurturing approach. It's great for situations that call for kindness or when healing people or animals.

Resource
Millburn, Naomi. "The Origin of Nail Polish." Classroom. Accessed August 21, 2019. https://classroom.synonym.com/origin-nail-polish -9845.html.

Magickal Sewing: Draft Blocker for Home Protection

Raechel Henderson

In the summer of 2018 I found myself having to pack up my home of sixteen years and leave it behind. I was only given a few weeks to pack up. It was a time of quick reckoning: sorting through all my and my family's possessions to decide what to take, what to toss, and what to leave behind. We filled a storage unit full, sold or gave away what we could, and in the end abandoned so much: beds, shelves, rugs, paintings. There was just no way we could bring it all.

And during all this hectic back-and-forth between the storage unit and the house, I was attempting to make my goodbyes with the house itself and the land it sat on. I had cultivated a relationship with the plants and rocks there, most of which I had installed over the years. I was familiar with the creatures that had taken up residence in the garden and in my converted-garage workshop. There was a family of cardinals I had known for years who had brought their children, who in turn brought their own children, to the bird feeder we had set up off the back porch. There were spirits I had worked with that lived there. I didn't want to sever those ties so abruptly, but I couldn't organize the kind of proper leave-taking ritual that I wanted.

Losing the house was just the beginning of a period of instability for my family. For six weeks, we were homeless and separated. My husband and son stayed with relatives two thousand miles away while my daughter and I stayed with friends. Those six weeks, adrift and uncertain, took a toll on all of us. As I worked on my book, *Sew Witchy*, I spent days looking for a place for my family to land together. And while we eventually landed in a new and lovely home, I still felt unsettled. I couldn't get comfortable in this place that was supposed to shelter me.

I turned to magick for an answer.

House Spirits

In many different Western cultures, there is a concept of spirits that take the form of snakes. For the Greeks, this was the *agathodaemon*, a spirit that was a personal or familial daemon who provided luck, health, and wisdom. This spirit was depicted as a serpent. In Russia, the *domovoy*, a household spirit, could take on the form of a snake as well.

But it is in many Eastern European mythologies and folklore where the idea of a household spirit in the form of a snake was most common. The house snake, called *žaltys*, provided good fortune and prosperity to the home that gave it welcome. Sometimes this was a real snake, kept as a pet, which had the added benefit of killing mice and rats. To kill such an animal was to bring misfortune on one's family.

The house snake could be present in the land before a house was built, or it could be attracted into the home after construction through gifts, rituals, and magick. Alternatively, it could be carried to the new home from the old. House snakes were traditionally kept near the hearth, in keeping with the idea that it was a spirit of home protection and that the hearth was the heart of the home.

My old home had played host to many spirits—house gnomes, Arachne, genus locii that resided in the plants and stones—but not a house snake. I was going to have to go about inviting one into my home. As it is a type of house spirit, the ways to attract its attention were simple: make my home inviting (keeping it neat and tidy), set out offerings, and then invite the spirit to move in.

As I was already reaching out to the local spirits of this new place, I worked the invitation into my meditations.

This addressed the magickal aspect of the house snake. But there was still a physical reality to attend to. We didn't have mice to get rid of (and if we did, we had three resident house cats who would take care of that). I wanted a physical representation of the house snake, and I wanted it to have a job to do, because the stories and mythology pointed to a relationship, a partnership rather than worship.

As I went through my list of "Things to Make for the House When I Have Time," my eye caught on the entry for a draft blocker. A draft blocker is a stuffed fabric tube that is placed along the bottom of doors or in windowsills to, as the name states, block drafts. Our previous house was poorly built and extremely drafty, making for freezing winters if we didn't want to crank up the heat (which we didn't). I had made blockers for various doors and windows,

A LITTLE BIT OF MAGIC

If you are new to sewing, don't get caught up on being perfect. Any "imperfections" will be visible to you alone. Everyone else will see quirks and style and magick.

but they had not made the move with us. I didn't know how this new house would fare once the temperature dropped, and so I had planned to make a few just in case.

As I looked over that project, it occurred to me that it had the same shape as a snake, and that was all I needed for the plan to click into place. I modified the pattern for a more snakelike appearance, sewed it up, and consecrated it to my needs.

The snake now keeps watch over the door to the garage, the only drafty one in the new abode. Each month on the Full Moon, I set out an offering of milk and thank it for its help. Going in and out of the house daily gives me the opportunity to interact with it, to thank it for its aid, and to generally be conscious and grateful for the roof over my head. Over the months I've felt a settledness from the draft blocker, a knowingness in its button eyes that speaks to a partnership forged. "Give me a place in your home, take care of me, honor me, and I will guard your house and bring you good fortune," it says. Along with the pictures on the walls and the linens on my bed, this little tube of stuffed fabric makes this house a home.

If you would like to make your own snake draft blocker/house guardian, follow these instructions.

Fabric and Other Materials

Choose heavy-weight fabric like corduroy, denim, and canvas. Not only will these better hold up to being pushed and kicked around when it comes to opening and closing doors, but they tap into the groundedness of earth and the hearth. You can choose colors that correspond to what magickal task your house snake will be doing. Earth tones are good for protection, blues for bringing harmony into the house, reds for warmth, gold or yellows for prosperity, and so on. I used a piece of brown drill not only for the protective energies but also because it wouldn't show dirt as easily as a lighter color. (Again, practicality can be magickal as well.)

I wanted to add in more color magick to my snake, so I raided my ribbon stash. With them, I added jaunty stripes. I chose orange, red, and yellow ribbons. (The end result was a snake that looks like a cartoon turkey. As Thanksgiving is my most favorite and revered holiday, I was okay with that.) You can also bring number magick into your snake through the number of ribbons you use. I used a pattern of four bands of ribbon, orange-yellow-red-orange, that was repeated three times. The three repetitions brought in the active energy of the number; I wanted to get comfortable in this new house quickly. The four stripes called in the stability of the number and also reflected the number of members of my family (me, my husband, and our two children).

Choosing your materials, ribbon decorations, and the buttons to use for eyes is something you should spend a little time on. Sit down and think about what you want your house snake to look like. Draw it out and color it in. Perhaps even meditate and consult with any spirit helpers or deities you work with. The physical representation of your house snake can be as simple or complex as you wish.

This project allows another layer of magickal working in that you can include herbs and crystals with the fiberfill stuffing. For example, you could include some dried mugwort and a piece of black tourmaline to enhance the protective qualities of your house snake. If you wanted to emphasize the prosperity- and fortune-bringing aspects of the house snake, you could include dried chamomile and a piece of citrine.

As this is a very personal bit of magick, taking the time to plan it out will add another layer of will to your finished project.

Snake Draft Blocker

Preparation:
Measure the width of the door or window you want to block. Add 1 inch to this measurement for the seam allowance.

Materials:
1 piece of fabric that is 10 inches by your width measurement from above
Small bowl or large cup

Tailor's chalk or a quilting pencil
Ruler
2 buttons
Your choice of ribbons
Sewing machine and needle or a hand-sewing needle
Thread
Fiberfill

1. Fold the fabric in half widthwise so that the wrong side faces out. On one of the short sides, mark out a curve by placing a small bowl or large cup and tracing it with chalk or pencil. This will be

the head end of the draft blocker. Cut out the curve on the line you traced.

2. Unfold the fabric and lay it right-side up. Measure 5 inches from the short edge of the head end of the fabric. Starting there, use the chalk or pencil and a ruler to mark the ribbon placement by drawing straight lines across the width of the fabric.

3. Now mark button placement for the eyes on the right side of the fabric. You can lay the buttons on the fabric where you like, then mark the spot with the chalk or pencil.

4. Attach ribbons along the lines you drew on the snake body using a sewing machine or by hand-sewing them. Attach the buttons at the marks you made with a needle. Fold the fabric in half widthwise, right sides together. Match up the ribbons and pin the sides together.

5. Sew a ½-inch seam on the short square end, the long end, and the curved end. Leave a 3-inch gap in the middle of the long edge for turning.

6. Trim the corners of the short square end and clip the curve of the head end. This reduces bulk.

7. Turn the body right-side out.

8. Fill the body with fiberfill and your prepared herbs, stones, rice, and so on.

9. Close the opening using a ladder stitch.

When you have finished your draft blocker, you can consecrate it. Give it a name and make a connection to it. Leave it offerings of milk regularly. This will be a spiritual ally in defense of your home, bringing you luck and good fortune.

Seeking Hecate:
The Wise Self Within

Danielle Blackwood

In these times of uncertainty, it can be difficult to know which way to proceed. Navigating our way through the fear, grief, rage, and confusion that saturates the collective at this juncture in history can be a daunting experience. The collective itself is in a place of liminality, as the dying gasps of the patriarchy give way to a new paradigm that is still finding its feet. It's challenging enough making our way through the very real crossroads in our personal lives, but when the overculture is also at a crossroads, it takes all our courage, our creativity and our heart to find our way through. Many of us long for a guide to help us through times of transition, both collective and personal. Grounding, centering, and contemplation can bring us important insight if we would but listen and allow our intuition to be our guide. However, the ability to differentiate between intuition and endless mind chatter rooted in anxiety can be elusive.

Another way to access wisdom when you find yourself at a crossroads is to connect with deity. The triple-form goddess Hecate has long been associated with liminal spaces and those places in between such as gateways, entrances, midnight, and crossroads. She is also associated with the night, the Moon, the underworld, the spirits of the dead, both medicinal and baneful plants, and Witchcraft. Hecate is known as the Keeper of the Keys and is a light bearer, unlocking the secret portals of wisdom and carrying a pair of blazing torches that can illuminate our path ahead.

We can connect with Hecate for her guidance, much the way Demeter received her help when Hades abducted Persephone. Demeter had wandered for nine days lost in the wilderness, grieving the disappearance of her daughter, when Hecate appeared on the tenth day, carrying a pair of torches to accompany Demeter on her search. The myth tells us that no god or mortal would tell Demeter the truth of what had befallen Persephone, but Hecate says to Demeter in the Homeric *Hymn to Demeter*, "I am telling you the whole truth." Like Demeter, we too can feel lost, bewildered, and in need of someone to walk beside us through times of darkness and confusion. Sometimes we need someone to simply tell us the truth of a situation so that we may begin to work with what is. Working with Hecate can help us decide which way to turn when we find ourselves unable to decide whether to turn left or right. Her voice is that whisper we hear at the edge of our consciousness that lets us know the basic truth of a matter so that we may find the best way forward.

Although some Witches work with Hecate during the New Moon, I have always associated her with the waning Moon, or fourth quarter Moon—the time when the shadows are deepening, and the light diminishes. The fourth quarter Moon is a time of endings and letting go and therefore is a natural time to work magick for banishing, cord cutting, and release. It is a time for turning within and exhaling after the peak of lunar energy that coincides with the Full Moon. During the waning/fourth quarter Moon, we may be feeling more reflective, receptive, and contemplative. The waning fourth quarter Moon is between the apex of the last Full Moon and the quiet new beginnings of the next New Moon. It is therefore a liminal time that facilitates trancework, pathworking, and magick. I find this the most potent time to connect with Hecate for guidance.

I recently led a retreat where we called on Hecate to be our guide for the deep work we were about to dive into. Many of

the participants were there because they had reached a crossroads in their lives and were looking for insight. As we gathered on the waning Moon in an old growth forest in the Pacific Northwest, we were all receptive to the subtle magick of Hecate. We walked in silent procession down a winding path until we reached a yurt in the darkening woods. One by one, before entering, the participants were purified at the threshold with the smoke of herbs sacred to Hecate. Once inside, we sat in circle, and a gentle rain began pattering on the canvas roof. In the stillness, a raven croaked directly overhead, as though signalling it was time to begin. We passed an old key (as a symbol of Hecate) on a length of weathered silk as a talking stick, and each of us had the opportunity to speak a few words of intention for the days ahead. Some shared their private grief, while others voiced their confusion about what their next steps should be. We then began our dream-tea ceremony, with tea made from mugwort (an herb sacred to Hecate) that I had harvested from my Witch's garden on the last Full Moon. Each of us drank deeply from an earthenware cup as we prepared to begin our journey. I played a slow, rhythmic beat on my drum, and people stretched out comfortably with pillows and blankets, ready to enter the dreamtime and receive guidance from Hecate. It was a powerful experience, and many found the answers they were seeking when the Sun rose the next morning.

If you are trying to make a difficult decision or are unsure of your next steps, perhaps the time has come to seek wisdom from the goddess Hecate. The following pathworking is best done at night on the waning Moon, preferably when the Moon is in Scorpio, Pisces, or Capricorn. If you wish to facilitate lucid dreaming after the pathworking, consider taking mugwort (*Artemisia vulgaris*) tea approximately forty-five minutes before you begin. Mugwort tea is available in many natural foods stores and online. Follow usage recommendations. Do not take mugwort if you are pregnant or think you might be pregnant, as it can bring on menstruation. If you are unsure, consult your doctor before taking any herb that you are unfamiliar with.

The following pathworking can be done with or without the dream-tea.

Seeking Hecate: Guidance at the Crossroads

Find a quiet place where you will be undisturbed for about fifteen to twenty minutes. Turn off your phone. Ground and center in your preferred way and consider clearing the space by burning essential oil or incense associated with Hecate, such as myrrh, storax, spikenard, or patchouli. Wear unrestrictive clothing and get into a comfortable position. Use pillows for support if needed and a blanket to keep warm and comfortable. It can be helpful to record yourself reading the pathworking before doing it, or have a friend read it to you. Have a journal and a pen ready to record what comes up for you after the journey.

You are walking along a gently winding footpath that leads you up the side of a forested hill. The last rays of the setting Sun shine through the canopy of leaves overhead, dappling the approaching shadow with flashes of gold. You deeply inhale the scent that comes with twilight as night-blooming flowers begin to release their perfume. A thrush begins her evening song, and not far away, you hear the distinctive call of a barred owl echoing through the trees.

You have been walking for some time. You are at a place of transition and have come to the woods for insight. You arrived here hoping for a message, some medicine to help you get out of your own way and connect with the forest of your inner landscape. The path diverges, and you suddenly find yourself standing at a crossroads. You pause, not sure if you should continue on the path you are on, go left, go right, or turn around and go back the way you came. It is getting dark, and the first stars begin to twinkle in the luminous twilight sky.

Your eye catches something glittering, and you see a key tied on a length of weathered ribbon tangled in a low branch. You reach out and take the key in your hand. Putting it into your pocket, you decide to take the left-hand path. Darkness is falling quickly now, and if you were to turn back, you're not sure you could even find your way back to the path that you started on. A soft breeze stirs, the air is charged, and everything in the forest shimmers; the dark silhouettes of the trees each seem to have their own presence.

You come upon a thatch-roof cottage surrounded by a small, tangled garden. In the pale light of the waning Moon, datura gleams, white as wax, emitting its nocturnal fragrance. Henbane, belladonna, and other nightshades nod gently in the soft breeze alongside healing mugwort, comfrey, and yarrow. A yew tree guards the entrance, and warm golden light spills out into the night from the windows.

You make your way toward the cottage and try the gate, but it is locked. You remember the key in your pocket and try it. The gate opens easily, and you walk into the garden and up to the front steps. The door is slightly ajar, and you knock tentatively. A woman's voice, rich and low, comes from within: "Be welcome and enter." You pause for a moment, take a deep breath, and step across the threshold.

The only light is coming from a fire burning in the grate and a single candle on an old wooden table. The room is scented with herbs hanging in bunches from the rafters. As your eyes adjust to the flickering firelight, you notice a figure draped in a dark cloak bent over the work in her lap. She raises her head and takes your measure. "What is it you seek?" You realize that seated before you is Hecate, Goddess of the Crossroads and Keeper of the Keys.

For a moment you are confused. The first thought that comes to you is to ask how to get back on the path that you left. But you realize the question is more than it seems. She gestures to an empty chair before the fire, and you sit. You have been walking a long time.

You gaze into the fire and lose yourself in the flames. You close your eyes and slip into a comfortable waking dream.

You hear her voice again, from far away: "Your quest is to find the key that will unlock the door to the guidance you are searching for. To find that door, you must journey inward. Your inner knowing already has all the answers you seek."

In your mind's eye you retrace all the steps that have brought you here to this moment.

You rise above the specifics of your mundane world, and your vision clears. You gain an overview. Do you see any patterns? What is the first thing that arises?

What message does Hecate have for you? It can be a word, an image, or a feeling.

What is the basic truth of the matter?

Hecate rises and appears before you in all her glory. While she is Goddess of the Crossroads and Keeper of the Keys, Hecate is also known as the Light Bearer, and in her hands, she holds a pair of blazing torches that illuminate the path before you.

She speaks: "Are you ready to cross the threshold and enter liminal space? Can you trust that you are exactly where you are meant to be on your journey?" Hecate places something in your hand that will be a talisman to help you make a decision or guide you on your next steps.

With talisman in hand, you see the path before you, take a deep breath, and step across the threshold.

• • • 🌙 • • •

Take a few moments to open your eyes, stretch, and come back to the room. What message did you receive from Hecate? What did the goddess give to you? Write down anything that comes up for you in your journal and take some time to reflect on your next steps.

Resource

Rayor, Diane J., trans. *The Homeric Hymns*. Berkeley: University of California Press, 2004. Line 58.

Being Rooted:
Grounding and Centering Using Your Five Senses

Monica Crosson

As I step into the shadows of the twisted maples and moss-laden fir, I leave behind my worldly self—the woman whose life is dictated by the ever ticking of the clock. Within my Greenwood temple, there is no schedule to hold to, no meals to prepare or calls to be made. It is also to the forest where I go to worship my deities: I pound my drum and allow the tendrils of my spirit to reach deep into the soil. There are only the slow stirrings of my soul as I feel the roots of the earth intertwining with the calling of my heart. Here I am one with the earth—here I am home.

This is one way I ground myself after a long day dealing with a world full of people who aren't quite like me, and this is how I release excess energy on those days when anxiety has me in its stronghold. Before spellwork or ritual, it is a good bet that I am grounding and finding my center with the beat of a drum.

But, like many of us, I am a busy Witch who doesn't always have the time to gather my supplies and wander to the forest, so there is a chance that if you stumble upon my door I will be in a pair of overalls and bent over in the dirt. For I am as connected to my cultivated bit of land as I am to the wild spaces that call to me. Both give me balance; both reinforce my connection to the land. I am writing this piece in response to a couple of questions I was asked not so very long ago: "Are grounding and centering the same thing?" and "Is there more than one way to ground yourself?"

Grounding and Centering 101

For those of you who aren't quite sure or just need a very simple explanation for what grounding and centering are, *grounding* is the way we draw upon our connection to the earth by tapping into the earth's natural reserves and drawing or releasing energy as needed. *Centering* is how we reinforce a connection with ourselves. It is a way of stabilizing and bringing ourselves into a positive state of being.

Grounding and centering are fundamental when practicing Witchcraft as part of the preparation for spellwork or for tapping into psychic abilities. Magickally, it helps balance and equalize the flow of energy and helps you avoid the negative side effects unbalanced energy can have on your spellwork. But grounding and centering are not activities that you need to reserve for spiritual or magickal activities. In fact, they are actions you should be trying to do every day, as they have a calming effect that may lower stress, help improve sleep, and bring you back to a place of balance and peace.

When you're not grounded, you are a bit like a leaf that has fallen from the tree—very vulnerable and thrown off balance. You may feel disorientated, restless, anxious, or out of touch with family, friends, or coworkers. Being grounded is more like being the tree itself: you are rooted, at peace, and balanced in your daily life.

One of the most common ways of grounding is through visualization. It is a method that is best done in bare feet and standing somewhere on grass, sand, or soil. With eyes closed, you imagine your energy extending down through your legs (like roots) and burrowing deep into the soil. Feel the earth's energy as it flows upward into your body and cycles through, clearing away all negativity and restoring your sense of balance.

This is one of my favorite ways of finding my center and reinforcing my connectedness to nature, but there are other ways that are quicker or more convenient for our busy lives. I have put together ways to ground and center that incorporate the use of our five senses. And why not? We are delighted by things of beauty, the sound of music, or the scent of a favorite flower. Think of the gentle touch of the breeze against your skin or the sweetness of a berry straight off the vine. The stimulation of each of our five senses plays an important part in connecting with the sacred, and we can use all our senses in different ways in balancing our personal energies. The senses are the gateway to our soul.

Grounding and Centering Using Hearing

Music is a sacred tool for finding our own voice and connecting heart and soul. There is music that opens and heals our hearts, like many love songs do. There is music that connects our spirits and souls—think of lovely harp melodies. We teach small children songs for play and learning, and we use songs with a raucous beat to invoke strength and bravery. We need to sing to open our hearts, call in our good intentions, and bless the sacred space of ourselves. It is essential for us to find and use our own unique voice to bring healing to ourselves as well as to the earth.

Sing Out or Chant

Sing out or chant words of power at the top of your lungs. It doesn't matter the song or what the words are—open your heart and call in your good intentions for yourself.

The Sound of Silence

We can be fulfilled by silence too. Meditate in that space in nature or in your own personal sanctuary that is quiet and let the soft silence gently beckon you inward.

Drumming

Just as nature's rhythms affect our bodies (think of the ever-waxing and ever-waning of the Moon), musical rhythms awaken our soul. As we move with the rhythm of the drum, the beat synchs with the soundings of our heartbeat, and it is within that synchronization that we feel our spirit unite with the rhythm of the earth.

Windchimes, Bells, or Garden Fountains

Place beautiful-sounding windchimes (or bells) in or around your garden or balcony or just outside your window. Let the lingering vibrations of their harmonic sound resonate deep within your soul. If you are lucky enough to have a small (or large) fountain in your garden or even a tabletop version, simply sit by the fountain and let the trickling sound of water cleanse and equalize your spirit.

Grounding and Centering Using Sight

To truly see the beauty of every nuance of light, color, and texture in our intimate sacred surroundings is to bring the essence of that sacredness deep within us. We have the opportunity to develop our vision to know both the visible and invisible worlds. With practice, we can have intimate insights (much like a macro lens) for detail not noticed by mundane eyes.

Go for a Walk

In a study published in *Enviromental Health and Preventative Medicine,* Japanese researchers conducted experiments in which they measured cortisol, heart rate, blood pressure, and pulse of volunteers before and after a walk. Part of the group walked through the forest, while the other walked through the city, and what the researchers found was not surprising. In test after test, a walk through the forest lowered blood pressure, heart rate, parasympathetic nerve activity, and cortisol. They also found that the presence of antimicrobial oil emitted by plants and trees (phytoncides) appear to boost the immune system. Taking a walk in your favorite natural location is a sure way to help you keep grounded.

Watch a Sunset or Sunrise

Just being in the presence of something beautiful can make us feel better and more connected to ourselves and our emotions. So whether you are standing atop a mountain, watching a sunset or sunrise, or gazing up at a particularly beautiful Moon, watching natural beauty will help unite you to the earth's rhythms.

Grounding and Centering Using Touch

It is said in some cultures that trees are the medicine people of the plant world. The roots are associated with the past, ancestors, and dream work. The trunk is the present and, like the heart, connects the deep-rooted ancient knowing with the far-reaching dreams and goals of the crown. The trunk is an effective transmitter of energy and support for both realms. When we use our sense of touch in the natural world (especially by touching trees), we make an intimate connection to it and tap into its ancient medicine. Using touch is our most intimate form of expression, and when used correctly, it can evoke a sense of comfort and a sense of well-being.

Forest Bathing

If just taking a walk in nature and experiencing it with your sight can create a sense of calm within your spirit, think of all that can be gained by literally bathing yourself in nature! Forest bathing is attuning yourself to the forest's surroundings. It's being mindful of every drop of misty rain, every leaf that falls, and the quiet, distant sound of our Mother's earth beat. Balance your energy by dipping your feet in a stream, lake, or other body of water. How about tilting your face to the breeze? Let the element of air blow away negativity and stimulate your creativity. Dance in the rain or make snow angels on a winter's day.

Play in the Dirt

Plunging your witchy hands into the soil is a great earthing technique. In fact, a study by UK scientists published in the journal *Neuroscience* shows that there is a soil microbe called *Mycobacterium vaccae* that has the same mood-enhancing effect as antidepressants. After a long day at work or before ritual, go to your garden and just spend some time working the soil. If you live in an apartment or have a small yard, plant a few pots of herbs and let the healing power of earth help you find your center.

Go Barefoot

Barefooting is another way to make that contact with earth's balancing energy. Wiggling your toes in fresh upturned soil or walking on fresh spring grass are great ways to ground and create a sense of ease. Go to the park and slip off your shoes. If you live near water, walk along the beach and enjoy the sand between your toes.

Stones for Grounding

One easy way to keep grounded is to carry a stone with you in your pocket as a very tangible reminder of your connectedness with the earth. When you feel anxiety or stress begin to creep in, take your stone and just roll it around in your hand until you feel a sense of well-being begin to envelop you. Try these:

Amber: Balances and purifies
Black Tourmaline: Balances and dispels negativity
Bloodstone: Restores energy and guards against negativity
Carnelian: Motivates and helps overcome fear
Citrine: Boosts confidence and provides calm
Hematite: Helps create a protective environment, provides clarity, and helps with anxiety
Jade: Aids in spiritual thinking and self-discovery
Red Jasper: Provides strength and balance and helps alleviate stress
Smoky Quartz: Offers mental calm and absorbs negative energy
Tiger's Eye: Offers warmth and stable energy and relieves fear and anxiety

Grounding and Centering Using Taste

Our sense of taste can easily be stimulated by the fruits, vegetables, herbs, and edible flowers we find in our gardens or local farmer's markets. This is an especially direct connection between nature and our entire body. I have the pleasure and the privilege of having a very large garden, and there is no better communion than standing among the fruit and vegetables and savoring every flavor-filled bite of a fresh berry or tomato.

Savor Favorite Healthful Foods

Our bodies are our temples and should be treated as such. Fresh locally grown food is a wonderful way to manifest a real connection between you and our Mother the earth. Practice eating slowly, savoring every bite.

Eat Seasonally

Enjoying food that is at its peak in your region is a great way to awaken your connection to the sacred. Better yet, if you can, gather the food from nature yourself, either by growing it or by utilizing U-pick farm stands, as this really makes a connection between nature and your physical and spiritual bodies.

Enjoy Some Chocolate

Every once in a while, give in to the delights of chocolate. This sinful treat releases endorphins in the brain that gives one the feeling of happiness. Take a few pieces of your favorite dark chocolate and sit somewhere tranquil to indulge.

Grounding and Centering Using Smell

Taking in air brings us energy, and exhaling releases tensions and promotes letting go and trusting in the next breath. The simple rhythm of successive breaths is both life-sustaining and transformative, connecting us to the element of air as well as the universe. When there is a pleasant fragrance in the air, our sense of smell is awakened. Scent is the strongest connection to memory, and our individual memories are the treasures of life. Think of the smell of chocolate chip cookies warm from the oven or the scent of an heirloom rose riding the breeze. What are some favorites scents for you, and what kind of feelings do they evoke?

Use Aromatherapy

The most primitive of all our senses, the sense of smell is linked to some of the oldest and deepest parts of the brain, triggering emotional and physical responses and allowing vivid memory recall. We can use this to stimulate a sense of groundedness anytime and anywhere. Use scents that trigger a sense of well-being and connectedness. You can do this by burning candles, burning incense, or using an essential oil diffuser. Listed here are a few essential oils that are especially suited for grounding and centering:

Birch: Use birch oil for connection to ancestors or for strength in self.

Buddha Wood: Use this soothing oil when in need of self-acceptance.

Clary Sage: Use this oil for mental and emotional support.

Frankincense: Use if feeling a spiritual disconnect.

Ginger Root: Use when feeling a disconnect in your interpersonal relationships.

Lavender: Use for calm and to release stuck energy.

Marjoram: Use for balance and calm.

Myrrh: Use for security and a sense of connectedness.

Patchouli: Use for relaxation and clarification of thought.

Sandalwood: Use to regain connection to spirit.

Vetiver: Use for self-awareness and emotional well-being.

Ground and Center on the Go!

Take the transformative powers of the earth along with you with this great roll-on.

You will need:

10 milliliter glass roller bottle (available in most craft stores or online)

Carrier oil (I suggest fractionated coconut oil)

4–6 drops of any of the oils in the essential oil list or a combination of several

Remove the roller and fill the bottle with carrier oil and essential oils. My favorite is a blend of 3 drops of sandalwood, 2 drops of lavender, and 1 drop of patchouli. Replace the roller, and it's ready to go.

When you are finished using your roll-on, the bottle can be cleaned and used again.

Resources

Lowry, C. A., J. H. Hollis, A. de Vries, B. Pan, L. R. Brunet, J. R. F. Hunt, J. F. R. Paton, et al. "Identification of an Immune-Responsive Meso-limbocortical Serotonergic System: Potential Role in Regulation of Emotional Behavior." *Neuroscience* 162, no. 2 (May 2007): 756–72. doi:10.1016/j.neuroscience.2007.01.067.

Park, Bum Jin, Yuko Tsunetsugu, Tamami Kasetani, Takahide Kagawa, and Yoshifumi Miyazaki. "The Physiological Effects of *Shinrin-yoku* (Taking in the Forest Atmosphere or Forest Bathing): Evidence from Field Experiments in 24 Forests across Japan." *Enviromental Health and Preventative Medicine* 15, no. 1 (January 2010): 18–26. doi:10.1007/s12199-009-0086-9.

Air Magic

Around the World
with Oracles

Tiffany Lazic

In the twenty-first century, we are lucky to have access to a wealth of divination tools, with more coming onto the market all the time. We live in a time in which we benefit from an abundance of possibilities for connecting with the Divine, the ineffable, that which is greater than ourselves. We may currently have ample opportunity for connection, but the roots of each of these methods have a long and rich history, much of it informed by historical era and geography.

The word *oracle* itself means "mouthpiece" and refers to the means through which we can "speak" with the gods. In ancient Greece from about 1400 BCE to the beginning of the Common Era, oracles were associated with certain locations and carried strong associations with a particular god. Delphi is well known for being the home of the oracle of Apollo, as was Delos. Zeus had oracles at Olympus, Dodona, and Ammon. Even certain demigods (who have one divine parent and one mortal parent), such as Asclepius and Heracles, had oracles. The Asclepian oracle at Epidaurus was dedicated to healing. People threw dice at Heracles's oracle in Bura to receive their guidance, but the term *oracle* could also refer to a person. The Pythia of Delphi was the priestess through whom Apollo spoke. The Libyan Sibyl of Ammon spoke for Zeus. As famous and reputable as these oracles were, they already stood on the shoulders of far older traditions as well as provided a solid foundation for the oracular avenues that followed.

In the timeline of history, the first human lineage from the primate line appeared between eight and six million years ago. The shift to what can be identified as "modern humans" occurred about 800,000 years ago. The shift in evolution to encompass a similar brain capacity to modern humans occurred about 600,000 years ago. There is archeological evidence that places the oldest known *Homo sapiens* at 300,000 years ago based on a skull found in a cave in Morocco along with stone tools. There is further evidence that the earliest known form of divination may have started around 30,000 years ago in sub-Saharan Africa. It seems that, relatively speaking, closely on the heels of learning to craft tools to ease our existence, we humans have sought methods for connecting with the Divine.

As our ancestors moved to different geographic locations, it is not a stretch to imagine that the response to the environment caused culture and tradition to develop in different ways. If you live in a place that is abundant with elephants, they are going to find a way into your understanding and celebration of place: your mythology, your art, your ceremonies. One would imagine that the mechanisms for connecting with the Divine would follow similar influences.

Let us take a journey. Imagine yourself in a magical hot air balloon that will take us on a time-traveling journey to discover the different oracles from around the world in the places from whence they came. We may learn something of ourselves and the nature of our relationship to the ethereal and ephemeral along the way.

Bone Divination (Africa)

Thought to be the oldest-known example of divination, bone divination has a wide range of approaches and has survived practically unchanged for millennia. Some approaches use as few as four bones, while others can include a variety of natural objects, such as stones and shells. Traversing the ocean during a terrible and painful part of our history, bone divination found its way to the Americas, particularly in the Hoodoo tradition of "throwing the bones."

I Ching (China)

Though there is archeological evidence of the tradition of bone divination also in China dating from the Shang dynasty (1600–1050 BCE), the I Ching (The Book of Changes), which is so closely associated with China, has its roots thousands of years earlier. The foundational structure is said to have been invented by Fu Hsi, the first emperor of China, who ruled between 2852 and 2737 BCE. Working with a binary system of yang (solid line) and yin (broken line), Fu Hsi created the eight trigrams (of three lines each) that form the basic spatial and qualitative structure of existence: heaven, earth, fire, river, mountain, wind, lake, and thunder. Wen Wang, the founder of the Chou dynasty (1150–249 BCE), is said to have crafted the basic form that we are familiar with today: sixty-four hexagrams formed when you place one trigram above another. Further, he gave each of the sixty-four hexagrams their identifying names and wrote the initial text for each. The last significant ancient contribution to the *I Ching* as we know it today came from Confucius (551–479 BCE). His thorough study of the *I Ching* gifted us with the interpretive text that is still used today.

The Palm-Leaf Prophecies (India)

Said to be one of the oldest oracular texts in history, the palm-leaf prophecies are like both a divine mirror of the individual's current circumstances and future advice-giving rolled into one. I was introduced to this oracle during a trip to India by a tour organizer whose family home is near a museum where the prophesies are stored. The author is said to have been Brighu (alternately spelled Bhrigu), a mythological hero who lived around 5000 BCE. Brighu is said to have written the lives of 80,000 individuals on these leaves, which were collected into about 1,600 bundles of about fifty leaves each. These bundles are currently preserved in Indian palm-leaf libraries and can be accessed with the aid of a specially trained palm leaf reader, or Nadi reader.

The procedure for determining whether you are one of the 80,000 individuals with a palm leaf is fascinating. It all starts with a thumbprint: right for men, left for women. Although each thumbprint is unique, they can be categorized into 108 different types. Each thumb type has about fourteen bundles associated with it and each of the fifty leaves in the bundle has ten to fifteen identifying statements. The seeker must respond in the positive to each of the statements in order to be considered for that leaf. If even one statement is not applicable, the reader moves on to the next leaf until the perfect match is found or it becomes evident that the person does not have a leaf. For those who do, the remaining information may reveal karma that needs to be released, give advice on problems that are being faced, or offer guidance on how to achieve your best life. Each leaf is specific to the person's situation and circumstance. Amazing for something written thousands of years ago!

Svyatki (Russia)

In a quick, more contemporary touchdown in the majestic beauty of Russia, we find the resurgence of an ancient divination tradition that has more to do with time frames than technique. *Svyatki* refers to a particularly auspicious time when the veil between the worlds is said to be thin, during which it is deemed possible to access information about the future. *Svyatki* actually means "yuletide" and encompasses the period between the Russian Christmas Eve, January 7, and the Epiphany, January 19 (in the Julian calendar). This was considered the best time to seek general information regarding one's future, insight into the harvest for the year to come, and, as is so very often the case with divination, issues of love and partnership. Working with any form of divination during these times would be beneficial, but tradition tended toward forms of scrying such as gazing into a fire or reading the shapes of melted candle wax.

Psephoi (Greece)

Heading back in time once more and traveling westward to the edge of ancient Anatolia (modern-day Turkey), we find that the ancient approach to divination begins to take a turn. Moving from a focus on the depth that comes through the interpretation of text as seen in China and India, divination here at the edge of the ancient Western world focuses on the meaning inherent in letters themselves. *Psephoi* means "pebble" in Greek and refers to the tiles, pot shards, and dice upon which the twenty-four letters of the Greek alphabet were etched. Each letter represents the first letter of the first word of an oracular sentence. Much of the focus of these messages seems to be aimed toward encouraging hard work and reflecting what is necessary in order to achieve success in any endeavor.

Runes (Northern Europe)

Floating gently in our balloon to the more northerly climes of ancient Western Europe, we find another application of a writing system that is also used for divination. There was much cultural cross-pollination in Europe from around 400 BCE to 400 CE, mainly due to the inexorable progress of the Roman legions. Customs, gods, and language were carried with the soldiers and impacted most parts of the ancient world. To the ancient Germanic

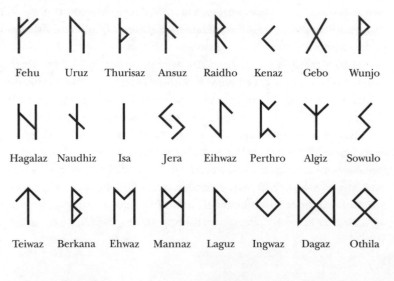

| Fehu | Uruz | Thurisaz | Ansuz | Raidho | Kenaz | Gebo | Wunjo |

| Hagalaz | Naudhiz | Isa | Jera | Eihwaz | Perthro | Algiz | Sowulo |

| Teiwaz | Berkana | Ehwaz | Mannaz | Laguz | Ingwaz | Dagaz | Othila |

people north of the Alps, however, the *Futhark*, as the alphabet is more accurately called, was Odin's inspiration and his gift to the people. As a language, the earliest runic inscriptions have been found dating to around 150 CE. As a divination tool, the Elder Futhark consists of twenty-four almost pictorial letters that can be placed on tiles or carved into wood.

These letters fall into three *ættir* (rows or groupings) of eight runes (letters), which represent the qualities or challenges of each of three realms: the human realm, which begins with the rune for wealth; the challenging underworld realm, which begins with the rune for obstacle or disaster; and the timeless upper realm, which begins with the rune that signifies the great Father God Tyr. A more modern addition of the blank rune that invites us to surrender to divine mystery brings the total number of runes to twenty-five.

Ogham (Celtic Europe)

Similar to the Futhark and following a similar time frame of usage, *Ogham* is also both an alphabet and a divination system that has roots both in historical development and mythological inspiration in the Celtic tradition. It is said to be both the gift of the god Ogma and possibly a quasi–sign language used to subversively communicate beneath the Roman gaze. Originally consisting of twenty symbols divided into four sets (*aicme*) of five letters (*fedha*), representing three sections of consonants and one of vowels, there was a later addition of an additional five diphthongs (*forfedha*), bringing the total number of letters to twenty-five.

Unlike the more representational Futhark, the Ogham letters consist of a certain number of horizontal straight lines (from one to five lines) carved in relation to a central vertical line: to the right, diagonally across, to the left, and straight across. The additional five letters are represented by more complex designs, still carved in relation to the central line. A marked feature of the Ogham that opens us to a greater understanding of the Celts is its connection with the trees. Each letter represents a tree, and if you have a sense for the qualities, particularities, and strength of the tree, you are well able to hear the divinatory message from the Ogham.

Tarot (Italy)

Though there are many theories regarding the origins of the tarot, the most solid ground we have places the origins in Milan, Italy. The oldest surviving deck, known as the Visconti-Sforza, was commissioned by Francesco Sforza, the Duke of Milan, in 1415 (a solid thousand years after the fall of the Roman Empire and our explorations of the roots of the Futhark and Ogham). The earliest archeological evidence of playing cards dates from twelfth-century China; however, it is the addition of the twenty-two trumps (major arcana cards) that is found in these Italian cards that marks the shift to the tarot as we know it today.

These cards were first used for entertainment, however, including the card game *tarocchi*. It was the Frenchman Eugene Court de Gébelin in the late eighteenth century who proposed that these cards contained esoteric wisdom, and it was his contemporary countryman Jean-Baptiste Alliette (better known as Etteilla) who popularized the tarot as a divination system. It is a testament to the influence of both these men that the tarot is still explored through both of these lenses today.

Lenormand (France)

Following the scent of the tarot from fifteenth-century Italy and eighteenth-century France, we meet another extraordinary person, Marie Anne Lenormand. A famous cartomancer and fortune-teller during the period that includes the French Revolution, Lenormand is credited with having created this divination system based on or inspired by the German card game *Das Spiel der Hoffnung* (The Game of Hope). There are two versions of the Lenormand: *Le Petit Jeu,* which consists of thirty-six cards, and *Le Grand Jeu,* which is based on a full deck of cards and has a male card and female card. Considering both versions were first published at least two years after her death in 1843, Lenormand would have been far more than merely a gifted fortune-teller had she actually been responsible for popularizing this system!

The Lenormand is an excellent approach for those looking for "cut to the chase" answers in their readings. Different from any other divination system, the Lenormand includes a wonderful, all-encompassing technique called *Le Grand Tableau,* which utilizes all thirty-six cards.

Kipper (Germany)

Right on the heels of the Lenormand and bringing the inspiration back again to Germany, we find the Kipper cards first coming on the market in the 1890s. The deck is attributed to a remarkable woman, Susanne Kipper, though there is scant tangible information to support this. There are further similarities between the Lenormand and the Kipper: both have thirty-six cards and both are more practically than symbolically focused. However, whereas the Lenormand has a preponderance of objects (such as fish, whip, clover, ring, anchor), the Kipper has a lot of people cards (Small Child, Younger Woman, Main Female, Community).

Tasseomancy (British Isles)

Typically utilizing tea, *tasseomancy* (from the French *tasse* meaning "cup" and the Greek suffix *-mancy* meaning "divination") can be performed with any type of liquid that leaves sediment, including coffee and wine. As a general rule, the preferred beverage, culturally speaking, will inform the divination approach found in a given country. Though tea-leaf reading was practiced in England, Scotland, Wales, and Ireland from the time tea was introduced in the seventeenth century, it was the nineteenth century when Victorians' passion for the approach inspired pottery manufacturers to craft specially designed cups for the purpose. These exquisite cups are marked with predetermined symbols for ease of interpretation. In contrast, the basic approach involves a plain teacup in which one reads the shapes that are formed by the sodden leaves that remain once the tea has been drunk.

Corn Divination (Mexico and the Americas)

Leaving the Victorian tearooms and braving a long voyage across the waters to the Americas, we discover yet another tradition that connects us to the Divine through the gifts of the natural world. Maize was massively important to the people of South and Central America. There are still around sixty-four different strains, and corn found its way into all areas of culture, including divination and healing. Some methods of divining with corn include the use of copal, a gorgeously scented resin used to connect one more acutely with the Divine. Recalling our experience with bone divination,

this approach has similar resonance. After passing kernels through the smoke of the copal, the kernels are tossed, and the patterns they create are interpreted to reveal the guidance or message.

Shaman Stones (Hawaii)

Coming close to the end of our global travels, we cross the waters once again to discover yet another reflection of that most ancient of divination methods: the casting of stones, or *hailona* in Hawaiian. Using one white stone as the foundation, one brings a question to one brings a question to the stones and reads the response depending on which of the remaining six stones lands closest to the white one. If the white stone represents awareness, the remaining six reflect qualities of freedom, focus, persistence, love, confidence, and flexibility.

Telesthesia (Australia)

We have traveled far. It seems there is quite a stash of stones, corn, cards, and twigs in the bottom of our hot air balloon basket. As we float once more across a great expanse of water to our final destination, we have the opportunity to let all these go and use our bodies as our means for communication with the Divine. *Telesthesia* (or *punka-punkara* as it is known in the Western Desert language of the Australian Indigenous people) is the method of interpreting physical sensations for meaning. It is a more formalized presentation of information such as the folk belief that if your palm is itchy, you will receive money, or if your ear is tingly, someone is talking about you. Tingling or throbbing in certain body parts indicates that certain members of the family are thinking of you. The body itself is the oracle, highly portable and always accessible.

· · · ☽ · · ·

As our trusty time-traveling vehicle touches down on solid ground in the twenty-first century, we do well to recall an inscription from the ancient Greek alphabet oracle:

Apollo, Lord, and Hermes, lead the way!
And thou, who wanders, this to thee we say:
Be still; enjoy the oracle's excellence,
for Phoebus Apollo has given it to us,
this Art of Divination from our ancestors.

Ultimately, the method chosen through which to communicate with the Divine matters less than the communication itself, but we are lucky indeed to live in such lush divination times.

Selected Resources

Douglas, Wilf. *Illustrated Topical Dictionary of the Western Desert Language: Based on the Ngaanyatjarra Dialect.* Perth, Australia: Edith Cowan University, 2001.

Opsopaus, John. "A Greek Alphabet Oracle." *Circle Network News* 57 (Fall 1995), 12–13. Online reproduction. Last modified November 7, 2015. http://opsopaus.com/OM/BA/GAO.html.

Mandrake or Mayapple?
Defining Magic and Failing

Thorn Mooney

The very first spell I ever did was a love spell out of a popular book for new Witches. I was freshly fourteen, I had just seen *The Craft*, and there was no time to lose. Yeah, you know those warnings in magic books that say things like "Don't skip the introduction and go straight to the spells, magic takes focus and self-knowledge, blah, blah, blah . . ."? Those warnings are there because of people like me: I am that very Witch. I mean, I was young, excitable, and anxious to get to the good stuff! Who could blame me? Don't worry—the spell didn't work. Not only did I not land the boyfriend I wanted, I also managed to set my pressboard bookcase on fire with the candle and—I swear this is true—lost my homework to the tiny blaze that ensued. I spent the next four years of high school hiding the marred furniture from my parents with a colorful sarong until it was time to move out. This was my initiation into magic.

So why didn't my spell work? And why did it malfunction so spectacularly? The rest of the book—which I eventually read cover to cover about a dozen times—cautioned me to consider several factors. Had I set my intention clearly? Was the Moon in the most conducive phase? Was it the right day of the week? Other books I would discover later in my self-training would advise me to consider the type of oil I'd used to dress the candle, the direction my altar was facing, how I cast a circle (did I?), what entities I'd invoked, the position of the planets, the hour of the day, and six hundred other minute things depending on tradition, perspective, and what the popular Witch community was into that year. There are, it turns out, an infinite number of ways to screw up a spell.

As to why I nearly burned the house down and subsequently got a D in English, adult me thinks I just needed to make better choices about where to leave burning candles (i.e., not on a middle shelf surrounded by paper). But there are plenty of magical traditions out there that would say it was retribution for being manipulative in my magic by focusing on a specific person (because of course I did). I told the story in a Wiccan chat room the week after I'd done the spell, and someone sternly suggested that I had opened some doorway and channeled too much power. Didn't I know magic was serious business?

Dauntless in the face of that first of many fires (ask my coven-mates . . . I am constantly on fire), I pursued magic more fervently, and it didn't take me long to notice something confusing: practically every book would open with some statement about how magic is everywhere and available to everyone—if only we would just learn to appreciate it—but then go on to include

complicated correspondence tables, precise instructions, unsettling warnings about consequences for messing up, and often lengthy shopping lists. Right next to warm encouragement about magic being my birthright would be admonishment that magic shouldn't be used lightly or in the place of mundane efforts. Magic was serious business, yes, but it was also just a question of changing perspective, shifting my vibes, or coming to understand the natural rhythms of the universe.

Well, which is it?

Is magic a hard-earned skill or a natural part of being human, accessible to everyone? Is it psychology repackaged—changing the world by changing our thinking—or is it the fantastical stuff we were promised as children? Does only my intention matter, or do I really need to worry about what phase the Moon is in and whether I've got real European mandrake or the false mayapple so commonly packaged and sold in its place here in the United States?

I wrestled with this conundrum for years, especially as a Witch. There are many kinds of magic in the world, and Witchcraft is widely known for being one of the more practical and accessible forms. So often the domain of the marginalized, Witchcraft didn't seem like it should require so many tools, so much book knowledge, so much additional effort on top of all the hard stuff that comes with just getting through the day to day of life.

In many spaces, this is the distinction between what is often called "high magic" and "low magic." High magic is ceremonial, bookish, and concerned with matters of the soul, the divine will, and higher consciousness. It is exacting, requires specialized training and study, and has historically been tied to the wealthy and the masculine. High magic was the realm of Elizabethan court magician John Dee, the notorious Aleister Crowley, and modern Golden Dawn luminary Israel Regardie. Witchcraft, in contrast, is a type of "low magic," in company with things that we often call "folk magic" or "spellcraft." This type of magic is immediate, practical, concerned with daily life—money, health, love, legal matters—and historically associated with country people, the poor, and women.

Was this the distinction I was wrestling with? The explanation for why magic seemed to always be presented in such conflicting ways? Was it really a simple matter of perspective?

Years and years after my first teen Witch forays, I've seen a great deal more of magic. An increasingly serious pursuit of Wicca led me to seek initiation into a Gardnerian coven. A deepening desire to explore the origins of my tradition led me to the Golden Dawn and the Ordo Templi Orientis. The demands of adulthood, the fallout of an abusive relationship, and frustration with the state of the world led me to the ruthlessly pragmatic, visceral magic of still other kinds of Witchcraft. I even learned a few close-up magic tricks along the way, just to keep things interesting at parties. Different experiences, in short, called for different kinds of magic.

Defining Magic

So what kind of magician am I? As students of magic, do we have to choose a particular model to follow? Is magic everywhere and in everything, or do we have to work at it?

You Are Allowed to Believe Conflicting Things at Once

One of the beautiful things about being a modern magician—whether you're a Witch or a ceremonialist or something in between—is that the world is full of more possibility than most other people can imagine. We know that there is more to the world than we can see, which means that where other people see walls and boxes and lines in the sand, we tend to see opportunities, loopholes, or downright illusions masquerading as fact. Just because someone says, "That's the way it is," that doesn't mean you have to accept it. As a magician, I work to know my own Will—my own purpose, divine intention, or destiny—and I

claim the power to exert that in the world. Part of that means that I can operate within different paradigms or ways of thinking at once, moving back and forth as the situation and my needs demand. So can you. The dichotomy of "high" versus "low" magic is a false one, because you can flow between them and work them at the same time, just by shifting perspective. In the same way that we are all individuals, yet all connected, multiple things may be true at once. The gods are both present and transcendent, within us and without. Water may be solid or gaseous as well as liquid. Magic is both an inborn ability that you can awaken and one that you must develop and practice.

Magic Gets Better with Practice

Like anything, magical skill can be developed. Just because something is innate and inherent in the world around us doesn't mean that we don't sometimes have to work to use it. It's true that you can work magic with minimal supplies or training (if any) and that skilled Witches and magicians know how to improvise regardless of what they have at hand, but it's equally true that the more you know and practice, the more flexible you can be. Think of it like dance or music. You don't have to be a trained musician or spend your time mastering historical waltzes in order to enjoy strumming a tune around a campfire or gettin' down at a nightclub. It's okay to enjoy something and use it to improve your life without devoting yourself to mastery. However, no one could mistake what I do on a dance floor for the Russian Ballet. Instinctive, natural ability cannot be confused with years of practice and study. Some types of magic come easily and are available to all with minimal effort. Others may require quite a bit more. No matter what path interests you, you are sure to improve as you continue to practice over time.

What You Think about Magic Will Change as You Grow

This has been the most important lesson I've learned over the years. Every time I've thought I had something totally figured out or I got too dogmatic in my approach to something, the target has moved. While it may be an interesting intellectual exercise, it's never done me a lot of good to try to pin down in concrete terms exactly how magic works. New experiences always come along to challenge my assumptions. I no longer believe in true mastery—to practice magic is to perpetually be a student, no matter how high you may rise in any given tradition and no matter how many years tick by. You can cling as hard as you like to any one model of how magic works or how it should be practiced, but growth means periodically calling those things into question and being open to changing your mind.

So when you find yourself conflicted and trying to muddle truth out of seemingly contrary ideas in books or spouted by teachers, remind yourself that magic is a difficult (maybe impossible) thing to pin down. Our traditions and histories overlap, and that exchange of ideas causes our language and perspectives to evolve from generation to generation of practitioners. Furthermore, our individual experiences create even more variation. Most of us progress in cycles rather than linearly, circling back around to old lessons, experiencing lulls, and then having epiphanies and leaping forward again. Different periods in your life will call for different types of magic, and those boundaries will probably blur as you gain experience.

Magic is more than one thing, and the skilled practitioner can sometimes change the rules. So if the spell calls for European mandrake and you find you only have access to its American imitator, all is not lost. The mayapple has just as much to offer.

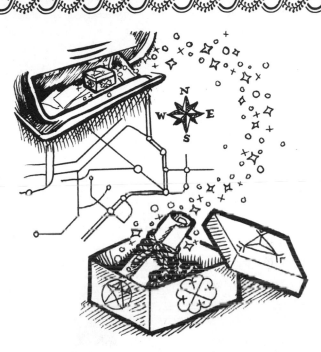

Two-Point Location Spells: Magic in Two Places at Once

Diana Rajchel

Magic doesn't multitask well. In many situations, one piece of assigned energy can do one job. But there are circumstances when you need to do two things at once or be two places at once. This is where two-point location spells come in handy. These take two pieces of paired energy, put them in separate places, and let them do their jobs through one energy always seeking its mate. While traditionally people use variations of this in love spells the most, it has a host of other applications—and can vastly expand the multitasking capabilities of spells and charms for small-scale life stuff.

"Ack, My Kid's a Driver!" Spell

Let's say you have a teenager. That teenager just got her license, and, as an enterprising young woman, she also fixed up an old jalopy to claim as her chariot. What's a terrified witchy parent to do? You can't be everywhere she is, and constantly burning protection candles in a house full of asthmatics causes other problems. Since part of raising a teenager demands you let them loose on their own (meaning you can't go with her everywhere, every living minute), you can give yourself a little peace of mind by creating a two-part charm object. It lets you send her protection—while she also enjoys a little independence.

You will need:
2 boxes or containers
Protective symbol
Markers to decorate the box
1 lodestone pair (1 receptive and 1 projective)
2 slips of paper
Pen
Red yarn

Choose two containers. Two muslin bags can work, but small boxes tend to spill fewer herbs. Decorate the boxes with related protective symbols, images, and words. You might even want to glue charms on the inside if you feel especially ambitious. Hold the lodestones in your hand, imagining a cord forming between them that expands and contracts as you pull them apart and push them together.

Place each lodestone in a separate box. Then on the slips of paper, write down an intention, sigil, spell, or keyword that you can say whenever you are worried about your young driver. Write this down on two pieces of paper. Roll them up like tiny scrolls, wrap the red yarn around each, and drop each in a respective box.

Take one of the boxes and tuck it away in the car's glove compartment. Take the other and put it somewhere safe. Whenever your teen is out with their car and you are worried, you can open your own box and speak spells of protection into it or add protective items as the situation changes and as your child gets older. You may even repeat the words on the scroll. As needs change, you can add new little scrolls (for instance, spells to find easy parking spots and ones to prevent break-ins). Dedicate each tiny scroll to only one purpose at a time; magic multitasks poorly, but the container allows multiple small spells to work together at once.

This two-point car charm is just one example of how to use this "pairing" technique, which relies on the interconnectedness of all things—the fact that everything is part of a whole. When one thing is split from the other, it calls back to that other. Think about those "best friends" lockets that break a single heart into two chains. It represents the link of friendship and a bond between two people. A witchy pair of friends might use such a locket to pass energy to each other when on long trips away. Advanced practitioners might use these lockets to send each other messages.

Pairing spells can work through energy alone but often it's easier to use two physical objects as anchors. Every use of this technique involves an energy link between two points that remains even when the objects are brought to different locations. Both objects and energies have a link between them. The simplest such link: paired lodestones. One mate calls to the other, so you can then add other items, sigils, scrolls, and so on to one lodestone, which transports energy to its partner. You can use other links: two pieces of someone's hair, a pair of magnets, or a piece of paper cut in half. The principle is that each must be a half that calls to the other half.

Two-Point Location Charm for New Love

Let's say you want to have a hot new romance but can't really stray too far from your usual haunts because of circumstances beyond your control. (If you can control those circumstances, take a chance! Love doesn't find itself!) Since you want to draw someone to you, send out an energy beacon. Make it a little stronger by giving it a place where it can draw energy to put out a continuous signal, so

this way new potential lovers can come to you. An added side benefit is that this spell can help local businesses by making your favorite
places to linger more attractive to passersby in general.

You will need:
Slip of paper
Pen
Sigil or 2-part phrase that bespeaks your intent
Love-drawing oil (optional)
Scissors
Some poster tacky

On a piece of paper, write a phrase or create a sigil that is recursive.
Examples of such a phrase are "Love, come to me; come to me,
love" and "The seeker is sought, I sought the seeker." Use something
that speaks to your heart and feels playful. Pour as much desire and
playful energy as you can into the paper. As you work, imagine your
feelings when you have your desired partner. Once the paper seems
to vibrate or glow with the power of your desire, anoint it with two

drops on each side of any love- or lust-drawing oil. You may also choose a general attraction oil if you want an added benefit to go to the business where you plant one of the halves.

Carefully cut the paper in half, down the center of the sigil or in between the two phrases. Put one slip of paper in your wallet. Put a little poster tacky on the back of the other one. Don't use chewing gum; that's just gross and cruel to people stuck cleaning it up. When you visit your hangout next, carefully affix the tacky in a hidden place—behind a picture, underneath a restaurant bench, or, if all else fails, under a window frame.

Then all you need do is keep hanging out there. You can reinforce the spell by meditating with or playing with the slip of paper that you keep in your person. Also, act in accord: brave some dating apps, and see about hosting an event at your hangout. The key to this spell is to keep showing up—eventually that other magical person will show up too.

Land of My Birth Spell

It can be a little difficult for people who work heavily with land and city spirits to get some time away from them. Some spirits need reassurance. For those that form caretaking relationships with these entities, these relationships need the same consideration given to close friends and family. Sometimes there is some suffering involved when the spirit worker travels, especially if said human forgets to inform the spirits of their leave of absence. Fortunately, there are already traditions for such situations, and here is one variation of it.

It's common for Witches to collect a little dirt from places they visit and then leave an offering behind. We use this dirt for lots of things. Phoning home, so to speak, is just one of many options.

You will need:
Trowel
Small jar

Water to pour out as an offering
2 dimes or 2 pennies

Pick an area outdoors where you really feel your connection to the land or city spirit. Explain out loud about how you're going on a trip but you don't want it to feel out of touch just because you're away. Tell it that you want to take some dirt with you so that it can call you if it needs you. Establish some boundaries around this—that you can't come back to the place right away, but you can send energy while you are preoccupied with human business. Pour the water as an offering. Place a small amount of soil in the jar. Lay one of the coins in the ground and one in the jar of soil. This is how the spirit can transmit to you, and you back to it.

Pack the jar in your bags when you travel. When you arrive at your destination, take it out and set up a small altar. Take a few minutes every day to check in with the feeling from the soil and to receive any thoughts and impressions through it. You can do small things to feed that soil as a means of nourishment. Some people might give reiki to the soil or give it a little water every day. You might feed it seeds, pennies, fertilizer, or even a little coffee. Listen to it for requests. When you return home, return the soil to its home. You have done your job in caring for it and can return to your usual interactions.

If you forget the jar, don't fret. That soil will integrate with where it was left. You can leave the coins where you dug. Eventually, grass and other plants can recycle that energy.

• • •) • • •

These are just a few examples of working with two-point location spells. There are two principles these spells operate from: either opposites attract, as in the driving protection spell; or two halves form a whole, as in the love and land spirit spells. Consider which approach best serves your purposes, and from there, enjoy covering more ground!

Organizing Group Rituals over the Internet

Ash W. Everell

For many Witches in rural areas, Witches who travel frequently, or Witches who simply usually work alone, getting together in a group with other Witches or magic practitioners can be a complicated and daunting task. For instance, in my small coven, many of our members frequently travel for work on important dates, such as sabbats and Full Moons. Organizing a group ritual via video chat or passing along our planned rituals beforehand to perform simultaneously is a great way for all of us to stay connected and perform magic as a group!

Coordinating a ritual over the internet can be a powerful tool. When you're unable to work magic within a group in person, using the internet, video chat, messaging, or social media can be an efficient way to connect and cast with other Witches.

Types of Internet Rituals

There are multiple options for conducting a group ritual with the aid of the internet, depending on how much you'd like the ritual participants to get involved. I like to categorize these ritual types as follows: group rituals, wherein ritual participants perform the ritual together, much like in real life but with the aid of video chat or instant messaging; and mass rituals, wherein ritual instructions and texts are passed around and performed simultaneously, but the participants do not directly interact with each other. The former also includes "Skyping in" or bringing a member of a group ritual to the ritual setting using FaceTime, video chat, or other modern marvels.

In this article, we'll explore both ritual types as well as the practical information needed to get started planning your own group rituals over the internet.

Group Rituals over Video Chat

If you regularly practice with a group, circle, or coven, you might
like to explore conducting rituals over video chat. That way, even
if you're scattered all over the world, you can still perform magic
as a group! Even if in real life you don't have a group you practice
magic with, video chat is a great way to engage in rituals with other
Witches you've made friends with from forums, chat servers, and
other sites around the internet.

When performing a group ritual via video chat, there are a few
basic tools you'll need. First, you'll need a phone or a computer
with a functioning webcam. Every member of your group ritual will

need to be able to communicate and be seen by the other members, so, if you've got a phone with video chat capability or a camera you can hook up to your computer or laptop, you're all set!

Second, you'll need an app or program with which to connect to your group members. FaceTime is a great idea if you're all using iPhones to connect, but I've found Skype and other similar apps to be very useful. You'll have to start a new "group chat" using the function in your app, and you'll be able to add in all your group members so everyone can see and talk to each other in real time.

Planning a Group Ritual

Once you've decided on which ritual your group is going to perform, you'll want to make plans about when and "where" you want to do it.

In order for everyone to perform a ritual over video chat, you'll need to pick an app or method with which to meet up and a time. Don't forget to add the time zone so all your coven members are on the same page! Test out your connection beforehand, and link up a few minutes before the designated ritual time so that you all can start your magic-making at the appropriate hour.

It's also important that each person holds the responsibility for creating the proper sacred space in their own, real-life space that would be conducive to magic. Instead of working together to form a circle, participants in a group ritual over video chat may like to first set up their working space by cleansing, banishing, and preparing their space on their own.

Once you've prepared your ritual space, you'll need to bring your laptop or phone into your circle before you draw it. That way, you'll ensure you're connected with your coven-mates and won't need to break your ritual state to go and grab your device or web cam. You might like to prop or place your laptop or phone directly on your altar, or, if that seems a little bit sacrilegious, you can bring in an extra folding table or bar cart on which to place your phone. Once you're all set up, proceed to draw your circle and join the group chat.

Mass Rituals

A mass ritual is a ritual conducted at a specific time by as many people as can access the ritual's text, but the Witches who perform the ritual may not even know the others are there. For instance, many Witches who use the same text for their esbat rituals as their fellow tradition-mates aren't necessarily performing a coordinated ritual en masse. However, if one tradition shares the exact text and ritual actions with their coven-mates and everyone in the coven always performs the ritual at the same time, in the same way, regardless of location or physical proximity to their fellow coven-mates (but without communicating directly with each other), this would qualify as a mass ritual.

Famously, during the Second World War, mass rituals and group rituals were both used to combine the powers of many occultists and practitioners to protect the city of London during the Blitz. During this time, the ritual used was conducted by practitioners in person after sharing information via secrecy and whispers, but nowadays, rituals can be much more easily disseminated via the internet, rather than through the grapevine.

The difference between mass rituals and group rituals is that members participating in a mass ritual may not necessarily know the others are there. The advantage to this model is that anyone can jump in and participate in a mass ritual, such as healing the earth on Litha or riding to the sabbat, no matter their path, their tradition, or whether they're a solitary or work with a group. It's infinitely scaleable, which means that one could write and coordinate a mass ritual and have its participants number in the thousands without the original author ever knowing.

Another advantage to the mass ritual model is, of course, the combined power of possibly thousands of Witches performing a ritual at the same time. Unlike the group ritual model, Witches in a mass ritual don't necessarily need to know each other beforehand, which means anyone can participate.

Plan a Mass Ritual

Mass rituals require quite a bit of prep on the initiator's part, because once the information is out there, it's up to the reader to

successfully complete it. This means that you'll need to include as much information as possible when planning your mass ritual, as it will surely attract Witches from all levels of experience, from those who can cast a circle with their eyes closed and their hands tied behind their back to Witches who've just picked up an athame for the first time.

All mass rituals start with a document: this document contains all the key information needed in order to execute the ritual. It should be clear enough that anyone can pick it up and perform the ritual at the correct time. You're going to need to be pretty specific when you write your ritual document, as you can't be certain that everyone practices the same way or assumes they'll have to cast a circle.

The following are some key elements to include in your ritual document:

Timing: Deciding on the timing of a mass ritual is key. First, you'll want to determine the best time to cast the ritual based on traditional

Witchcraft methods: What is the ritual for, and which phase of the Moon best suits it? Should the ritual rely on Moon phases, planetary hours, or different timing? When you've decided the time and date of the ritual, make a note of it, especially the time zone. Ritual participants hail from all over the world—performing a ritual at 3 a.m. UTC could have very different consequences than performing it five hours earlier at 3 a.m. EST!

Preparation and Tools: Be as specific as possible about the tools and reagents needed to perform the ritual, as well as what they're used for. Certain participants may not be able to find an acorn top to represent security, for instance, but if you explain what it's for, they can substitute the ingredient for something more accessible in their corner of the world, such as a lock or some dirt from their property.

Complete Ritual Text: Not only will you want to write out the step-by-step instructions, including circle drawing, benedictions, offerings, and any deities to be invoked, but you'll want to write down any recited texts or incantations used, word by word. Ritual is always more effective when everyone's on the same page!

After you've written up your ritual, you'll want to put it up on the internet for any interested Witches to peruse and choose to participate in. If you're reading this, you're probably already involved in a Witchcraft community, social media group, forum, or newsletter. You can post your ritual up on the internet for anyone interested to see and participate in by pasting the ritual document into a post, or perhaps create a shareable Google Doc that interested Witches can pass around the link to.

The mass ritual format could also be used by smaller groups who aren't able to connect via video chat or otherwise in real time too. Simply send the ritual text to your coven-mates via email, letter, or text message, and make magic as you're used to at the agreed-upon time!

The Benefits and Joy
of Freeform Spiritual Dance

Kerri Connor

Dance has been an expression of spirituality for thousands of years. The ancient whirling dervishes of Sufism and Turkey, Middle Eastern belly dance, and the tribal dances of indigenous peoples the world over, along with the more recent 5Rhythms and trance dance, all share a connection with spirituality.

Music is the universal language that accompanies dance. From the midnight margaritas of *Practical Magic* to the stone circle dance of the fictional Craigh na Dun of *Outlander*, Pagans are often depicted in media as having a strong connection to music. That is because music guides us to connect to one another, ourselves, and spirit. Dance engages the body, mind, and soul for a one-of-a-kind spiritual experience. Dance allows you to ascend to a higher consciousness. It transcends space and time, bringing you fully into the present. Dance is a type of meditation that plants you into the here and now. It empties the mind of distractions and worries and allows one to commune with the universe at peace.

Benefits of Freeform Spiritual Dance

While many forms of dance require a teacher and learning steps and poses, freeform is just what its name implies. Freeform spiritual dance encourages the dancer to do what feels good, to move in ways that stretch the body, mind, and spirit all at the same time. There are no set steps, moves, or patterns to learn. It is only about doing what feels right to you, the dancer.

There are great physical, emotional, and mental benefits to adding spiritual dance to your life, the most obvious being it gives you physical exercise, which helps promote good health. Adding dance to my life not only helped me subtract pounds, but it helped

tone my muscles and increased my stamina, strength, and flexibility. This in turn helps create more body positivity, and the act of exploring movements to increase pleasure also promotes body positivity.

Dance is an aerobic exercise that helps build coordination and balance, muscles, and strong bones, to fight osteoporosis. It helps loosen and lubricate joints. It helps keep our bodies young and can aid in turning back the clock to heal previous damage.

It also improves mental and emotional health as well as relieves tension and stress. By increasing the endorphins and adrenaline your body releases, it brings happiness. Adding in dance as a normal part of your spiritual practice produces long-term positive effects by improving your state of mind and overall mental health. It's hard to be miserable when you are dancing!

Dance can allow you to connect deeply to your inner self or to the outer universe—to the life force that connects us all to the

Divine. It allows you to connect to your primal life energy. It is natural. It is instinctive. Even babies old enough to stand but not yet walk instantly know that bending their knees to a rhythm feels good. It brings them joy and laughter.

Approaching Spiritual Dance

When participating in freeform spiritual dance, you can either choose to be fully present in the here and now with heightened senses, or you may choose to get lost in the moment and escape from the mundane world.

Like other forms of meditation, freeform spiritual dance is an easy aspect to add to your practice. It can literally be done any place where you have room. It can be done alone or in groups with other people. It can be done indoors or outdoors. Dance works in a multitude of locations.

You also do not need any experience. At all. I had dabbled in belly dance years ago, and while I loved it, I didn't keep with it. Life got in the way, and that was a mistake I can now remedy.

My Path to Spiritual Dance

My path to spiritual dance was an interesting, twisted one. It began in New Orleans at Mardi Gras.

While I don't live in New Orleans, I do love to visit and try to go as often as I can. A few years ago, I finally made it to my first Mardi Gras, and after a week of walking and catching beads and tons of other assorted goodies, I was in so much pain that it was obvious what terrible shape I was in. I was also at my highest weight ever. I decided then it was time to make some serious changes in my life. I was still a recovering cancer survivor, not yet considered in full remission, and I decided I'd had enough medical scares. It was time to lose weight and get into better shape.

Oddly, I found a lot of assistance from the internet. Through Facebook ads, I actually discovered options that helped me. I was highly skeptical, but what did I have to lose? I tried different meal kits—not diet programs, but ones that supplied healthy recipes and foods for you to put together and cook yourself. It gave me a whole new outlook on food, and not only did it allow me to cut down on how much I ate at one time, it also helped introduce me to new recipes and foods I had never had. I cut most meat out of my daily diet as I learned how sluggish it made me feel. I tried out a program that awards you for losing weight. It worked. I made over $900 after completing my first weight loss goal. I quadrupled my daily steps with the help of my Fitbit app and increased my daily active minutes 900 percent.

I also found Misty Tripoli of Body Groove. Body Groove is about getting a good workout by doing what works for you. It teaches very simple dance moves that are repeated throughout an entire song. Topped with Misty's fun personality and inviting ideas, I got off the couch and started moving again. Her freeform dance plan was a springboard for ideas of my own.

I began my own themed night dance-a-thons. Sometimes it was the Beatles, eighties hair bands, nineties pop—whatever I felt like dancing to that night. If it was cold or raining, I would dance in my living room or bedroom. But when it was nice outside, I would head out to my deck in the evening hours as the sun set, and the stars would come out. As I was surrounded by the trees and lightning bugs with the stars and Moon up above, it should be no surprise I eventually changed the music to a more spiritual playlist. My spiritual dance practice was born.

I lost weight and loved the way dance made me feel and the connection I felt to the universe around me. It brought a happiness and joy into my life I didn't even realize was missing. Life became far more livable and lovable. It helped me deal with negative people and situations.

Forming My Own Group

I decided I wanted to share the experience with others. If I was able to find such pleasure and feel my life change from simply dancing, maybe others could too.

My first women's spiritual Full Moon dance went better than I could have anticipated. I admit, I was nervous. There weren't any events like this in my community, so I had to start my own. (This is something we Pagans need to do more of—if something doesn't exist in your area, create it!) I thought people might think I was crazy. I thought some people (living in a highly Catholic area) might make nasty comments. I thought if other people wanted to do this, then surely someone else would have started it. I thought I had little chance of finding others that would be interested, but I knew I wouldn't find anyone without trying.

I posted an event on Facebook through my Spiral Labyrinth page and invited women to come dance under the Full Moon with me. I was very surprised at the number of women in my local area who not only responded but were just as excited about the idea as I was. I had set the cap at twenty-five and it filled up. Hundreds more had clicked the "interested" option.

Very few of those who responded knew one another. I, myself, only knew three of the women who had confirmed attendance. A few of the women brought a friend with, but for the most part, we were a group of complete strangers. We spent the first hour introducing ourselves and getting to know each other a little. As we readied to begin our dance, we stood in a circle in the middle of the labyrinth and held hands.

As the song *There Is No Time* by Kellianna played, we swayed back and forth and sang along. We then spent the next hour or so dancing to different types of music in freeform dance to a playlist I spent weeks constructing. We began at sunset. Eventually, the Moon came up in the distance and peeked through the trees. Candles, solar lighting, and glow stones helped guide our way and added to the ambiance of the evening. We had an assortment

A LITTLE BIT OF MAGIC

You don't have to take my word for it. You can turn some music on right now, wherever you are, and spend the next few minutes finding out the benefits of dance for yourself.

of handheld percussion instruments—tambourines, maracas, and rain sticks—to add to the experience. For those who wanted to wear them, coin hip scarves and veils were also available.

We talked, we danced, we drank wine. It was truly an incredible experience. A group of strangers, none of whom had ever done anything like this before, came together under the Moon and built a bond between women. While a few had dance experience and others had drum circle experience, dancing with others under the Full Moon was a first for all. The memories created that night will last a lifetime. We made the commitment to be open to one another and to share with one another as we celebrated sisterhood and our connection to the Moon.

Add Spiritual Dance to Your Practice

While dancing with a group is an incredible experience, you don't have to start there (though you can if you want!). Feel free to start simple and build your practice.

Not in great shape? Start with just a song or two. The next week add a third. Build your "repertoire" as you go. When you are starting off, you may need more flowy, ethereal music to get you going. As you become more experienced and adept, add in more drumming or tribal-type songs to get your heart pumping. Eventually, you can build a playlist that includes different music at different tempos to give you a warmup, workout, and a cooldown. Maybe you want to keep your playlist all light and flowy. Perhaps you want it all drumming.

Fit your music to what your goals are for your practice. There are no right or wrongs; it is about what suits you. Make different playlists for different occasions or atmospheres. I do different ones for each of the sabbats and another one for the Full Moons. Personalize your lists to work best for you. Services like YouTube, Spotify, Amazon Music, and Pandora are extremely helpful for finding new music. (These services are also a great way to find Pagan artists to support!)

If you decide to pursue establishing a group, be sure you have a space where people will be able to dance freely without running or bumping into each other. In the Spiral Labyrinth we have a rule: if you want to be by yourself, dance on the outskirts of the spiral. The closer to center means the more open you are to having others near you. This has worked very well for us, and it keeps people from encroaching on others who do not welcome it. Providing this border allows for everyone to have what they need to create their own sacred safe space.

In a group setting, you will also want to keep an area off to the side for dancing breaks. We used benches and camp chairs for a

seating area where dancers could take a break, enjoy the fire pit, have some water or wine, relax, and recuperate before jumping back into the spiral for another round of songs.

Whatever you do, do what works for you.

I have a more relaxed daily practice, which is more of a meditative time. For special occasions, however, I treat my spiritual dance time as more of a ritual. For a Full Moon dance, I wear a white flowy dress with white ballet flats. For a New Moon dance, I dress in black. For sabbat dances, I customize my clothing to the specific holiday. I also use slightly different playlists. While there are staple songs that can go on any of my playlists, I look for others that are specific to the sabbat, Full Moon, or New Moon too. I use candles and incense to help set the mood. You can be as simple or as elaborate as you want with your preparations and can easily customize your practice to what your needs are.

I truly hope everyone reading this gives spiritual dance a try. If dance weren't supposed to be a part of our lives, it would not produce the pleasure-giving hormones it does. It wouldn't give us joy. It wouldn't relieve stress and make us happy. It feels good and makes us happy because it *is* good.

Dance was given to us as a gift from whichever Creator you believe in. When we accept the gift and put it to use, we can connect with the Creator and the rest of the universe, as was intended.

Who's Got the Word?

Chic and S. Tabatha Cicero

Abracadabra! is the word uttered by countless stage magicians and crafty sorcerers on television and in the movies. The strangeness of the word itself is part of its appeal: it sounds like two parts gibberish and one part occult power. It may surprise some readers to learn that the word is not the by-product of some nineteenth-century snake-oil salesman from a traveling carnival show but was considered a traditional word of power dating from ancient times. The earliest known mention of the word *abracadabra* is found in a pharmacological recipe called *Liber Medicinalis* (*The Medical Book*) written by Roman physician Quintus Serenus Sammonicus in the second century CE. To cure fevers and malaria, Sammonicus suggested creating a healing amulet by writing the word several times on a piece of parchment, dropping the last letter at each new rendition until only a single letter *A* remains at the bottom of an inverted cone. This was to be tied around the neck of the patient with linen thread. The fever, like the magic word, was intended to gradually fade out and disappear.

```
ABRACADABRA
 ABRACADABR
  ABRACADAB
   ABRACADA
    ABRACAD
     ABRACA
      ABRAC
       ABRA
        ABR
         AB
          A
```

In more recent times, magician Aleister Crowley altered the spelling of this ancient word to fit his own magical system of Thelema, changing it to *abrahadabra* so that *Had* (or *Hadit*), the second deity of the Thelemic trinity, would be located at the center of the word.

Certain words have long been associated with magical power. In Eastern mysticism, mantras or sacred names and syllables are used to effect changes in consciousness. A mantra can represent a cosmic force, a deity, Buddha, God, or a specific aspect of Buddha or God. Combined with meditation, this mantra is repeated or chanted in order to clarify the mind and bring enlightenment. The best known Hindu mantra is *OM,* which signifies the ultimate reality, supreme god-consciousness, and the vibrational sound that resulted in the creation of the universe.

Western traditions have also employed words of power in magic and mysticism. Chief among these are the names of deities. The ancient Egyptians gave tremendous importance to the knowledge of names. A name was considered as much a part of an individual's being as was his body and his soul. Likewise, the name of a god was considered the god himself. In the Egyptian *Book of the Dead*, the deceased who desires a favorable verdict in the Hall of Judgment must declare to know the names of all deities he will encounter in the underworld, as well as the names of all manner of objects in the Hall itself: "Homage to thee, O Great God, thou Lord of Maāti . . . I know thee, and I know thy name, and I know the names of the two and forty gods who exist with thee in this Hall of Maāti" (Budge, 1971, 163). Today's magicians will recognize the influence of this Egyptian practice in various initiation ceremonies of the Golden Dawn, such as when the Hiereus first tells the candidate, "Thou canst not pass by me, saith the Guardian of the West, unless thou canst tell me my Name" (Regardie 2003, 152).

Royal and divine Egyptian names were often inscribed within the symbol of the cartouche or *shenu*, which represented a type of name amulet fashioned to resemble a rope, tied together at the bottom. To record a name within the magic circle of a cartouche was to ensure that the person or power behind it would live on in the afterlife.

The Papyrus of Turin contains a story of how the great goddess Isis tricked the Sun god Rê into revealing his "Secret Name" to her in order that she heal him of an affliction that she herself had covertly caused. As a result, Isis gained mastery over Rê and became "Great in Magic" (Budge 1994, xxxiii). The Egyptians believed that knowing the secret name of a deity conferred great power to the magician who knew it. Another papyrus records how the god Set attempted to trick his nephew Horus into revealing the younger god's secret name in order to gain power over him, but Horus defeated his uncle by inventing a number of absurd names.

A good many names of power were formulated for magical rites in the ancient world. Many of these made their way into magical texts and grimoires that became part of the literary corpus of Western magic. The exact origins and meanings of many such words have become lost or distorted over time. Examples of this can be readily found in a collection known as the *Greek Magical Papyri*, a series of papyrus scrolls from Greco-Roman Egypt, dating from the second century BCE to the fifth century CE. They contain a number

A LITTLE BIT OF MAGIC

The word abracadadra *has acquired new meanings and is even used as a verb for the act of creation: "Sort out the jigsaw pieces of problems, then abracadabra them into brilliant solutions."* —Linda Goodman's Star Signs

of magical spells, hymns, and rituals. Some of the most intriguing aspects of these ancient spells are what have become known to modern magicians as the Barbarous Names of Evocation. Some of these names made their way into the Golden Dawn's Bornless Ritual, a forceful invocation and technique for godform assumption. Examples include these: *AROGOGO ROBRAO SOCHOU MODORIO PHALARCHAO OOO.*

The word *barbarous* comes from the Greek term *barbaros,* which simply meant people who were foreign or did not speak Greek. Barbarous names were nonsensible words that probably sounded like "bar-bar-bar" (or "blah-blah-blah"!) to the Greeks. A number of these words are obviously based on Egyptian, Babylonian, Hebrew, Gnostic, and Arabic divine names that have become corrupted over time to the point that some of them are completely unrecognizable. However, the Greeks understood that such words had intrinsic power that could be released through controlled vibration or intonation of them.

The very strangeness of these names contributed to their cryptic mystique. They are often called *verba ignota,* or "unknown words." According to a medieval grimoire known as *The Notary Art,* unknown words are expressly intoned in their original language because they would lose their power if translated (Peterson 2001, 155–220). The power of unknown words was not thought to come from knowledge but rather their vocalization and the fervor exhibited by the magician intoning them. In the Practicus Ritual of the Golden Dawn, the student is told, "Change not the barbarous Names of Evocation, for

they are Names Divine, having in the Sacred Rites a power ineffable"
(Regardie 2003, 213).

Godnames

However, the words of power most commonly used by Western
magicians are associated with the Qabalah, particularly the divine
names assigned to the ten *sephiroth* (singular *sephirah*). These are
emanations of deity and reservoirs of divine energy on the Tree of
Life. Each successive sephirah became denser than its predecessor,
acquiring substance as energy descended into physical manifestation. Names assigned to the sephiroth are referred to as "godnames," and they are composed of various names given to God by
the ancient Hebrews: *Yah, El, YHVH, Elohim, Adonai,* and so on.

Foremost in this list is the name *YHVH* (pronounced by magicians
in Hebrew letter by letter as יהוה, "Yod Heh Vav Heh"). Known as
the tetragrammaton, or "four-lettered name," YHVH is considered a
stand-in for the highest name of the transcendent God whose true
name is unknown and unpronounceable. Such reverence is given to
the ineffable name that whenever the letters YHVH occur in the Hebrew scriptures, substitute words are used in its place, such as Elohim
or Adonai. This veneration was undoubtedly the catalyst behind the
third commandment: "Thou shalt not take the name of the Lord thy
God in vain." In the words of Christian humanist François Rabelais, "If
time would permit us to discourse of the sacred Hebrew writ, we might
find a hundred noted passages evidently showing how religiously they
observed proper names in their significance" (Rabelais 18—?, 478).
Early Christians and Gnostics were heavily influenced by the Hebrew
tradition of sacred words as shown in the Gospel of St. John: "In the
beginning was the Word, and the Word was with God, and the Word
was God" (1:1). During the Middle Ages, certain rabbis were known by
the title *Ba'alai Shem,* or "Masters of the Name," and were said to have
the ability to heal illness, cast out demons, and see the future.

YHVH, the highest divine name, is comprehensive in scope.
The letters contained in it are used to define the four basic elements in magic (fire, water, air, and earth) as well as the four Qabalistic worlds of existence that lie between the infinite Divine and
the physical realm. In magical terms, the totality of the universe is
contained in this name of power.

The power of sacred words is extended to the spiritual beings who exist between the Divine Source and the world of human beings—namely, angels and archangels. The names of most Qabalistic angels are composed of a Hebrew root word that denotes the angel's main attribute, followed by a suffix that is actually a holy godname. For example, the name of the archangel Raphael is formed from the word *raph*, meaning "heal," and the divine name *El*, which means "God," indicating that Raphael is the "healer of God." Names of other angels, such as the Shem ha-Mephoresh angel *Amemiah*, are composed of the word *auhmam*, meaning "hidden," and the godname *Yah*, which also means "God" and is sometimes equated with "Lord." By the suffixes attached to their names, such angels are understood to be holy emissaries "of God."

The Qabalah includes another tradition for creating words of power: *gematria*. This was a method for ascribing numbers to the letters of the Hebrew alphabet and for deriving hidden meanings and esoteric perspectives from the numerical value of words. Words which share the same numerical value, such as *achad* ("unity") and *ahevah* ("love") both add up to thirteen and are said to have a significant relationship to one another.

Another technique used by the Qabalists was to create sacred acronyms called *notariqons*. An expansive notariqon uses every letter in a single word to create the first letter of a word in a sentence. The first word in the book of Genesis, *berashith*, meaning "in the beginning," is a perfect example. In Hebrew it is spelled *Beth Resh Aleph Shin Yod Tau*. Every letter in berashith can be made an abbreviation of another word, yielding the sentence *Berashith Rahi Elohim Sheyequebelo Israel Torah*, which means "In the Beginning God(s) saw that Israel would accept the law."

A *contractive notariqon* uses the first letter of each word in a sentence to create a single word that is the synthesis of the entire sentence. One example of this is *agla*, which is found in the Golden Dawn's Lesser Ritual of the Pentagram. The letters of AGLA are taken from the sentence *Atah Gibor Le-Olahm Adonai*, which means "Thou art great forever, my Lord." The word *amen* spoken at the end of countless prayers is another example: it is written in Hebrew as *Aleph, Mem, Nun*, which stands for the phrase *Adonai Melekh Na'amon* or "Lord, Faithful King."

Vibration

Energized vocalization of words of power has long been an important feature of magic. One Assyrian text dating to the period of Esarhaddon (680 BCE) describes a king who prayed to the Sun god that any ritual performed by the king's enemy would fail: "May the lips of the priest's son hurry and stumble over a word" (Clodd 1921, 139). The idea in ancient times was that any mistake in the ritual formula and recitation of sacred words destroyed their power. Contemporary magicians understand that successful magic is accompanied by thoughtful preparation, fortified visualization, and energized *vibration* of sacred godnames.

All matter is vibratory energy. There is a well-established phenomenon known as harmonic resonance that shows that if one object starts to vibrate strongly enough, another object nearby will begin to vibrate or resonate with the first, if both objects share the same natural vibratory rate. Vibration is a method employed by magicians by which divine names and words of power are intoned forcefully in a strong "vibration" meant to attract the specific energies that are associated with them. The magician vibrates a godname in order to effect a harmonic resonance between deity as it exists within his or her own psychic microcosm and within the macrocosm of the greater universe. The aim is to have the magician's psyche "resonate" with the Divine. A properly performed vibration should be felt throughout the entire body and imagined to be vibrated throughout the universe. It is often accompanied by a tingling sensation in the hands or face.

Vibration Exercise: IAO

IAO (pronounced "ee-ah-oh") was the name of the supreme deity of the Gnostics. It is derived from the tetragrammaton of the Hebrew God embodied by the letters YHVH (sometimes pronounced in the ancient world as *Yahweh, Yeho,* or *Yahu*). In the Golden Dawn the letters of the name IAO are used to represent a triad of Egyptian deities Isis, Apophis, and Osiris—or the cycle of life, death, and rebirth. Hermetic magicians often vibrate the name IAO as the Western equivalent of the Eastern mantra *om.* Vibrating this name of power can bring a sense of inner peace and clarity as well as renewed energy.

Stand up straight with your feet hip width apart, parallel to each other, arms at your sides. Alternatively, you could sit upright in a straight-backed chair with your feet flat on the ground and your thighs parallel to the floor, placing your hands on top of your thighs. Close your eyes.

Begin a pattern of rhythmic breathing in which the exhalation is twice as long as the inhalation. There are no pauses between inhalation and exhalation. Inhale slowly to the count of three, and exhale slowly to the count of six.

When ready, take a deep inhale. Slowly intone each syllable of the name IAO with no pauses between them: "Eeeee—Aaahh—Ooohh." At the end of the final syllable, take another slow, deep inhale. Then vibrate the name again. Repeat this vibration ten times.

Variations

Building Energy: Start vibrating with a low note (tone) and end with a high note.

Releasing Energy: Start vibrating with a high note and end with a low note.

Modulating Force: Vibrate in one tone but start out softly. Then intone loudly, then softly again at the end.

Visualized Vibration: Bring your hands above your head, and as you vibrate "I," start with a higher note. As you vibrate "A," bring your hands slowly down to the level of your throat and deepen the note, visualizing it in your vocal chords. As you vibrate "O," bring your hands slowly down to your heart center and deepen the note, visualizing it in your diaphragm, where it spreads out to your entire body.

Silent Vibration: Start with a loud tone and gradually lower the volume until you withdraw the vibration into your mind and hear it psychically. When you want to end the silent vibration, externalize it by softly vibrating "IAO" aloud a number of times before bringing the exercise to a close.

Take note of how you feel and any insights that you may have experienced during these exercises.

Finally, divine names are not the only words that have a powerful influence—human speech has the ability to start conflicts or mend fences. Words can hurt or heal. We would all do well to remember the tremendous capacity to cause change through our words and deeds and act accordingly.

Resources

Budge, E. A. Wallis. *Egyptian Magic.* New York: Dover Publications, 1971.

———. *Legends of the Egyptian Gods.* New York: Dover Publications, 1994.

Clodd, Edward. *Magic in Names and In Other Things.* New York: E. P. Dutton & Co., 1921.

Peterson, Joseph H., ed. "Ars Notoria: The Notary Art of Solomon." In *The Lesser Key of Solomon.* York Beach, ME: Weiser, 2001.

Rabelais, François. *The Works of Rabelais, faithfully translated from the French with variorum notes, and numerous illustrations by Gustave Doré.* Nottingham: 18—?.

Regardie, Israel. *The Golden Dawn: An Account of the Teachings, Rites and Ceremonies of the Order of the Golden Dawn.* 7th ed. St. Paul, MN: Llewellyn Publications, 2003.

Color Magic

Charlie Rainbow Wolf

It's no secret that color influences us in many ways. When I worked in marketing, it was understood that yellow made people cheery and likely to spend more. Warm colors inspired urgency and created impulse purchases, while cool colors appealed to the budget-conscious shoppers. Have you ever noticed that most clearance labels are red, yellow, or orange?

Colors in your environment affect you too. Single colors and monotones might be perceived by the brain as being dull or boring, causing the mind to wander when studying or concentrating on a task. Too many colors are jarring, giving the brain too much stimulation. It's not an accident that most hospitals are decorated in fairly bland tones.

Color is taken for granted; it's expected that grass and foliage are usually green, for example. In nature, red is associated with danger. The bright red and white toadstools that permeate video games and cartoons are actually quite toxic. Yellow tells a tale of caution: the bold coloring of the poison dart frog is warning that all may not be as cute and innocent as it looks.

When you start to understand color and the way it influences you, you can start to use it in more than just a mundane way. Adding color to your magical spells can enhance their potency, from the colored candles you burn, to the food you feast on, to the ritual garb you choose to wear. Magic happens when you blend your intent with the right tools. What better tool than the colors of the rainbow?

You Are a Rainbow

I know *I'm* a rainbow—it's right there in my name! The truth is that everyone is a rainbow, because of the colors that permeate through your subtle body. This is the energy field that surrounds your physical body. You use your physical senses of sight, sound, smell, taste, and touch to communicate and experience your life. But what animates that meat suit? What brings you your emotions, your wellness, your highs and lows? That's the job of the subtle body.

It's easy to tell when your physical body is ailing. You will have physical symptoms such as a runny nose, upset stomach, cough, fever, or more. It's somewhat harder to tell when the subtle body is out of balance. This is where practices like energy healing, chakra balancing, and reiki are valuable. The physical body cannot function at its best if the subtle body is out of whack.

The Chinese have long understood this. Their word for the energy that animates you and makes you who you are is *chi*. When this energy is disrupted in any way, that is when illness or disease may occur. You've perhaps heard the old saying "as above, so below"? Well, in this case, it's the counterpart "as within, so without"!

Chakras

I can't write an article on color without giving a nod to chakras. These are the energy centers associated with the different layers of the subtle body. Each chakra influences you in a different way and each one has its own color. When you are doing energy work, you might wear the color of the chakra you are working on or surround yourself with it in some way. Eating food of the associated color is also appropriate, as is listening to music in the key that resonates with that color. Sound odd? It's not! Sound is a frequency, and so is color. They resonate either harmoniously or discordantly with each other.

Muladhara

This is the root chakra, and it is found at the base of your spine. It's an earth element, its color is red, and it is associated with your sense of smell and making sure that your basic needs are met. When it's out of balance, you will feel restless and anxious about what's happening in your life. It's easy to hold grudges and lose your cool.

When it is balanced, you'll feel happy, with no unhealthy attachments to negative habits or things from the past. When working with this chakra, utilize red and listen to or chant in the sound of C.

Svadhisthana

This is also called the sacral chakra because of its location just above your pubic bone. Its color is orange, and its element is water. It has a big influence on your moods and is aligned with your sense of taste. When this area is out of sync, you'll have a lot of nervous energy. You could become unnecessarily critical of yourself, or you'll go completely the opposite direction and act conceited and arrogant. When the sacral chakra is balanced, you know how to ask for your needs to be met in a confident but not narcissistic way. There's joy in your life and you have healthy relationships with others. When you work with this chakra, focus on orange and seek out chants in the sound of D.

Manipura

This is the solar plexus chakra, and it's located at your navel. It resonates with yellow and the note E. Its element is fire, and it's associated with the sense of sight. This is where you form your opinions and criticisms. If you have ever been bullied or even perhaps bullied someone yourself, those feelings came from this chakra. When it is imbalanced you focus that judgment on yourself and others. Apathy and frustration might take over. When it's balanced, you focus on your own development rather than scrutinizing the situations and people around you. You are able to face the future without apprehension and look forward to what new experiences are coming your way.

Anahata

This is the heart chakra, and its colors are both pink and green. Not surprising, really: pink is the color of rose quartz and many Valentine's Day hearts, but when that love is out of whack, it can turn green with envy in a hurry! Obviously, this chakra is located right in the center of your chest at heart level. This has nothing to do with the do-you-love-me-how-much-do-you-love-me-will-you-always-love-me need that comes through ego; this is pure unconditional love. Its element is air, it resonates with the note F, and it's associated with your sense of touch. If you're feeling jealous, lonely, or bitter, then your heart chakra probably needs a tweak. When this area is balanced, you will be filled with understanding and compassion, both for yourself and for others.

Vishuddha

This is the throat chakra, located (obviously) in your throat. Its color is blue, and it resonates to the note C. It governs the way that you communicate—and remember, not all communication is verbal. It's aligned with your sense of sound, and when it's out of balance, you'll know about it. Everything you say will come out the wrong way, and it will be easy for you to jump to conclusions and to misunderstand others. When it's balanced, conversation flows easily, you enjoy listening to others, and there are few misunderstandings. Surrounding yourself in blue will assist you in creating harmony around this chakra.

Ajna

This is the third-eye or brow chakra, and it is the one that is the most often misunderstood. It's associated with the color indigo and the musical note A, but more than that, it deals with dreams, premonitions, and psychic gifts. When this area is imbalanced, everything seems just plain crazy. It doesn't take much to become deluded, or believe distorted versions of the truth, and the issue here is that—because you're in the thick of things—you will totally believe you are right, no matter how outlandish your thinking becomes. When this area is balanced, you're able to remain open-minded while easily discerning between what is fantasy and what has validity.

Sahasrara

This is the crown chakra, located at the top of your head. There are many colors associated with it, but the most prominent are violet and white. It resonates with the music note B and influences your perceptions and thought process. When this area has issues, you'll feel like you don't fit in, as though you're not good enough, or perhaps you'll become vain and egotistical. Either way, everything starts to get too serious and lose its fun. Breathing, meditation, and surrounding yourself in the colors of this chakra will go a long way toward bringing you back to a place of happiness, self-acceptance, and the ability to live with appreciation.

The Colors

Now that you know what color goes with what chakra and what area of your life your chakras influence, you can start applying color to your life to bring things into harmony and to steer your destiny in the direction that you want it to take. Some of the colors below are not in the rainbow, and that's okay. Earth is brown, and you won't find brown in a color prism, but if you take green and orange, guess what color you make! Look at the colors of the rainbow as the ingredients, and then cook up what you need based on the qualities they have to offer.

Pink

Pink is a heart chakra color associated with love, friendship, and innocence. Use pink in your magic spells when you want to restore harmony between people who have fallen out. Wear pink to nurture compassion and understanding and attract new friends. Rose quartz jewelry invites pure and untainted love into your life, while burning pink candles helps heal heartache or encourage new partnerships to grow strong and true.

Red

Red is a sign of danger but also passion and courage. It's the courageous who face danger. People can be passionate in anger as well as in lust. Red adds energy, courage, and intensity to your spellwork. Wear red when you need to make a power play, and burn red candles when you want a boost of energy. Red in the bedroom can spice up your sex life, from red lingerie and bedding to aphrodisiac herbs wrapped in a red cloth placed under the bed. Just like on traffic signals, red is a wonderful color to use if you need to stop something. If you have a particularly challenging day ahead of you, wrap yourself in red energy when you do your grounding, centering, and shielding.

Orange

Orange is the color to use when you want encouragement and opportunities, when you hope to create something that's fun and festive, or when you're hoping to really stand out from the crowd. This is a very creative color, and if you need inspiration when writing your rituals or even just planning things on a mundane level, surround yourself with orange and cultivate a new mindset. It's a sacral chakra color and helps you form boundaries when it comes to your emotional connections with other people, enabling you to establish healthy relationships with those who are an asset to your well-being and to avoid attachments with those who are too challenging. Invoke orange whenever you're trying to break a habit or sever a link with something—or someone—no longer serving a purpose in your life.

Yellow

Yellow pertains to anything that deals with communication, travel, education, and day-to-day interactions. Yellow has been proven in marketing to spread optimism, so it's a good color to use when you want to do the same! Wear it and smile; it will enhance your personal

power. Essential oils from yellow flowers and fruits are said to stimulate the mind. Yellow is also used when you want to send someone off on safe travels. Tying a yellow ribbon around a tree or a pole to ensure someone's safe return from war is established in folk history and pop culture alike—who remembers Tony Orlando?

Gold

Gold is associated—as you might think—with financial gain, success, and abundance. Wearing gold jewelry or carrying something gold when doing business deals, conducting legal transactions, or working prosperity magic is said to add positive energy to the outcome. Apart from that, gold is elegant and refined and will help draw favorable attention your way.

Green

Green is one of the two heart chakra colors. Because many countries have currency notes that are green, it's also associated with prosperity and affluence. There's certainly a wealth of green in many natural settings, with it being the color of much vegetation. It's a soothing and calming color promoting peace and tranquility. Use green in spells when you want to encourage peace, abundance, and progress—and for love spells of all kinds, whether romantic, platonic, or concerning forgiveness and understanding. Nothing says "go" quite like the green light on the traffic signals!

Blue

All blues are throat chakra colors and will help you communicate efficiently. Effective communication involves listening, observing, and hearing what isn't said as well as what is vocalized. Light blue is gentle and soothing (and seen in many hospitals and schools), while bolder blue is more self-assured. The indigo shade of blue is associated with the brow chakra and psychic work. Use the lighter blues when doing cleansing work, or restoring calm and serenity after an upheaval of any sort. Use the heavier blues when you want to enhance your divination skills, open your third eye, and create a path for the truth—from all realms and realities—to be heard.

Purple

Because this is a crown chakra color, the magic that can be worked with purple is phenomenal, from elevating your own spirit so that you can step into the destiny your soul took this lifetime to live, to contacting the ascended masters, and more. It's a good color when connecting with your ancestors or seeking out the traditions of your chosen spiritual path. Shades of violet and purple are regal and royal and used when ambition and power are needed. Wear purple accessories to a business meeting when you want people to take you seriously—it is, after all, the color of the queen of England's regal robe!

Brown

I often feel brown gets a bad rap for being dull and uninteresting, but that may be because I'm an avid gardener. I love to get my hands in the brown soil or see the different colors of brown in the clay as I form it into pots and plates. There's something magical about the earth: you plant a seed, and it grows into something amazing, which then provides seeds before it dies so that the cycle of life is continued. To me, the earth is a tangible connection to the past and a promise for the future. Use brown when you want to connect with the cycle of life, honor your ancestors, or ground yourself in your workings—whether they be mundane or magical.

Black

This is a very strong color and is used in protection and banishment work. Tourmaline, obsidian, and jet are among the most protective stones I've used. Carry them with you when dealing with negative people or entering into challenging situations, or put them on your workstation. Use the dark of the Moon to banish unwanted situations from your life, and cloak your magical tools in black cloth to help them from leaking their power or absorbing unwanted energies.

Gray

This is another color that is often overlooked and labeled as bland or uninspiring, but it's another one of which I'm rather fond. I see gray as completely neutral, a clean slate, waiting for something to happen. It's where the past and the future meet in the present. It's a wonderful color to use when you're not sure what you want—when you know you need something and you're waiting for a sign to appear. It's also the color of dignity (watch how many times the Dowager Countess wears gray on *Downton Abbey*). The big stones in many rivers are gray, standing strong and secure while the weather rages over them and the river rushes around them.

White

This is the color of purity and one of the crown chakra colors. When you need to work a particular spell and haven't got the color you really need, substituting with white will work. White is a consecration color, and in many ceremonies it signifies a rite of passage, with the initiate wearing white at the start of the proceedings, and donning another color once the ritual has been performed.

Conclusion

It was Issac Newton who first discovered that if you shine a single ray of light through a prism, it breaks down into the individual colors of the rainbow. Red blends to orange, orange blends to yellow, and so on. The cycle has no beginning and no end. It can be seen in the skies after showers in the beautiful arcs of the rainbow. Color has a lot to teach us—not just about its use in magic or its influence in our daily lives, but also about harmony, unity, and how blending together individual vibrations really can create something beautiful.

2021 Almanac

The Date

The date is used in numerological calculations that govern magical rites. Below is a calendar for 2021.

JANUARY						
					1	2
3	4	5	6	7	8	9
10	11	12	13	14	15	16
17	18	19	20	21	22	23
24	25	26	27	28	29	30
31						

FEBRUARY						
1	2	3	4	5	6	
7	8	9	10	11	12	13
14	15	16	17	18	19	20
21	22	23	24	25	26	27
28						

MARCH						
1	2	3	4	5	6	
7	8	9	10	11	12	13
14	15	16	17	18	19	20
21	22	23	24	25	26	27
28	29	30	31			

APRIL						
				1	2	3
4	5	6	7	8	9	10
11	12	13	14	15	16	17
18	19	20	21	22	23	24
25	26	27	28	29	30	

MAY						
						1
2	3	4	5	6	7	8
9	10	11	12	13	14	15
16	17	18	19	20	21	22
23	24	25	26	27	28	29
30	31					

JUNE						
	1	2	3	4	5	
6	7	8	9	10	11	12
13	14	15	16	17	18	19
20	21	22	23	24	25	26
27	28	29	30			

JULY						
				1	2	3
4	5	6	7	8	9	10
11	12	13	14	15	16	17
18	19	20	21	22	23	24
25	26	27	28	29	30	31

AUGUST						
1	2	3	4	5	6	7
8	9	10	11	12	13	14
15	16	17	18	19	20	21
22	23	24	25	26	27	28
29	30	31				

SEPTEMBER						
		1	2	3	4	
5	6	7	8	9	10	11
12	13	14	15	16	17	18
19	20	21	22	23	24	25
26	27	28	29	30		

OCTOBER						
					1	2
3	4	5	6	7	8	9
10	11	12	13	14	15	16
17	18	19	20	21	22	23
24	25	26	27	28	29	30
31						

NOVEMBER						
1	2	3	4	5	6	
7	8	9	10	11	12	13
14	15	16	17	18	19	20
21	22	23	24	25	26	27
28	29	30				

DECEMBER						
		1	2	3	4	
5	6	7	8	9	10	11
12	13	14	15	16	17	18
19	20	21	22	23	24	25
26	27	28	29	30	31	

The Day

Each day is ruled by a planet that possesses specific magical influences:

MONDAY (MOON): Peace, sleep, healing, compassion, friends, psychic awareness, purification, and fertility.

TUESDAY (MARS): Passion, sex, courage, aggression, and protection.

WEDNESDAY (MERCURY): The conscious mind, study, travel, divination, and wisdom.

THURSDAY (JUPITER): Expansion, money, prosperity, and generosity.

FRIDAY (VENUS): Love, friendship, reconciliation, and beauty.

SATURDAY (SATURN): Longevity, exorcism, endings, homes, and houses.

SUNDAY (SUN): Healing, spirituality, success, strength, and protection.

The Lunar Phase

The lunar phase is important in determining the best times for magic.

THE WAXING MOON (from the New Moon to the Full) is the ideal time for magic to draw things toward you.

THE FULL MOON is the time of greatest power.

THE WANING MOON (from the Full Moon to the New) is a time for study, meditation, and little magical work (except magic designed to banish harmful energies).

The Moon's Sign

The Moon continuously "moves" through the zodiac, from Aries to Pisces. Each sign possesses its own significance.

ARIES: Good for starting things, but lacks staying power. Things occur rapidly, but quickly pass. People tend to be argumentative and assertive.

TAURUS: Things begun now last the longest, tend to increase in value, and become hard to alter. Brings out appreciation for beauty and sensory experience.

GEMINI: Things begun now are easily changed by outside influence. Time for shortcuts, communication, games, and fun.

CANCER: Stimulates emotional rapport between people. Pinpoints need, supports growth and nurturance. Tends to domestic concerns.

LEO: Draws emphasis to the self, central ideas, or institutions, away from connections with others and other emotional needs. People tend to be melodramatic.

VIRGO: Favors accomplishment of details and commands from higher up. Focuses on health, hygiene, and daily schedules.

LIBRA: Favors cooperation, social activities, beautification of surroundings, balance, and partnership.

Scorpio: Increases awareness of psychic power. Precipitates psychic crises and ends connections thoroughly. People tend to brood and become secretive.

Sagittarius: Encourages flights of imagination and confidence. This is an adventurous, philosophical, and athletic Moon sign. Favors expansion and growth.

Capricorn: Develops strong structure. Focus on traditions, responsibilities, and obligations. A good time to set boundaries and rules.

Aquarius: Rebellious energy. Time to break habits and make abrupt changes. Personal freedom and individuality is the focus.

Pisces: The focus is on dreaming, nostalgia, intuition, and psychic impressions. A good time for spiritual or philanthropic activities.

Color and Incense of the Day

The color and incense for the day are based on information from *Personal Alchemy* by Amber Wolfe, and relate to the planet that rules each day. This information can be taken into consideration along with other factors when planning works of magic or when blending magic into mundane life. Please note that the incense selections listed are not hard and fast. See page 273 for a list of color correspondences. If you cannot find or do not like the incense listed for the day, choose a similar scent that appeals to you.

Holidays and Festivals

Holidays and festivals and many cultures and nations are listed throughout the year. The exact dates of many ancient festivals are difficult to determine; prevailing data has been used.

Time Zones

The times and dates of all astrological phenomena in this almanac are based on **Eastern Standard Time (EST)**. If you live outside of the Eastern time zone, you will need to make the following adjustments:

PACIFIC STANDARD TIME: Subtract three hours.

MOUNTAIN STANDARD TIME: Subtract two hours.

CENTRAL STANDARD TIME: Subtract one hour.

ALASKA: Subtract four hours.

HAWAII: Subtract five hours.

DAYLIGHT SAVING TIME (ALL ZONES): Add one hour.

Daylight Saving Time begins at 2 am on March 14, 2021 and ends at 2 am on November 7, 2021.

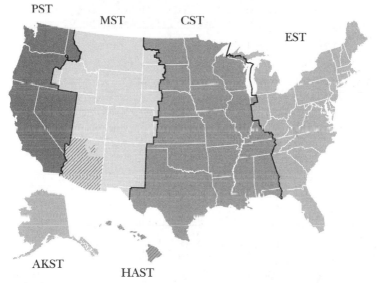

Please refer to a world time zone resource for time adjustments for locations outside the United States.

2021 Sabbats
and Full Moons

January 28	Leo Full Moon 2:16 pm
February 2	Imbolc
February 27	Virgo Full Moon 3:17 am
March 20	Ostara (Spring Equinox)
March 28	Libra Full Moon 2:48 pm
April 26	Scorpio Full Moon 11:32 pm
May 1	Beltane
May 26	Sagittarius Full Moon 7:14 am
June 20	Midsummer (Summer Solstice)
June 24	Capricorn Full Moon 2:40 pm
July 23	Aquarius Full Moon 10:37 pm
August 1	Lammas
August 22	Aquarius Full Moon 8:02 am
September 20	Pisces Full Moon 7:55 pm
September 22	Mabon (Fall Equinox)
October 20	Aries Full Moon 10:57 am
October 31	Samhain
November 19	Taurus Full Moon 3:57 am
December 21	Yule (Winter Solstice)
December 18	Gemini Full Moon 11:36 pm

All times are Eastern Standard Time (EST)
or Eastern Daylight Time (EDT)

2021 Sabbats in the Southern Hemisphere

Because Earth's Northern and Southern Hemispheres experience opposite seasons at any given time, the season-based sabbats listed on the previous page and in this almanac section are not correct for those residing south of the equator. Listed here are the Southern Hemisphere sabbat dates for 2021:

February 2	Lammas
March 20	Mabon (Fall Equinox)
May 1	Samhain
June 20	Yule (Winter Solstice)
August 1	Imbolc
September 22	Ostara (Spring Equinox)
November 1	Beltane
December 21	Midsummer (Summer Solstice)

Birthstone Poetry

Birthstone poetry in the monthly calendar
reprinted from
The Occult and Curative Powers of Precious Stones
by William T. Fernie, M.D.
Harper & Row (1981)

Originally printed in 1907 as
*Precious Stones: For Curative Wear; and Other Remedial Uses;
Likewise the Nobler Metals*

January

1 Friday
New Year's Day • Kwanzaa ends
Waning Moon
Moon phase: Third Quarter
Color: Rose

Moon Sign: Leo
Incense: Vanilla

2 Saturday
First Writing Day (Japanese)
Waning Moon
Moon phase: Third Quarter
Color: Indigo

Moon Sign: Leo
Moon enters Virgo 8:13 pm
Incense: Ivy

3 Sunday
St. Genevieve's Day
Waning Moon
Moon phase: Third Quarter
Color: Amber

Moon Sign: Virgo
Incense: Heliotrope

4 Monday
Kamakura Workers' Festival (Japanese)
Waning Moon
Moon phase: Third Quarter
Color: White

Moon Sign: Virgo
Incense: Hyssop

5 Tuesday
Bird Day
Waning Moon
Moon phase: Third Quarter
Color: Gray

Moon Sign: Virgo
Moon enters Libra 12:42 am
Incense: Geranium

◐ Wednesday
Epiphany
Waning Moon
Fourth Quarter 4:37 am
Color: Brown

Moon Sign: Libra
Incense: Honeysuckle

7 Thursday
Tricolor Day (Italian)
Waning Moon
Moon phase: Fourth Quarter
Color: Green

Moon Sign: Libra
Moon enters Scorpio 3:53 am
Incense: Clove

January

8 Friday
Midwives' Day (Bulgarian)
Waning Moon
Moon phase: Fourth Quarter
Color: Rose

Moon Sign: Scorpio
Incense: Orchid

---

9 Saturday
Feast of the Black Nazarene (Filipino)
Waning Moon
Moon phase: Fourth Quarter
Color: Blue

Moon Sign: Scorpio
Moon enters Sagittarius 6:15 am
Incense: Patchouli

---

10 Sunday
Feast of St. Leonie Aviat
Waning Moon
Moon phase: Fourth Quarter
Color: Yellow

Moon Sign: Sagittarius
Incense: Frankincense

---

11 Monday
Carmentalia (Roman)
Waning Moon
Moon phase: Fourth Quarter
Color: Lavender

Moon Sign: Sagittarius
Moon enters Capricorn 8:30 am
Incense: Neroli

---

12 Tuesday
Revolution Day (Tanzanian)
Waning Moon
Moon phase: Fourth Quarter
Color: Maroon

Moon Sign: Capricorn
Incense: Cinnamon

🌑 Wednesday
Twentieth Day (Norwegian)
Waning Moon
New Moon 12:00 am
Color: White

Moon Sign: Capricorn
Moon enters Aquarius 11:44 am
Incense: Lilac

---

14 Thursday
Feast of the Ass (French)
Waxing Moon
Moon phase: First Quarter
Color: Turquoise

Moon Sign: Aquarius
Incense: Apricot

January

15 Friday
Korean Alphabet Day
Waxing Moon
Moon phase: First Quarter
Color: Coral

Moon Sign: Aquarius
Moon enters Pisces 5:17 pm
Incense: Rose

---

16 Saturday
Teachers' Day (Thai)
Waxing Moon
Moon phase: First Quarter
Color: Gray

Moon Sign: Pisces
Incense: Sage

---

17 Sunday
St. Anthony's Day (Mexican)
Waxing Moon
Moon phase: First Quarter
Color: Orange

Moon Sign: Pisces
Incense: Hyacinth

---

18 Monday
Martin Luther King Jr. Day
Waxing Moon
Moon phase: First Quarter
Color: Ivory

Moon Sign: Pisces
Moon enters Aries 2:07 am
Incense: Clary sage

---

19 Tuesday
Edgar Allan Poe's birthday
Waxing Moon
Moon phase: First Quarter
Color: Black

Moon Sign: Aries
Sun enters Aquarius 3:40 pm
Incense: Ylang-ylang

☽ Wednesday
Vogel Gryff (Swiss)
Waxing Moon
Second Quarter 4:02 pm
Color: Topaz

Moon Sign: Aries
Moon enters Taurus 1:56 pm
Incense: Marjoram

---

21 Thursday
St. Agnes's Day
Waxing Moon
Moon phase: Second Quarter
Color: Purple

Moon Sign: Taurus
Incense: Jasmine

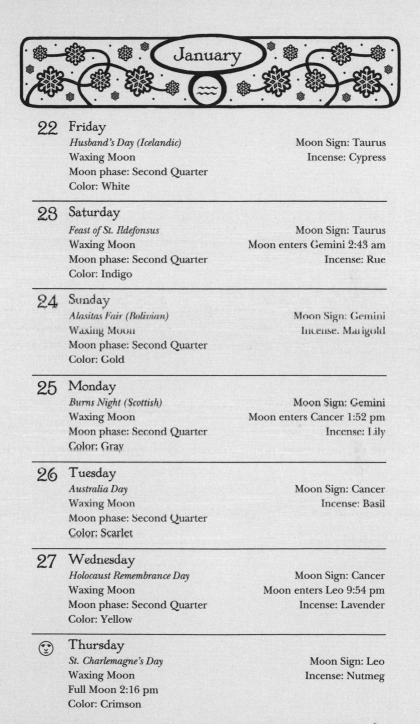

January

22 Friday
Husband's Day (Icelandic)
Waxing Moon
Moon phase: Second Quarter
Color: White

Moon Sign: Taurus
Incense: Cypress

---

23 Saturday
Feast of St. Ildefonsus
Waxing Moon
Moon phase: Second Quarter
Color: Indigo

Moon Sign: Taurus
Moon enters Gemini 2:43 am
Incense: Rue

---

24 Sunday
Alasitas Fair (Bolivian)
Waxing Moon
Moon phase: Second Quarter
Color: Gold

Moon Sign: Gemini
Incense: Marigold

---

25 Monday
Burns Night (Scottish)
Waxing Moon
Moon phase: Second Quarter
Color: Gray

Moon Sign: Gemini
Moon enters Cancer 1:52 pm
Incense: Lily

---

26 Tuesday
Australia Day
Waxing Moon
Moon phase: Second Quarter
Color: Scarlet

Moon Sign: Cancer
Incense: Basil

---

27 Wednesday
Holocaust Remembrance Day
Waxing Moon
Moon phase: Second Quarter
Color: Yellow

Moon Sign: Cancer
Moon enters Leo 9:54 pm
Incense: Lavender

☺ Thursday
St. Charlemagne's Day
Waxing Moon
Full Moon 2:16 pm
Color: Crimson

Moon Sign: Leo
Incense: Nutmeg

January

29 Friday
Feast of St. Gildas
Waning Moon
Moon phase: Third Quarter
Color: Purple

Moon Sign: Leo
Incense: Yarrow

30 Saturday
Gasparilla Pirate Festival (Floridian)
Waning Moon
Moon phase: Third Quarter
Color: Blue

Moon Sign: Leo
Moon enters Virgo 3:02 am
Incense: Magnolia

31 Sunday
Independence Day (Nauru)
Waning Moon
Moon phase: Third Quarter
Color: Yellow

Moon Sign: Virgo
Incense: Almond

January Birthstones

By her in January born
No gem save Garnets should be worn;
They will ensure her constancy,
True friendship, and fidelity.

Modern: Garnet   Zodiac (Capricorn): Ruby

February Birthstones

The February-born shall find
Sincerity, and peace of mind,
Freedom from passion and from care,
If they the Amethyst will wear.

Modern: Amethyst   Zodiac (Aquarius): Garnet

February

1 **Monday**
St. Brigid's Day (Irish)
Waning Moon
Moon phase: Third Quarter
Color: Silver

Moon Sign: Virgo
Moon enters Libra 6:25 am
Incense: Rosemary

2 **Tuesday**
Imbolc • Groundhog Day
Waning Moon
Moon phase: Third Quarter
Color: Red

Moon Sign: Libra
Incense: Ginger

3 **Wednesday**
St. Blaise's Day
Waning Moon
Moon phase: Third Quarter
Color: Topaz

Moon Sign: Libra
Moon enters Scorpio 9:15 am
Incense: Bay laurel

○ **Thursday**
Independence Day (Sri Lankan)
Waning Moon
Fourth Quarter 12:37 pm
Color: White

Moon Sign: Scorpio
Incense: Balsam

5 **Friday**
Constitution Day (Mexican)
Waning Moon
Moon phase: Fourth Quarter
Color: Coral

Moon Sign: Scorpio
Moon enters Sagittarius 12:16 pm
Incense: Thyme

6 **Saturday**
Bob Marley's birthday (Jamaican)
Waning Moon
Moon phase: Fourth Quarter
Color: Brown

Moon Sign: Sagittarius
Incense: Sandalwood

7 **Sunday**
Feast of St. Richard the Pilgrim
Waning Moon
Moon phase: Fourth Quarter
Color: Orange

Moon Sign: Sagittarius
Moon enters Capricorn 3:52 pm
Incense: Juniper

February

8 Monday
Prešeren Day (Slovenian)
Waning Moon
Moon phase: Fourth Quarter
Color: Ivory

Moon Sign: Capricorn
Incense: Narcissus

9 Tuesday
St. Maron's Day (Lebanese)
Waning Moon
Moon phase: Fourth Quarter
Color: White

Moon Sign: Capricorn
Moon enters Aquarius 8:20 pm
Incense: Bayberry

10 Wednesday
Feast of St. Scholastica
Waning Moon
Moon phase: Fourth Quarter
Color: Brown

Moon Sign: Aquarius
Incense: Lilac

☽ Thursday
National Foundation Day (Japanese)
Waning Moon
New Moon 2:06 pm
Color: Purple

Moon Sign: Aquarius
Incense: Myrrh

12 Friday
Lunar New Year (Ox)
Waxing Moon
Moon phase: First Quarter
Color: Rose

Moon Sign: Aquarius
Moon enters Pisces 2:23 am
Incense: Alder

13 Saturday
Parentalia
Waxing Moon
Moon phase: First Quarter
Color: Gray

Moon Sign: Pisces
Incense: Pine

14 Sunday
Valentine's Day
Waxing Moon
Moon phase: First Quarter
Color: Gold

Moon Sign: Pisces
Moon enters Aries 10:54 am
Incense: Eucalyptus

February

15 Monday
Presidents' Day
Waxing Moon
Moon phase: First Quarter
Color: Lavender

Moon Sign: Aries
Incense: Clary sage

---

16 Tuesday
Mardi Gras (Fat Tuesday)
Waxing Moon
Moon phase: First Quarter
Color: Scarlet

Moon Sign: Aries
Moon enters Taurus 10:12 pm
Incense: Cedar

---

17 Wednesday
Ash Wednesday
Waxing Moon
Moon phase: First Quarter
Color: White

Moon Sign: Taurus
Incense: Lavender

---

18 Thursday
St. Bernadette's Third Vision
Waxing Moon
Moon phase: First Quarter
Color: Green

Moon Sign: Taurus
Sun enters Pisces 5:44 am
Incense: Carnation

☾ Friday
Flag Day (Turkmenian)
Waxing Moon
Second Quarter 1:47 pm
Color: Pink

Moon Sign: Taurus
Moon enters Gemini 11:04 am
Incense: Mint

---

20 Saturday
World Day of Social Justice
Waxing Moon
Moon phase: Second Quarter
Color: Indigo

Moon Sign: Gemini
Incense: Rue

---

21 Sunday
Feralia (Roman)
Waxing Moon
Moon phase: Second Quarter
Color: Amber

Moon Sign: Gemini
Moon enters Cancer 10:53 pm
Incense: Marigold

22 Monday

Caristia (Roman)
Waxing Moon
Moon phase: Second Quarter
Color: White

Moon Sign: Cancer
Incense: Hyssop

23 Tuesday

Mashramani Festival (Guyana)
Waxing Moon
Moon phase: Second Quarter
Color: Maroon

Moon Sign: Cancer
Incense: Basil

24 Wednesday

Regifugium (Roman)
Waxing Moon
Moon phase: Second Quarter
Color: Brown

Moon Sign: Cancer
Moon enters Leo 7:23 am
Incense: Honeysuckle

25 Thursday

St. Walburga's Day (German)
Waxing Moon
Moon phase: Second Quarter
Color: Turquoise

Moon Sign: Leo
Incense: Mulberry

26 Friday

Purim begins at sundown
Waxing Moon
Moon phase: Second Quarter
Color: Purple

Moon Sign: Leo
Moon enters Virgo 12:07 pm
Incense: Violet

Saturday

Independence Day (Dominican)
Waxing Moon
Full Moon 3:17 am
Color: Blue

Moon Sign: Virgo
Incense: Ivy

28 Sunday

Kalevala Day (Finnish)
Waning Moon
Moon phase: Third Quarter
Color: Yellow

Moon Sign: Virgo
Moon enters Libra 2:17 pm
Incense: Heliotrope

March

1 **Monday**
Matronalia (Roman)   Moon Sign: Libra
Waning Moon   Incense: Lily
Moon phase: Third Quarter
Color: Gray

---

2 **Tuesday**
Read Across America Day   Moon Sign: Libra
Waning Moon   Moon enters Scorpio 3:38 pm
Moon phase: Third Quarter   Incense: Cinnamon
Color: Scarlet

---

3 **Wednesday**
Doll Festival (Japanese)   Moon Sign: Scorpio
Waning Moon   Incense: Marjoram
Moon phase: Third Quarter
Color: Yellow

---

4 **Thursday**
St. Casimir's Fair (Polish and Lithuanian)   Moon Sign: Scorpio
Waning Moon   Moon enters Sagittarius 5:43 pm
Moon phase: Third Quarter   Incense: Jasmine
Color: Crimson

◑ **Friday**
Navigium Isidis Festival (Roman)   Moon Sign: Sagittarius
Waning Moon   Incense: Yarrow
Fourth Quarter 8:30 pm
Color: Purple

---

6 **Saturday**
Alamo Day (Texas)   Moon Sign: Sagittarius
Waning Moon   Moon enters Capricorn 9:20 pm
Moon phase: Fourth Quarter   Incense: Magnolia
Color: Black

---

7 **Sunday**
Vejovis Festival (Roman)   Moon Sign: Capricorn
Waning Moon   Incense: Almond
Moon phase: Fourth Quarter
Color: Gold

8 Monday
International Women's Day
Waning Moon
Moon phase: Fourth Quarter
Color: White

Moon Sign: Capricorn
Incense: Rosemary

9 Tuesday
Teachers' Day (Lebanese)
Waning Moon
Moon phase: Fourth Quarter
Color: Red

Moon Sign: Capricorn
Moon enters Aquarius 2:41 am
Incense: Cedar

10 Wednesday
Tibet Uprising Day
Waning Moon
Moon phase: Fourth Quarter
Color: Brown

Moon Sign: Aquarius
Incense: Lilac

11 Thursday
Maha Shivaratri
Waning Moon
Moon phase: Fourth Quarter
Color: Green

Moon Sign: Aquarius
Moon enters Pisces 9:44 am
Incense: Myrrh

12 Friday
Girl Scouts' birthday
Waning Moon
Moon phase: Fourth Quarter
Color: Pink

Moon Sign: Pisces
Incense: Orchid

Saturday
Feast of St. Leander of Seville
Waning Moon
New Moon 5:21 am
Color: Blue

Moon Sign: Pisces
Moon enters Aries 6:44 pm
Incense: Patchouli

14 Sunday
Blue Dragon Festival (Chinese)
Waxing Moon
Moon phase: First Quarter
Color: Yellow

Moon Sign: Aries
Incense: Frankincense
Daylight Saving Time begins at 2 am

15 Monday

Fertility Festival (Japanese)
Waxing Moon
Moon phase: First Quarter
Color: Silver

Moon Sign: Aries
Incense: Neroli

16 Tuesday

St. Urho's Day (Finnish-American)
Waxing Moon
Moon phase: First Quarter
Color: Maroon

Moon Sign: Aries
Moon enters Taurus 6:56 am
Incense: Ginger

17 Wednesday

St. Patrick's Day
Waxing Moon
Moon phase: First Quarter
Color: Topaz

Moon Sign: Taurus
Incense: Honeysuckle

18 Thursday

Sheila's Day (Irish)
Waxing Moon
Moon phase: First Quarter
Color: Turquoise

Moon Sign: Taurus
Moon enters Gemini 7:47 pm
Incense: Clove

19 Friday

Denver March Powwow (ends Mar. 21)
Waxing Moon
Moon phase: First Quarter
Color: Coral

Moon Sign: Gemini
Incense: Alder

20 Saturday

Ostara • Spring Equinox
Waxing Moon
Moon phase: First Quarter
Color: Brown

Moon Sign: Gemini
Sun enters Aries 5:37 am
Incense: Sandalwood

☽ Sunday

Juarez Day (Mexican)
Waxing Moon
Second Quarter 10:40 am
Color: Orange

Moon Sign: Gemini
Moon enters Cancer 8:18 am
Incense: Juniper

March

22 Monday
World Water Day
Waxing Moon
Moon phase: Second Quarter
Color: Lavender

Moon Sign: Cancer
Incense: Narcissus

23 Tuesday
Pakistan Day
Waxing Moon
Moon phase: Second Quarter
Color: Gray

Moon Sign: Cancer
Moon enters Leo 5:56 pm
Incense: Geranium

24 Wednesday
Day of Blood (Roman)
Waxing Moon
Moon phase: Second Quarter
Color: White

Moon Sign: Leo
Incense: Lavender

25 Thursday
Tolkien Reading Day
Waxing Moon
Moon phase: Second Quarter
Color: Purple

Moon Sign: Leo
Moon enters Virgo 11:25 pm
Incense: Carnation

26 Friday
Prince Kuhio Day (Hawaiian)
Waxing Moon
Moon phase: Second Quarter
Color: Rose

Moon Sign: Virgo
Incense: Cypress

27 Saturday
Passover begins at sundown
Waxing Moon
Moon phase: Second Quarter
Color: Indigo

Moon Sign: Virgo
Incense: Sage

Sunday
Palm Sunday
Waxing Moon
Full Moon 2:48 pm
Color: Amber

Moon Sign: Virgo
Moon enters Libra 1:22 am
Incense: Hyacinth

March

29 Monday
Feast of St. Eustace of Luxeuil
Waning Moon
Moon phase: Third Quarter
Color: Ivory

Moon Sign: Libra
Incense: Hyssop

30 Tuesday
Seward's Day (Alaskan)
Waning Moon
Moon phase: Third Quarter
Color: Black

Moon Sign: Libra
Moon enters Scorpio 1:33 am
Incense: Ylang-ylang

31 Wednesday
César Chávez Day
Waning Moon
Moon phase: Third Quarter
Color: Gray

Moon Sign: Scorpio
Incense: Bay laurel

March Birthstones

Who in this world of ours, her eyes
In March first opens, shall be wise.
In days of peril, firm and brave,
And wear a Bloodstone to her grave.

Modern: Aquamarine
Zodiac (Pisces): Amethyst

April

1 Thursday

All Fools' Day • April Fools' Day
Waning Moon
Moon phase: Third Quarter
Color: Green

Moon Sign: Scorpio
Moon enters Sagitarrius 1:59 am
Incense: Nutmeg

2 Friday

Good Friday
Waning Moon
Moon phase: Third Quarter
Color: White

Moon Sign: Sagittarius
Incense: Vanilla

3 Saturday

Passover ends
Waning Moon
Moon phase: Third Quarter
Color: Black

Moon Sign: Sagittarius
Moon enters Capricorn 4:13 am
Incense: Pine

☽ 4 Sunday

Easter • Tomb-Sweeping Day (Chinese)
Waning Moon
Fourth Quarter 6:02 am
Color: Amber

Moon Sign: Capricorn
Incense: Eucalyptus

5 Monday

Children's Day (Palestinian)
Waning Moon
Moon phase: Fourth Quarter
Color: Silver

Moon Sign: Capricorn
Moon enters Aquarius 9:04 am
Incense: Rosemary

6 Tuesday

Tartan Day
Waning Moon
Moon phase: Fourth Quarter
Color: Maroon

Moon Sign: Aquarius
Incense: Bayberry

7 Wednesday

Motherhood and Beauty Day (Armenian)
Waning Moon
Moon phase: Fourth Quarter
Color: White

Moon Sign: Aquarius
Moon enters Pisces 4:30 pm
Incense: Marjoram

8 Thursday
Buddha's birthday
Waning Moon
Moon phase: Fourth Quarter
Color: Crimson

Moon Sign: Pisces
Incense: Jasmine

---

9 Friday
Valor Day (Filipino)
Waning Moon
Moon phase: Fourth Quarter
Color: Rose

Moon Sign: Pisces
Incense: Violet

---

10 Saturday
Siblings Day
Waning Moon
Moon phase: Fourth Quarter
Color: Blue

Moon Sign: Pisces
Moon enters Aries 2:11 am
Incense: Magnolia

Sunday
Juan Santamaria Day (Costa Rican)
Waning Moon
New Moon 10:31 pm
Color: Yellow

Moon Sign: Aries
Incense: Almond

---

12 Monday
Ramadan begins at sundown
Waxing Moon
Moon phase: First Quarter
Color: Gray

Moon Sign: Aries
Moon enters Taurus 1:44 pm
Incense: Clary sage

---

13 Tuesday
Thai New Year (ends April 15)
Waxing Moon
Moon phase: First Quarter
Color: Red

Moon Sign: Taurus
Incense: Cinnamon

---

14 Wednesday
Black Day (South Korean)
Waxing Moon
Moon phase: First Quarter
Color: Topaz

Moon Sign: Taurus
Incense: Lilac

April

15 Thursday
Fordicidia (Roman)
Waxing Moon
Moon phase: First Quarter
Color: Turquoise

Moon Sign: Taurus
Moon enters Gemini 2:35 am
Incense: Apricot

16 Friday
World Voice Day
Waxing Moon
Moon phase: First Quarter
Color: Purple

Moon Sign: Gemini
Incense: Thyme

17 Saturday
Yayoi Matsuri (Japanese)
Waxing Moon
Moon phase: First Quarter
Color: Brown

Moon Sign: Gemini
Moon enters Cancer 3:25 pm
Incense: Sage

18 Sunday
International Day for Monuments and Sites
Waxing Moon
Moon phase: First Quarter
Color: Orange

Moon Sign: Cancer
Incense: Hyacinth

19 Monday
Sechseläuten (Swiss)
Waxing Moon
Moon phase: First Quarter
Color: White

Moon Sign: Cancer
Sun enters Taurus 4:33 pm
Incense: Lily

◖ Tuesday
Drum Festival (Japanese)
Waxing Moon
Second Quarter 2:59 am
Color: Black

Moon Sign: Cancer
Moon enters Leo 2:11 am
Incense: Ginger

21 Wednesday
Tiradentes Day (Brazilian)
Waxing Moon
Moon phase: Second Quarter
Color: Yellow

Moon Sign: Leo
Incense: Honeysuckle

April

22 Thursday
Earth Day
Waxing Moon
Moon phase: Second Quarter
Color: Purple

Moon Sign: Leo
Moon enters Virgo 9:08 am
Incense: Balsam

23 Friday
St. George's Day (English)
Waxing Moon
Moon phase: Second Quarter
Color: Coral

Moon Sign: Virgo
Incense: Rose

24 Saturday
St. Mark's Eve
Waxing Moon
Moon phase: Second Quarter
Color: Indigo

Moon Sign: Virgo
Moon enters Libra 12:06 pm
Incense: Ivy

25 Sunday
Robigalia (Roman)
Waxing Moon
Moon phase: Second Quarter
Color: Gold

Moon Sign: Libra
Incense: Frankincense

☺ Monday
Chernobyl Remembrance Day (Belarusian)
Waxing Moon
Full Moon 11:32 pm
Color: Ivory

Moon Sign: Libra
Moon enters Scorpio 12:18 pm
Incense: Narcissus

27 Tuesday
Freedom Day (South African)
Waning Moon
Moon phase: Third Quarter
Color: Scarlet

Moon Sign: Scorpio
Incense: Ylang-ylang

28 Wednesday
Floralia (Roman)
Waning Moon
Moon phase: Third Quarter
Color: Brown

Moon Sign: Scorpio
Moon enters Sagittarius 11:42 am
Incense: Lavender

April

29 Thursday

Showa Day (Japanese)
Waning Moon
Moon phase: Third Quarter
Color: White

Moon Sign: Sagittarius
Incense: Mulberry

---

30 Friday

Orthodox Good Friday • Arbor Day
Waning Moon
Moon phase: Third Quarter
Color: Pink

Moon Sign: Sagittarius
Moon enters Capricorn 12:16 pm
Incense: Mint

April Birthstones

She who from April dates her years,
Diamonds shall wear, lest bitter tears
For vain repentance flow; this stone
Emblem for innocence is known.

Modern: Diamond
Zodiac (Aries): Bloodstone

May

1 Saturday
Beltane • May Day
Waning Moon
Moon phase: Third Quarter
Color: Blue

Moon Sign: Capricorn
Incense: Sandalwood

2 Sunday
Orthodox Easter
Waning Moon
Moon phase: Third Quarter
Color: Yellow

Moon Sign: Capricorn
Moon enters Aquarius 3:31 pm
Incense: Eucalyptus

3 Monday
Roodmas
Waning Moon
Fourth Quarter 3:50 pm
Color: Lavender

Moon Sign: Aquarius
Incense: Neroli

4 Tuesday
Teacher Appreciation Day
Waning Moon
Moon phase: Fourth Quarter
Color: Red

Moon Sign: Aquarius
Moon enters Pisces 10:09 pm
Incense: Basil

5 Wednesday
Cinco de Mayo (Mexican)
Waning Moon
Moon phase: Fourth Quarter
Color: Topaz

Moon Sign: Pisces
Incense: Marjoram

6 Thursday
Martyrs' Day (Lebanese and Syrian)
Waning Moon
Moon phase: Fourth Quarter
Color: Purple

Moon Sign: Pisces
Incense: Nutmeg

7 Friday
Pilgrimage of St. Nicholas (Italian)
Waning Moon
Moon phase: Fourth Quarter
Color: Rose

Moon Sign: Pisces
Moon enters Aries 7:52 am
Incense: Orchid

May

8 Saturday
White Lotus Day (Theosophical)
Waning Moon
Moon phase: Fourth Quarter
Color: Gray

Moon Sign: Aries
Incense: Patchouli

---

9 Sunday
Mother's Day
Waning Moon
Moon phase: Fourth Quarter
Color: Gold

Moon Sign: Aries
Moon enters Taurus 7:46 pm
Incense: Marigold

---

10 Monday
Independence Day (Romanian)
Waning Moon
Moon phase: Fourth Quarter
Color: Silver

Moon Sign: Taurus
Incense: Rosemary

---

11 Tuesday
Ramadan ends
Waning Moon
New Moon 3:00 pm
Color: White

Moon Sign: Taurus
Incense: Cedar

---

12 Wednesday
Florence Nightingale's birthday
Waxing Moon
Moon phase: First Quarter
Color: Brown

Moon Sign: Taurus
Moon enters Gemini 8:43 am
Incense: Lavender

---

13 Thursday
Pilgrimage to Fátima (Portuguese)
Waxing Moon
Moon phase: First Quarter
Color: Green

Moon Sign: Gemini
Incense: Myrrh

---

14 Friday
Carabao Festival (Spanish)
Waxing Moon
Moon phase: First Quarter
Color: Pink

Moon Sign: Gemini
Moon enters Cancer 9:30 pm
Incense: Cypress

May

15 Saturday

Festival of St. Dymphna
Waxing Moon
Moon phase: First Quarter
Color: Gray

Moon Sign: Cancer
Incense: Sage

16 Sunday

Shavuot begins at sundown
Waxing Moon
Moon phase: First Quarter
Color: Orange

Moon Sign: Cancer
Incense: Almond

17 Monday

Norwegian Constitution Day
Waxing Moon
Moon phase: First Quarter
Color: Lavender

Moon Sign: Cancer
Moon enters Leo 8:44 am
Incense: Lily

18 Tuesday

Battle of Las Piedras Day (Uruguayan)
Waxing Moon
Moon phase: First Quarter
Color: Maroon

Moon Sign: Leo
Incense: Geranium

◐ Wednesday

Mother's Day (Kyrgyzstani)
Waxing Moon
Second Quarter 3:13 pm
Color: Yellow

Moon Sign: Leo
Moon enters Virgo 4:59 pm
Incense: Bay laurel

20 Thursday

Feast of St. Aurea of Ostia
Waxing Moon
Moon phase: Second Quarter
Color: White

Moon Sign: Virgo
Sun enters Gemini 3:37 pm
Incense: Mulberry

21 Friday

Navy Day (Chilean)
Waxing Moon
Moon phase: Second Quarter
Color: Coral

Moon Sign: Virgo
Moon enters Libra 9:35 pm
Incense: Violet

May

22 Saturday
Harvey Milk Day (Californian)
Waxing Moon
Moon phase: Second Quarter
Color: Black

Moon Sign: Libra
Incense: Rue

23 Sunday
Tubilustrium (Roman)
Waxing Moon
Moon phase: Second Quarter
Color: Gold

Moon Sign: Libra
Moon enters Scorpio 11:00 pm
Incense: Juniper

24 Monday
Victoria Day (Canadian)
Waxing Moon
Moon phase: Second Quarter
Color: Gray

Moon Sign: Scorpio
Incense: Hyssop

25 Tuesday
Missing Children's Day
Waxing Moon
Moon phase: Second Quarter
Color: Scarlet

Moon Sign: Scorpio
Moon enters Sagittarius 10:39 pm
Incense: Bayberry

☺ Wednesday
Pepys's Commemoration (English)
Waxing Moon
Full Moon 7:14 am
Color: Brown

Moon Sign: Sagittarius
Incense: Honeysuckle

27 Thursday
Feast of St. Bede the Venerable
Waning Moon
Moon phase: Third Quarter
Color: Crimson

Moon Sign: Sagittarius
Moon enters Capricorn 10:23 pm
Incense: Apricot

28 Friday
St. Germain's Day
Waning Moon
Moon phase: Third Quarter
Color: Purple

Moon Sign: Capricorn
Incense: Rose

May

29 **Saturday**
Oak Apple Day (English)
Waning Moon
Moon phase: Third Quarter
Color: Blue

Moon Sign: Capricorn
Incense: Pine

---

30 **Sunday**
Canary Islands Day
Waning Moon
Moon phase: Third Quarter
Color: Amber

Moon Sign: Capricorn
Moon enters Aquarius 12:04 am
Incense: Eucalyptus

---

31 **Monday**
Memorial Day
Waning Moon
Moon phase: Third Quarter
Color: White

Moon Sign: Aquarius
Incense: Clary sage

May Birthstones

Who first beholds the light of day,
In spring's sweet flowery month of May,
And wears an Emerald all her life,
Shall be a loved, and happy wife.

Modern: Emerald
Zodiac (Taurus): Sapphire

June

1 Tuesday
Dayak Harvest Festival (Malaysian)
Waning Moon
Moon phase: Third Quarter
Color: Black

Moon Sign: Aquarius
Moon enters Pisces 5:07 am
Incense: Ginger

2 Wednesday
Republic Day (Italian)
Waning Moon
Fourth Quarter 3:24 am
Color: Topaz

Moon Sign: Pisces
Incense: Lavender

3 Thursday
Feast of St. Clotilde
Waning Moon
Moon phase: Fourth Quarter
Color: Green

Moon Sign: Pisces
Moon enters Aries 1:59 pm
Incense: Clove

4 Friday
Flag Day (Estonian)
Waning Moon
Moon phase: Fourth Quarter
Color: Pink

Moon Sign: Aries
Incense: Yarrow

5 Saturday
Constitution Day (Danish)
Waning Moon
Moon phase: Fourth Quarter
Color: Indigo

Moon Sign: Aries
Incense: Ivy

6 Sunday
National Day of Sweden
Waning Moon
Moon phase: Fourth Quarter
Color: Orange

Moon Sign: Aries
Moon enters Taurus 1:46 am
Incense: Hyacinth

7 Monday
Vestalia begins (Roman)
Waning Moon
Moon phase: Fourth Quarter
Color: Ivory

Moon Sign: Taurus
Incense: Neroli

June

8 Tuesday
World Oceans Day
Waning Moon
Moon phase: Fourth Quarter
Color: Red

Moon Sign: Taurus
Moon enters Gemini 2:47 pm
Incense: Basil

9 Wednesday
Heroes' Day (Ugandan)
Waning Moon
Moon phase: Fourth Quarter
Color: White

Moon Sign: Gemini
Incense: Marjoram

☽ Thursday
Portugal Day
Waning Moon
New Moon 6:53 am
Color: Turquoise

Moon Sign: Gemini
Incense: Carnation

11 Friday
Kamehameha Day (Hawaiian)
Waxing Moon
Moon phase: First Quarter
Color: Rose

Moon Sign: Gemini
Moon enters Cancer 3:29 am
Incense: Alder

12 Saturday
Independence Day (Filipino)
Waxing Moon
Moon phase: First Quarter
Color: Black

Moon Sign: Cancer
Incense: Sage

13 Sunday
St. Anthony of Padua's Day
Waxing Moon
Moon phase: First Quarter
Color: Gold

Moon Sign: Cancer
Moon enters Leo 2:22 pm
Incense: Juniper

14 Monday
Flag Day
Waxing Moon
Moon phase: First Quarter
Color: Lavender

Moon Sign: Leo
Incense: Lily

June

♊

15 Tuesday
Vestalia ends (Roman)
Waxing Moon
Moon phase: First Quarter
Color: Gray

Moon Sign: Leo
Moon enters Virgo 11:02 pm
Incense: Geranium

16 Wednesday
Bloomsday (Irish)
Waxing Moon
Moon phase: First Quarter
Color: Yellow

Moon Sign: Virgo
Incense: Honeysuckle

◑ Thursday
Bunker Hill Day (Massachusetts)
Waxing Moon
Second Quarter 11:54 pm
Color: Purple

Moon Sign: Virgo
Incense: Mulberry

18 Friday
Waterloo Day (British)
Waxing Moon
Moon phase: Second Quarter
Color: White

Moon Sign: Virgo
Moon enters Libra 4:54 am
Incense: Vanilla

19 Saturday
Juneteenth
Waxing Moon
Moon phase: Second Quarter
Color: Brown

Moon Sign: Libra
Incense: Magnolia

20 Sunday
Litha • Summer Solstice • Father's Day
Waxing Moon
Moon phase: Second Quarter
Color: Yellow

Moon Sign: Libra
Sun enters Cancer 11:32 pm
Moon enters Scorpio 7:58 am
Incense: Frankincense

21 Monday
National Day (Greenlandic)
Waxing Moon
Moon phase: Second Quarter
Color: White

Moon Sign: Scorpio
Incense: Clary sage

June

22 Tuesday
Teachers' Day (El Salvadoran)
Waxing Moon
Moon phase: Second Quarter
Color: Scarlet

Moon Sign: Scorpio
Moon enters Sagittarius 8:55 am
Incense: Bayberry

23 Wednesday
St. John's Eve
Waxing Moon
Moon phase: Second Quarter
Color: Brown

Moon Sign: Sagittarius
Incense: Lilac

Thursday
St. John's Day
Waxing Moon
Full Moon 2:40 pm
Color: Crimson

Moon Sign: Sagittarius
Moon enters Capricorn 9:05 am
Incense: Myrrh

25 Friday
Fiesta de Santa Orosia (Spanish)
Waning Moon
Moon phase: Third Quarter
Color: Coral

Moon Sign: Capricorn
Incense: Thyme

26 Saturday
Pied Piper Day (German)
Waning Moon
Moon phase: Third Quarter
Color: Blue

Moon Sign: Capricorn
Moon enters Aquarius 10:09 am
Incense: Sandalwood

27 Sunday
Seven Sleepers' Day (German)
Waning Moon
Moon phase: Third Quarter
Color: Amber

Moon Sign: Aquarius
Incense: Almond

28 Monday
Paul Bunyan Day
Waning Moon
Moon phase: Third Quarter
Color: Gray

Moon Sign: Aquarius
Moon enters Pisces 1:51 pm
Incense: Narcissus

29 Tuesday

Haro Wine Battle (Spanish)
Waning Moon
Moon phase: Third Quarter
Color: Red

Moon Sign: Pisces
Incense: Ylang-ylang

30 Wednesday

The Burning of the Three Firs (French)
Waning Moon
Moon phase: Third Quarter
Color: Yellow

Moon Sign: Pisces
Moon enters Aries 9:21 pm
Incense: Lavender

June Birthstones

Who comes with summer to this earth,
And owes to June her hour of birth,
With ring of Agate on her hand,
Can health, wealth, and long life command.

Modern: Moonstone or Pearl
Zodiac (Gemini): Agate

July

Thursday
Canada Day
Waning Moon
Fourth Quarter 5:11 pm
Color: White

Moon Sign: Aries
Incense: Balsam

---

2 Friday
World UFO Day
Waning Moon
Moon phase: Fourth Quarter
Color: Rose

Moon Sign: Aries
Incense: Yarrow

---

3 Saturday
Dog Days of Summer begin
Waning Moon
Moon phase: Fourth Quarter
Color: Black

Moon Sign: Aries
Moon enters Taurus 8:28 am
Incense: Patchouli

---

4 Sunday
Independence Day
Waning Moon
Moon phase: Fourth Quarter
Color: Orange

Moon Sign: Taurus
Incense: Heliotrope

---

5 Monday
Tynwald Day (Manx)
Waning Moon
Moon phase: Fourth Quarter
Color: Silver

Moon Sign: Taurus
Moon enters Gemini 9:24 pm
Incense: Rosemary

---

6 Tuesday
San Fermín begins (Spanish)
Waning Moon
Moon phase: Fourth Quarter
Color: Maroon

Moon Sign: Gemini
Incense: Geranium

---

7 Wednesday
Star Festival (Japanese)
Waning Moon
Moon phase: Fourth Quarter
Color: Brown

Moon Sign: Gemini
Incense: Bay laurel

July

8 Thursday
Feast of St. Sunniva
Waning Moon
Moon phase: Fourth Quarter
Color: Purple

Moon Sign: Gemini
Moon enters Cancer 9:51 am
Incense: Jasmine

☽ Friday
Battle of Sempach Day (Swiss)
Waning Moon
New Moon 9:17 pm
Color: Coral

Moon Sign: Cancer
Incense: Violet

10 Saturday
Nicola Tesla Day
Waxing Moon
Moon phase: First Quarter
Color: Gray

Moon Sign: Cancer
Moon enters Leo 8:21 pm
Incense: Pine

11 Sunday
Mongolian Naadam Festival (ends July 13)
Waxing Moon
Moon phase: First Quarter
Color: Yellow

Moon Sign: Leo
Incense: Marigold

12 Monday
Malala Day
Waxing Moon
Moon phase: First Quarter
Color: Ivory

Moon Sign: Leo
Incense: Hyssop

13 Tuesday
Feast of St. Mildrith
Waxing Moon
Moon phase: First Quarter
Color: Scarlet

Moon Sign: Leo
Moon enters Virgo 4:30 am
Incense: Ginger

14 Wednesday
Bastille Day (French)
Waxing Moon
Moon phase: First Quarter
Color: White

Moon Sign: Virgo
Incense: Honeysuckle

15 **Thursday**
St. Swithin's Day
Waxing Moon
Moon phase: First Quarter
Color: Green

Moon Sign: Virgo
Moon enters Libra 10:32 am
Incense: Carnation

---

16 **Friday**
Fiesta de la Tirana (Chilean)
Waxing Moon
Moon phase: First Quarter
Color: Purple

Moon Sign: Libra
Incense: Mint

○ **Saturday**
Gion Festival first Yamaboko parade (Japanese)
Waxing Moon
Second Quarter 6:11 am
Color: Indigo

Moon Sign: Libra
Moon enters Scorpio 2:38 pm
Incense: Sandalwood

---

18 **Sunday**
Nelson Mandela International Day
Waxing Moon
Moon phase: Second Quarter
Color: Orange

Moon Sign: Scorpio
Incense: Eucalyptus

---

19 **Monday**
Flitch Day (English)
Waxing Moon
Moon phase: Second Quarter
Color: Lavender

Moon Sign: Scorpio
Moon enters Sagittarius 5:08 pm
Incense: Lily

---

20 **Tuesday**
Binding of Wreaths (Lithuanian)
Waxing Moon
Moon phase: Second Quarter
Color: Red

Moon Sign: Sagittarius
Incense: Cedar

---

21 **Wednesday**
National Day (Belgian)
Waxing Moon
Moon phase: Second Quarter
Color: Topaz

Moon Sign: Sagittarius
Moon enters Capricorn 6:36 pm
Incense: Marjoram

July

22 Thursday

St. Mary Magdalene's Day
Waxing Moon
Moon phase: Second Quarter
Color: Crimson

Moon Sign: Capricorn
Sun enters Leo 10:26 am
Incense: Clove

Friday

Mysteries of St. Cristina (Italian)
Waxing Moon
Full Moon 10:37 pm
Color: Rose

Moon Sign: Capricorn
Moon enters Aquarius 8:12 pm
Incense: Alder

24 Saturday

Gion Festival second Yamaboko parade (Japanese)
Waning Moon
Moon phase: Third Quarter
Color: Blue

Moon Sign: Aquarius
Incense: Magnolia

25 Sunday

Illapa Festival (Incan)
Waning Moon
Moon phase: Third Quarter
Color: Gold

Moon Sign: Aquarius
Moon enters Pisces 11:30 pm
Incense: Frankincense

26 Monday

St. Anne's Day
Waning Moon
Moon phase: Third Quarter
Color: White

Moon Sign: Pisces
Incense: Clary sage

27 Tuesday

Sleepyhead Day (Finnish)
Waning Moon
Moon phase: Third Quarter
Color: Gray

Moon Sign: Pisces
Incense: Cinnamon

28 Wednesday

Independence Day (Peruvian)
Waning Moon
Moon phase: Third Quarter
Color: Yellow

Moon Sign: Pisces
Moon enters Aries 5:58 am
Incense: Lavender

July

29 Thursday
St. Olaf Festival (Faroese)
Waning Moon
Moon phase: Third Quarter
Color: Turquoise

Moon Sign: Aries
Incense: Nutmeg

---

30 Friday
Micman Festival of St. Ann
Waning Moon
Moon phase: Third Quarter
Color: Pink

Moon Sign: Aries
Moon enters Taurus 4:08 pm
Incense: Violet

○ Saturday
Feast of St. Ignatius
Waning Moon
Fourth Quarter 9:16 am
Color: Brown

Moon Sign: Taurus
Incense: Ivy

❖

July Birthstones

The glowing Ruby shall adorn
Those who in warm July are born;
Then will they be exempt and free
From love's doubt, and anxiety.

Modern: Ruby
Zodiac (Cancer): Emerald

August

1 Sunday
Lammas
Waning Moon
Moon phase: Fourth Quarter
Color: Yellow

Moon Sign: Taurus
Incense: Hyacinth

---

2 Monday
Porcingula (Pecos)
Waning Moon
Moon phase: Fourth Quarter
Color: Gray

Moon Sign: Taurus
Moon enters Gemini 4:46 am
Incense: Hyssop

---

3 Tuesday
Flag Day (Venezuelan)
Waning Moon
Moon phase: Fourth Quarter
Color: White

Moon Sign: Gemini
Incense: Basil

---

4 Wednesday
Constitution Day (Cook Islands)
Waning Moon
Moon phase: Fourth Quarter
Color: Topaz

Moon Sign: Gemini
Moon enters Cancer 5:17 pm
Incense: Bay laurel

---

5 Thursday
Carnival of Bogotá
Waning Moon
Moon phase: Fourth Quarter
Color: Green

Moon Sign: Cancer
Incense: Jasmine

---

6 Friday
Hiroshima Peace Memorial Ceremony
Waning Moon
Moon phase: Fourth Quarter
Color: Purple

Moon Sign: Cancer
Incense: Mint

---

7 Saturday
Republic Day (Ivorian)
Waning Moon
Moon phase: Fourth Quarter
Color: Blue

Moon Sign: Cancer
Moon enters Leo 3:31 am
Incense: Rue

🌙 **Sunday**
Islamic New Year begins at sundown
Waning Moon
New Moon 9:50 am
Color: Amber

Moon Sign: Leo
Incense: Almond

---

9 **Monday**
Nagasaki Peace Memorial Ceremony
Waxing Moon
Moon phase: First Quarter
Color: Ivory

Moon Sign: Leo
Moon enters Virgo 10:56 am
Incense: Rosemary

---

10 **Tuesday**
Puck Fair (ends Aug. 12; Irish)
Waxing Moon
Moon phase: First Quarter
Color: Red

Moon Sign: Virgo
Incense: Ylang-ylang

---

11 **Wednesday**
Mountain Day (Japanese)
Waxing Moon
Moon phase: First Quarter
Color: Brown

Moon Sign: Virgo
Moon enters Libra 4:08 pm
Incense: Lilac

---

12 **Thursday**
World Elephant Day
Waxing Moon
Moon phase: First Quarter
Color: Turquoise

Moon Sign: Libra
Incense: Clove

---

13 **Friday**
Women's Day (Tunisian)
Waxing Moon
Moon phase: First Quarter
Color: White

Moon Sign: Libra
Moon enters Scorpio 8:01 pm
Incense: Thyme

---

14 **Saturday**
Qixi Festival (Chinese)
Waxing Moon
Moon phase: First Quarter
Color: Gray

Moon Sign: Scorpio
Incense: Magnolia

August

○ Sunday
Bon Festival (Japanese)
Waxing Moon
Second Quarter 11:20 am
Color: Gold

Moon Sign: Scorpio
Moon enters Sagittarius 11:12 pm
Incense: Juniper

---

16 Monday
Xicolatada (French)
Waxing Moon
Moon phase: Second Quarter
Color: Silver

Moon Sign: Sagittarius
Incense: Lily

---

17 Tuesday
Black Cat Appreciation Day
Waxing Moon
Moon phase: Second Quarter
Color: Maroon

Moon Sign: Sagittarius
Incense: Cedar

---

18 Wednesday
St. Helen's Day
Waxing Moon
Moon phase: Second Quarter
Color: White

Moon Sign: Sagittarius
Moon enters Capricorn 1:58 am
Incense: Honeysuckle

---

19 Thursday
Vinalia Rustica (Roman)
Waxing Moon
Moon phase: Second Quarter
Color: Crimson

Moon Sign: Capricorn
Incense: Carnation

---

20 Friday
St. Stephen's Day (Hungarian)
Waxing Moon
Moon phase: Second Quarter
Color: Pink

Moon Sign: Capricorn
Moon enters Aquarius 4:49 am
Incense: Violet

---

21 Saturday
Consualia (Roman)
Waxing Moon
Moon phase: Second Quarter
Color: Indigo

Moon Sign: Aquarius
Incense: Sandalwood

☺ Sunday

Ghost Festival (Chinese)
Waxing Moon
Full Moon 8:02 am
Color: Orange

Moon Sign: Aquarius
Sun enters Virgo 5:35 pm
Moon enters Pisces 8:43 am
Incense: Heliotrope

---

23 Monday

National Day (Romanian)
Waning Moon
Moon phase: Third Quarter
Color: White

Moon Sign: Pisces
Incense: Neroli

---

24 Tuesday

St. Bartholomew's Day
Waning Moon
Moon phase: Third Quarter
Color: Gray

Moon Sign: Pisces
Moon enters Aries 2:57 pm
Incense: Bayberry

---

25 Wednesday

Liberation of Paris
Waning Moon
Moon phase: Third Quarter
Color: Yellow

Moon Sign: Aries
Incense: Lilac

---

26 Thursday

Heroes' Day (Namibian)
Waning Moon
Moon phase: Third Quarter
Color: Purple

Moon Sign: Aries
Incense: Balsam

---

27 Friday

Independence Day (Moldovan)
Waning Moon
Moon phase: Third Quarter
Color: Rose

Moon Sign: Aries
Moon enters Taurus 12:27 am
Incense: Cypress

---

28 Saturday

St. Augustine's Day
Waning Moon
Moon phase: Third Quarter
Color: Black

Moon Sign: Taurus
Incense: Sage

August

29 Sunday

St. John's Beheading
Waning Moon
Moon phase: Third Quarter
Color: Gold

Moon Sign: Taurus
Moon enters Gemini 12:42 pm
Incense: Marigold

 Monday

St. Rose of Lima Day (Peruvian)
Waning Moon
Fourth Quarter 3:13 am
Color: Lavender

Moon Sign: Gemini
Incense: Narcissus

---

31 Tuesday

La Tomatina (Valencian)
Waning Moon
Moon phase: Fourth Quarter
Color: Scarlet

Moon Sign: Gemini
Incense: Cinnamon

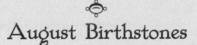

August Birthstones

Wear Sardonyx, or for thee
No conjugal felicity;
The August-born without this stone,
'Tis said, must live unloved, and lone.

Modern: Peridot
Zodiac (Leo): Onyx

September ♍

1 Wednesday
Wattle Day (Australian)
Waning Moon
Moon phase: Fourth Quarter
Color: Brown

Moon Sign: Gemini
Moon enters Cancer 1:26 am
Incense: Marjoram

2 Thursday
St. Mammes's Day
Waning Moon
Moon phase: Fourth Quarter
Color: Turquoise

Moon Sign: Cancer
Incense: Mulberry

3 Friday
National Feast of San Marino
Waning Moon
Moon phase: Fourth Quarter
Color: Coral

Moon Sign: Cancer
Moon enters Leo 11:58 am
Incense: Vanilla

4 Saturday
Feast of St. Rosalia
Waning Moon
Moon phase: Fourth Quarter
Color: Gray

Moon Sign: Leo
Incense: Patchouli

5 Sunday
International Day of Charity
Waning Moon
Moon phase: Fourth Quarter
Color: Yellow

Moon Sign: Leo
Moon enters Virgo 7:06 pm
Incense: Almond

☽ Monday
Labor Day • Rosh Hashanah begins at sundown
Waning Moon
New Moon 8:52 pm
Color: White

Moon Sign: Virgo
Incense: Hyssop

7 Tuesday
Independence Day (Brazilian)
Waxing Moon
Moon phase: First Quarter
Color: Black

Moon Sign: Virgo
Moon enters Libra 11:20 pm
Incense: Geranium

8 Wednesday

International Literacy Day
Waxing Moon
Moon phase: First Quarter
Color: Topaz

Moon Sign: Libra
Incense: Lavender

---

9 Thursday

Remembrance for Herman the Cheruscan (Asatru)
Waxing Moon
Moon phase: First Quarter
Color: Purple

Moon Sign: Libra
Incense: Apricot

---

10 Friday

National Day (Belizean)
Waxing Moon
Moon phase: First Quarter
Color: Pink

Moon Sign: Libra
Moon enters Scorpio 2:05 am
Incense: Alder

---

11 Saturday

Patriot Day
Waxing Moon
Moon phase: First Quarter
Color: Indigo

Moon Sign: Scorpio
Incense: Ivy

---

12 Sunday

Grandparents' Day
Waxing Moon
Moon phase: First Quarter
Color: Amber

Moon Sign: Scorpio
Moon enters Sagittarius 4:34 am
Incense: Juniper

◐ Monday

The Gods' Banquet
Waxing Moon
Second Quarter 4:39 pm
Color: Lavender

Moon Sign: Sagittarius
Incense: Lily

---

14 Tuesday

Holy Cross Day
Waxing Moon
Moon phase: Second Quarter
Color: Red

Moon Sign: Sagittarius
Moon enters Capricorn 7:34 am
Incense: Basil

September ♍

15 Wednesday

Yom Kippur begins at sundown
Waxing Moon
Moon phase: Second Quarter
Color: Yellow

Moon Sign: Capricorn
Incense: Bay laurel

16 Thursday

Independence Day (Mexican)
Waxing Moon
Moon phase: Second Quarter
Color: White

Moon Sign: Capricorn
Moon enters Aquarius 11:23 am
Incense: Nutmeg

17 Friday

Teachers' Day (Honduran)
Waxing Moon
Moon phase: Second Quarter
Color: Rose

Moon Sign: Aquarius
Incense: Yarrow

18 Saturday

World Water Monitoring Day
Waxing Moon
Moon phase: Second Quarter
Color: Blue

Moon Sign: Aquarius
Moon enters Pisces 4:22 pm
Incense: Pine

19 Sunday

Feast of San Gennaro
Waxing Moon
Moon phase: Second Quarter
Color: Orange

Moon Sign: Pisces
Incense: Eucalyptus

☺ Monday

Sukkot begins at sundown
Waxing Moon
Full Moon 7:55 pm
Color: Silver

Moon Sign: Pisces
Moon enters Aries 11:13 pm
Incense: Clary sage

21 Tuesday

Mid-Autumn Festival
Waning Moon
Moon phase: Third Quarter
Color: Maroon

Moon Sign: Aries
Incense: Cedar

22 Wednesday

Mabon • Fall Equinox
Waning Moon
Moon phase: Third Quarter
Color: White

Moon Sign: Aries
Sun enters Libra 3:21 pm
Incense: Lilac

23 Thursday

Feast of St. Padre Pio
Waning Moon
Moon phase: Third Quarter
Color: Green

Moon Sign: Aries
Moon enters Taurus 8:38 am
Incense: Myrrh

24 Friday

Schwenkenfelder Thanksgiving (German-American)
Waning Moon
Moon phase: Third Quarter
Color: Coral

Moon Sign: Taurus
Incense: Orchid

25 Saturday

Doll Memorial Service (Japanese)
Waning Moon
Moon phase: Third Quarter
Color: Black

Moon Sign: Taurus
Moon enters Gemini 8:36 pm
Incense: Magnolia

26 Sunday

Feast of Santa Justina (Mexican)
Waning Moon
Moon phase: Third Quarter
Color: Gold

Moon Sign: Gemini
Incense: Heliotrope

27 Monday

Sukkot ends
Waning Moon
Moon phase: Third Quarter
Color: Ivory

Moon Sign: Gemini
Incense: Rosemary

☽ Tuesday

Confucius's birthday
Waning Moon
Fourth Quarter 9:57 pm
Color: White

Moon Sign: Gemini
Moon enters Cancer 9:34 am
Incense: Basil

September

29 Wednesday

Michaelmas
Waning Moon
Moon phase: Fourth Quarter
Color: Yellow

Moon Sign: Cancer
Incense: Honeysuckle

---

30 Thursday

St. Jerome's Day
Waning Moon
Moon phase: Fourth Quarter
Color: Crimson

Moon Sign: Cancer
Moon enters Leo 8:53 pm
Incense: Balsam

September Birthstones

A maiden born when autumn leaves
Are rustling in September's breeze,
A Sapphire on her brow should bind;
'Twill cure diseases of the mind.

Modern: Sapphire
Zodiac (Virgo): Carnelian

October

1 **Friday**
Armed Forces Day (South Korean)
Waning Moon
Moon phase: Fourth Quarter
Color: Pink

Moon Sign: Leo
Incense: Mint

---

2 **Saturday**
Gandhi's birthday
Waning Moon
Moon phase: Fourth Quarter
Color: Gray

Moon Sign: Leo
Incense: Rue

---

3 **Sunday**
German Unity Day
Waning Moon
Moon phase: Fourth Quarter
Color: Amber

Moon Sign: Leo
Moon enters Virgo 4:38 am
Incense: Frankincense

---

4 **Monday**
St. Francis's Day
Waning Moon
Moon phase: Fourth Quarter
Color: Gray

Moon Sign: Virgo
Incense: Narcissus

---

5 **Tuesday**
Republic Day (Portuguese)
Waning Moon
Moon phase: Fourth Quarter
Color: Scarlet

Moon Sign: Virgo
Moon enters Libra 8:41 am
Incense: Cinnamon

 **Wednesday**
German-American Day
Waning Moon
New Moon 7:05 am
Color: Brown

Moon Sign: Libra
Incense: Bay laurel

---

7 **Thursday**
Nagasaki Kunchi Festival (ends Oct. 9)
Waxing Moon
Moon phase: First Quarter
Color: White

Moon Sign: Libra
Moon enters Scorpio 10:22 am
Incense: Jasmine

October

8 **Friday**
Arbor Day (Namibian)
Waxing Moon
Moon phase: First Quarter
Color: Coral

Moon Sign: Scorpio
Incense: Violet

---

9 **Saturday**
Leif Erikson Day
Waxing Moon
Moon phase: First Quarter
Color: Blue

Moon Sign: Scorpio
Moon enters Sagittarius 11:24 am
Incense: Patchouli

---

10 **Sunday**
Finnish Literature Day
Waxing Moon
Moon phase: First Quarter
Color: Orange

Moon Sign: Sagittarius
Incense: Hyacinth

---

11 **Monday**
Thanksgiving Day (Canadian)
Waxing Moon
Moon phase: First Quarter
Color: White

Moon Sign: Sagittarius
Moon enters Capricorn 1:15 pm
Incense: Hyssop

☽ **Tuesday**
National Festival of Spain
Waxing Moon
Second Quarter 11:25 pm
Color: Gray

Moon Sign: Capricorn
Incense: Cedar

---

13 **Wednesday**
Fontinalia (Roman)
Waxing Moon
Moon phase: Second Quarter
Color: Topaz

Moon Sign: Capricorn
Moon enters Aquarius 4:47 pm
Incense: Lavender

---

14 **Thursday**
Double Ninth Festival (Chinese)
Waxing Moon
Moon phase: Second Quarter
Color: Purple

Moon Sign: Aquarius
Incense: Mulberry

October

15 Friday
The October Horse (Roman)
Waxing Moon
Moon phase: Second Quarter
Color: Rose

Moon Sign: Aquarius
Moon enters Pisces 10:22 pm
Incense: Alder

16 Saturday
The Lion Sermon (British)
Waxing Moon
Moon phase: Second Quarter
Color: Gray

Moon Sign: Pisces
Incense: Pine

17 Sunday
Dessalines Day (Haitian)
Waxing Moon
Moon phase: Second Quarter
Color: Yellow

Moon Sign: Pisces
Incense: Marigold

18 Monday
Feast of St. Luke
Waxing Moon
Moon phase: Second Quarter
Color: Ivory

Moon Sign: Pisces
Moon enters Aries 6:04 am
Incense: Neroli

19 Tuesday
Mother Teresa Day (Albanian)
Waxing Moon
Moon phase: Second Quarter
Color: Red

Moon Sign: Aries
Incense: Ginger

☻ Wednesday
Feast of St. Acca
Waxing Moon
Full Moon 10:57 am
Color: White

Moon Sign: Aries
Moon enters Taurus 3:59 pm
Incense: Marjoram

21 Thursday
Apple Day (United Kingdom)
Waning Moon
Moon phase: Third Quarter
Color: Crimson

Moon Sign: Taurus
Incense: Myrrh

October

22 Friday
Jidai Festival (Japanese)
Waning Moon
Moon phase: Third Quarter
Color: Pink

Moon Sign: Taurus
Incense: Rose

---

23 Saturday
Revolution Day (Hungarian)
Waning Moon
Moon phase: Third Quarter
Color: Black

Moon Sign: Taurus
Sun enters Scorpio 12:51 am
Moon enters Gemini 3:57 am
Incense: Ivy

---

24 Sunday
United Nations Day
Waning Moon
Moon phase: Third Quarter
Color: Gold

Moon Sign: Gemini
Incense: Eucalyptus

---

25 Monday
St. Crispin's Day
Waning Moon
Moon phase: Third Quarter
Color: Silver

Moon Sign: Gemini
Moon enters Cancer 5:00 pm
Incense: Rosemary

---

26 Tuesday
Death of Alfred the Great
Waning Moon
Moon phase: Third Quarter
Color: Gray

Moon Sign: Cancer
Incense: Geranium

---

27 Wednesday
Feast of St. Abbán
Waning Moon
Moon phase: Third Quarter
Color: Yellow

Moon Sign: Cancer
Incense: Lilac

◐ Thursday
Ohi Day (Greek)
Waning Moon
Fourth Quarter 4:05 pm
Color: Green

Moon Sign: Cancer
Moon enters Leo 5:07 am
Incense: Clove

October

29 Friday

National Cat Day
Waning Moon
Moon phase: Fourth Quarter
Color: Purple

Moon Sign: Leo
Incense: Vanilla

---

30 Saturday

John Adams's birthday
Waning Moon
Moon phase: Fourth Quarter
Color: Blue

Moon Sign: Leo
Moon enters Virgo 2:09 pm
Incense: Sandalwood

---

31 Sunday

Halloween • Samhain
Waning Moon
Moon phase: Fourth Quarter
Color: Orange

Moon Sign: Virgo
Incense: Heliotrope

October Birthstones

October's child is born for woe,
And life's vicissitudes must know;
But lay an Opal on her breast,
And hope will lull those foes to rest.

Modern: Opal or Tourmaline
Zodiac (Libra): Peridot

November

1 Monday
All Saints' Day • Día de los Muertos
Waning Moon
Moon phase: Fourth Quarter
Color: Lavender

Moon Sign: Virgo
Moon enters Libra 7:11 pm
Incense: Lily

2 Tuesday
Election Day (general)
Waning Moon
Moon phase: Fourth Quarter
Color: Scarlet

Moon Sign: Libra
Incense: Ylang-ylang

3 Wednesday
Election Day (general)
Waning Moon
Moon phase: Fourth Quarter
Color: Topaz

Moon Sign: Libra
Moon enters Scorpio 8:52 pm
Incense: Honeysuckle

4 Thursday
Diwali
Waning Moon
New Moon 5:15 pm
Color: Turquoise

Moon Sign: Scorpio
Incense: Balsam

5 Friday
Guy Fawkes Night (British)
Waxing Moon
Moon phase: First Quarter
Color: White

Moon Sign: Scorpio
Moon enters Sagittarius 8:52 pm
Incense: Cypress

6 Saturday
St. Leonard's Ride (German)
Waxing Moon
Moon phase: First Quarter
Color: Brown

Moon Sign: Sagittarius
Incense: Magnolia

7 Sunday
Feast of St. Willibrord
Waxing Moon
Moon phase: First Quarter
Color: Gold

Moon Sign: Sagittarius
Moon enters Capricorn 8:03 pm
Incense: Hyacinth
Daylight Saving Time ends at 2 am

November

8 Monday
World Urbanism Day
Waxing Moon
Moon phase: First Quarter
Color: Ivory

Moon Sign: Capricorn
Incense: Narcissus

9 Tuesday
Fateful Day (German)
Waxing Moon
Moon phase: First Quarter
Color: Maroon

Moon Sign: Capricorn
Moon enters Aquarius 10:03 pm
Incense: Bayberry

10 Wednesday
Martin Luther's Birthday
Waxing Moon
Moon phase: First Quarter
Color: White

Moon Sign: Aquarius
Incense: Bay laurel

◖ Thursday
Veterans Day • Remembrance Day (Canadian)
Waxing Moon
Second Quarter 7:46 am
Color: Purple

Moon Sign: Aquarius
Incense: Apricot

12 Friday
Feast Day of San Diego (Tesuque Puebloan)
Waxing Moon
Moon phase: Second Quarter
Color: Rose

Moon Sign: Aquarius
Moon enters Pisces 2:54 am
Incense: Thyme

13 Saturday
Festival of Jupiter
Waxing Moon
Moon phase: Second Quarter
Color: Blue

Moon Sign: Pisces
Incense: Sandalwood

14 Sunday
Feast of St. Lawrence O'Toole
Waxing Moon
Moon phase: Second Quarter
Color: Yellow

Moon Sign: Pisces
Moon enters Aries 10:48 am
Incense: Almond

November
♏

15 Monday
Seven-Five-Three Festival (Japanese)
Waxing Moon
Moon phase: Second Quarter
Color: Silver

Moon Sign: Aries
Incense: Neroli

16 Tuesday
St. Margaret of Scotland's Day
Waxing Moon
Moon phase: Second Quarter
Color: Black

Moon Sign: Aries
Moon enters Taurus 9:18 pm
Incense: Cedar

17 Wednesday
Queen Elizabeth's Ascension Day
Waxing Moon
Moon phase: Second Quarter
Color: Brown

Moon Sign: Taurus
Incense: Lilac

18 Thursday
Independence Day (Moroccan)
Waxing Moon
Moon phase: Second Quarter
Color: Green

Moon Sign: Taurus
Incense: Jasmine

😊 Friday
Native American Heritage Day
Waxing Moon
Full Moon 3:57 am
Color: Coral

Moon Sign: Taurus
Moon enters Gemini 9:33 am
Incense: Yarrow

20 Saturday
National Adoption Day
Waning Moon
Moon phase: Third Quarter
Color: Gray

Moon Sign: Gemini
Incense: Pine

21 Sunday
Feast of the Presentation of Mary
Waning Moon
Moon phase: Third Quarter
Color: Amber

Moon Sign: Gemini
Sun enters Sagittarius 9:34 pm
Moon enters Cancer 10:33 pm
Incense: Juniper

22 Monday
St. Cecilia's Day
Waning Moon
Moon phase: Third Quarter
Color: White

Moon Sign: Cancer
Incense: Clary sage

---

23 Tuesday
St. Clement's Day
Waning Moon
Moon phase: Third Quarter
Color: Red

Moon Sign: Cancer
Incense: Geranium

---

24 Wednesday
Evolution Day
Waning Moon
Moon phase: Third Quarter
Color: Yellow

Moon Sign: Cancer
Moon enters Leo 10:59 am
Incense: Lavender

---

25 Thursday
Thanksgiving Day (US)
Waning Moon
Moon phase: Third Quarter
Color: White

Moon Sign: Leo
Incense: Nutmeg

---

26 Friday
Constitution Day (Indian)
Waning Moon
Moon phase: Third Quarter
Color: Pink

Moon Sign: Leo
Moon enters Virgo 9:12 pm
Incense: Violet

○ Saturday
Feast of St. Virgilius
Waning Moon
Fourth Quarter 7:28 am
Color: Indigo

Moon Sign: Virgo
Incense: Magnolia

---

28 Sunday
Hanukkah begins at sundown
Waning Moon
Moon phase: Fourth Quarter
Color: Gold

Moon Sign: Virgo
Incense: Frankincense

November

29 Monday

William Tubman's birthday (Liberian)
Waning Moon
Moon phase: Fourth Quarter
Color: Lavender

Moon Sign: Virgo
Moon enters Libra 3:55 am
Incense: Hyssop

---

30 Tuesday

St. Andrew's Day (Scottish)
Waning Moon
Moon phase: Fourth Quarter
Color: Gray

Moon Sign: Libra
Incense: Basil

November Birthstones

Who first come to this world below,
With drear November's fog, and snow,
Should prize the Topaz's amber hue,
Emblem of friends, and lovers true.

Modern: Topaz or Citrine
Zodiac (Scorpio): Beryl

December

1   Wednesday
Feast for Death of Aleister Crowley (Thelemic)
Waning Moon
Moon phase: Fourth Quarter
Color: Yellow

Moon Sign: Libra
Moon enters Scorpio 6:55 am
Incense: Bay laurel

2   Thursday
Republic Day (Laotian)
Waning Moon
Moon phase: Fourth Quarter
Color: Purple

Moon Sign: Scorpio
Incense: Jasmine

3   Friday
St. Francis Xavier's Day
Waning Moon
Moon phase: Fourth Quarter
Color: Rose

Moon Sign: Scorpio
Moon enters Sagittarius 7:13 am
Incense: Alder

☽   Saturday
Feasts of Shango and St. Barbara
Waning Moon
New Moon 2:43 am
Color: Black

Moon Sign: Sagittarius
Incense: Rue

5   Sunday
Krampus Night (European)
Waxing Moon
Moon phase: First Quarter
Color: Yellow

Moon Sign: Sagittarius
Moon enters Capricorn 6:31 am
Incense: Eucalyptus

6   Monday
Hanukkah ends
Waxing Moon
Moon phase: First Quarter
Color: Gray

Moon Sign: Capricorn
Incense: Rosemary

7   Tuesday
Burning the Devil (Guatemalan)
Waxing Moon
Moon phase: First Quarter
Color: White

Moon Sign: Capricorn
Moon enters Aquarius 6:49 am
Incense: Bayberry

December

---

8 Wednesday
Bodhi Day (Japanese)
Waxing Moon
Moon phase: First Quarter
Color: Brown

Moon Sign: Aquarius
Incense: Lilac

---

9 Thursday
Anna's Day (Sweden)
Waxing Moon
Moon phase: First Quarter
Color: Crimson

Moon Sign: Aquarius
Moon enters Pisces 9:53 am
Incense: Balsam

☽ Friday
Alfred Nobel Day
Waxing Moon
Second Quarter 8:36 pm
Color: Pink

Moon Sign: Pisces
Incense: Violet

---

11 Saturday
Pilgrimage at Tortugas
Waxing Moon
Moon phase: Second Quarter
Color: Indigo

Moon Sign: Pisces
Moon enters Aries 4:46 pm
Incense: Sandalwood

---

12 Sunday
Fiesta of Our Lady of Guadalupe (Mexican)
Waxing Moon
Moon phase: Second Quarter
Color: Orange

Moon Sign: Aries
Incense: Almond

---

13 Monday
St. Lucy's Day (Scandinavian and Italian)
Waxing Moon
Moon phase: Second Quarter
Color: Silver

Moon Sign: Aries
Incense: Lily

---

14 Tuesday
Forty-Seven Ronin Memorial (Japanese)
Waxing Moon
Moon phase: Second Quarter
Color: Red

Moon Sign: Aries
Moon enters Taurus 3:11 am
Incense: Ginger

December

15 Wednesday

Consualia (Roman)
Waxing Moon
Moon phase: Second Quarter
Color: White

Moon Sign: Taurus
Incense: Lavender

---

16 Thursday

Las Posadas begin (end Dec. 24)
Waxing Moon
Moon phase: Second Quarter
Color: Turquoise

Moon Sign: Taurus
Moon enters Gemini 3:43 pm
Incense: Nutmeg

---

17 Friday

Saturnalia (Roman)
Waxing Moon
Moon phase: Second Quarter
Color: Purple

Moon Sign: Gemini
Incense: Rose

☺ Saturday

Feast of the Virgin of Solitude
Waxing Moon
Full Moon 11:36 pm
Color: Blue

Moon Sign: Gemini
Incense: Pine

---

19 Sunday

Opalia (Roman)
Waning Moon
Moon phase: Third Quarter
Color: Gold

Moon Sign: Gemini
Moon enters Cancer 4:42 am
Incense: Heliotrope

---

20 Monday

Feast of St. Dominic of Silos
Waning Moon
Moon phase: Third Quarter
Color: White

Moon Sign: Cancer
Incense: Hyssop

---

21 Tuesday

Yule • Winter Solstice
Waning Moon
Moon phase: Third Quarter
Color: Maroon

Moon Sign: Cancer
Sun enters Capricorn 10:59 am
Moon enters Leo 4:54 pm
Incense: Ylang-ylang

December

22 Wednesday

Feasts of SS. Chaeremon and Ischyrion
Waning Moon
Moon phase: Third Quarter
Color: Topaz

Moon Sign: Leo
Incense: Honeysuckle

23 Thursday

Larentalia (Roman)
Waning Moon
Moon phase: Third Quarter
Color: Green

Moon Sign: Leo
Incense: Myrrh

24 Friday

Christmas Eve
Waning Moon
Moon phase: Third Quarter
Color: Coral

Moon Sign: Leo
Moon enters Virgo 3:24 am
Incense: Mint

25 Saturday

Christmas Day
Waning Moon
Moon phase: Third Quarter
Color: Gray

Moon Sign: Virgo
Incense: Sage

☾ Sunday

Kwanzaa begins (ends Jan. 1) • *Boxing Day*
Waning Moon
Fourth Quarter 9:24 pm
Color: Amber

Moon Sign: Virgo
Moon enters Libra 11:24 am
Incense: Marigold

27 Monday

St. Stephen's Day
Waning Moon
Moon phase: Fourth Quarter
Color: Ivory

Moon Sign: Libra
Incense: Neroli

28 Tuesday

Feast of the Holy Innocents
Waning Moon
Moon phase: Fourth Quarter
Color: Scarlet

Moon Sign: Libra
Moon enters Scorpio 4:16 pm
Incense: Cedar

29 Wednesday
Feast of St. Thomas à Becket
Waning Moon
Moon phase: Fourth Quarter
Color: Yellow

Moon Sign: Scorpio
Incense: Majoram

---

30 Thursday
Republic Day (Madagascan)
Waning Moon
Moon phase: Fourth Quarter
Color: White

Moon Sign: Scorpio
Moon enters Sagittarius 6:08 pm
Incense: Clove

---

31 Friday
New Year's Eve
Waning Moon
Moon phase: Fourth Quarter
Color: Pink

Moon Sign: Sagittarius
Incense: Orchid

December Birthstones

If cold December gives you birth,
The month of snow, and ice, and mirth,
Place in your hand a Turquoise blue;
Success will bless whate'er you do.

Modern: Turquoise or Blue Topaz
Zodiac (Sagittarius): Topaz

Fire Magic

Tales of a Brigidine Flametender

Mickie Mueller

I woke up this morning with an alert on my phone to remind me that tonight I'm tending a flame dedicated to the goddess Brigid at sundown. No, it's not Imbolc, Brigid's festival day—it's the end of August. I'm a flametender and abbess in a group, also known as a *cill* (pronounced kith or keeth), of diverse people who share the honor of tending Brigid's flame once every twenty days. If you aren't a member of one of these groups, you may be wondering what that entails. If you are flametender too, you know what I'm talking about . . . but read on. Let's discuss the practice of flametending!

In 2015 Brid, a friend of mine from the St. Louis Pagan community, reached out to me to ask if I would be interested in joining a group of women who tend sacred flames in honor of the Celtic goddess Brigid. At first I was a little hesitant because I had visions of robed and sequestered dedicants uttering prayers, invocations, and blessings for twenty-four hours straight, and it all seemed a bit overwhelming. Plus, I had just moved and had gone through a big life shift, and I was in an emotionally fragile place. I was also running a business and a home and had my publishing projects to write and illustrate. How in the world could I add one more thing?!

Brid assured me that it didn't have to be a challenging practice and that if I liked it, I could stay, but if it wasn't for me, there would be no hard feelings. Another concern of mine was that I work with many different deities in my magic and I also connect with them spiritually when I create my artwork. Although I worked with Brigid quite a bit at the time, working with other deities was going to have to be okay. She assured me that it was, and so with the click of a button I sent her my message agreeing to become a Brigidine flametender.

The group had a page on social media, and I found a schedule there with my name on it and the date for my shift. Every day the abbess posted the name of the next person in the rotation as a reminder. When my shift came around, I lit my candle at sundown, and I've been doing it every twenty days ever since. I really believe that Brigid inspired her to reach out to me. At the time it seemed like just one more thing on my plate, but what it really became was an opportunity to slow down occasionally and find the sacred in everything that I do. It was very healing. It's a beautiful practice and my friend was right; it wasn't difficult and it's a practice that can be adjusted to fit your life.

Cills of the Past, Present, and Future

Flametending in the name of the goddess Brigid is a tradition that goes back to pre-Christian times in Kildare, Ireland, where ritual fires were kept by priestesses of the goddess, and the tradition was carried over by nuns with the conversion to Christianity. It is believed that the flame was kept alight until possibly the sixteenth century, when the monasteries were suppressed under King Henry VIII. The flame was relighted in 1993 and is now a perpetual flame there.

Today there are many individuals and groups who carry on this tradition. At the time of this writing, most cills are exclusively female, but I see this changing and I'm sure the balance will be even more diverse than it is today by the time this is published. Essentially, each member takes turns lighting a candle at sunset in honor of the goddess Brigid. An invocation to her is recited either formally or informally, and that person keeps the flame going until the sunset of the following evening, when the next person on the shift lights their candle. The twentieth shift is held by Brigid herself in spirit.

I'm still a member of my original group of female flametenders, and Brid, who invited me, is now their abbess. I also formed a second group in 2019 with inclusive diverse membership, in which I serve as an abbess with cofounder and abbot Blake Octavian Blair. Blake is a fellow author as well; you've probably read his articles in various editions of the *Magical Almanac.* Blake worked with Brigid for years and knew other men who did also, but he discovered that it was challenging to find a group that welcomed all sexes and genders, so we decided to form our own. Brigid is a healing goddess who crosses boundaries, so it just made sense to forge our own inclusive group. Our new Brigidine cill has people of many backgrounds, inclucing New Age practitioners, tarot readers, Pagans, Druids, and Witches. It's an international fellowship of nineteen people, representing inclusion regardless of age, sex, sexual orientation, gender, or race. I created a logo and worked on the foundational written material since I had experience from my other group, and Blake edited and adjusted the texts. I also help field questions from people with less experience in the practice. Blake is usually the one to manage the schedule and posting on our group page. He enjoys it and, frankly, is really good at it. I step in if he's busy or away from technology due to travel. We make a good team.

A Day in the Life of a Flametender

So by now, you're probably wondering what exactly flametending entails. Well, the candle is only one element of the practice. Tending Brigid's flame can take many forms. If you wish, you can set up a small sacred space on a shelf, side table, or anyplace that speaks to you. It can be a permanent space or temporary. It can even be a single candle dedicated to the purpose. I often use a seven-day candle or a large jar candle of some kind, and I light several others when I invoke her at the beginning of my shift. I usually then do petitions for people to whom I send healing on a regular basis and then add any cill members requests in as well.

That being said, it's not a perfect world, so sometimes I'm literally right in the middle of preparing dinner at sunset. I might run in, light my candles as I invoke Brigid, and then I go back later with petitions and healing work. Brigid is a goddess of hearth and home—she totally gets it.

My altar for Brigid can vary. I have a permanent space dedicated to her in my bedroom on a wall shelf that was too high for my cats to jump onto but a good height for me to work at. I keep a statue of her there, several special candles, a small feather fan that I use to energetically clear the space, incense burner, crystals, and so on. Some days I prefer to set up an altar space to her in my dining room, which is usually a less formal altar. The least formal version of my flametending is a single candle on my kitchen windowsill. Brigid is a goddess of the hearth, so my kitchen is sacred space and a perfect place to honor her.

Flame choices can really vary, and of course safety is always a top concern. For many people, a flameless candle is a good choice because of safety, cats, children, and such. I usually light the flame at the beginning of my shift, and since I work at home, I can move my flame from its altar to my desk if I'm writing or doing art, both to keep an eye on it for safety and because this allows Brigid's energy to be part of the work I'm doing, since she is a goddess of inspiration. If I have to leave the house, I always use safety and turn on a flameless LED candle until I return. These flameless options are fine because they run on electricity and are aspects of the element of fire. Brigid is a goddess of inspiration; she appreciates your creative force and intention in your choice of "flame" as well as the importance of fire safety.

So you may wonder, is it all about the candles? The candles are a symbol, but there is much more that we do to honor Brigid during a flamekeeping shift. Ideally, a flametender tries to keep a flame burning from sunset on their shift to sunset on the next shift when they extinguish their flame. Some can only manage it for an hour or two, which is also just fine; as with all things spiritual, the intention is key. Activities in her honor can also be considered part of flamekeeping whether a candle is lit or not.

Thoughtfully bringing the sacred into everyday activities is a wonderful way to honor Brigid on a shift day. Many people like to do healing work at some point during their shift. You can add the names of people, places, or situations in need of healing energy to a small box, bag, dish, or cauldron and send Brigid's healing energy where it needs to go. If you are a reiki practitioner like I

am, your shift is a wonderful time to send reiki. You can spend a bit of time doing a special meditation or journeying. Caring for animals, nourishing others with food, making your home pleasing and comforting, giving love and compassion to yourself and others, supporting social justice, writing, music, poetry, knitting, any creative pursuit—these activities are all part of the many facets of Brigid. On a shift day, you can easily make these activities spiritual acts simply by mindfully acknowledging Brigid while performing everyday tasks that relate to her.

Brigid's Magical Correspondences

Included are both old-world and modern correspondences associated with Brigid. These can serve as inspiration for activities that can be done in her honor.

Elements of Fire and Water: Candles, fireplace, bonfire, light, sunlight, sparks, forge, stove, oven; springs, rivers, streams—all water including the kitchen sink or bathtub

Activities: Healing, poetry, music, whistling, all arts and crafts, teaching and learning, storytelling, herbalism, agriculture and livestock, caring for the home, the kitchen, cooking, childbirth and parenting, metalwork, beekeeping, magic, divination, justice, humanitarian efforts, protection of the earth and vulnerable people, caring for pets

Animals: Ewes and lambs, dairy cows, geese, swans, snakes, bees, owls, wolves, bears, badgers

Plants: Blackberry, violet, angelica, dandelion, snowdrop, rushes and grass, crocus, rowan, willow, oak, hazel, apples, rosemary, lavender, dill, chamomile, clover, oats, grain, and hops

Metals and Stones: Iron, silver, all white stones, quartz crystal, sandstone, amethyst, jasper, citrine

Colors: White, yellow, green, red, black

Other Symbols: Brigid's cross, triple spiral, triquetra, corn dollies, bells, dragons, the Milky Way, thresholds and doorways

Numbers: 3, 9, 19

Kindling Your Own Flame

If this sounds like a practice that's of interest to you, it's not hard to get started. All you really need is a representation of fire, some time, and your heart. Many people like the fellowship aspect of flamekeeping, so the first place to look is online. There are several organizations, such as Ord Brighideach, which is an interfaith order that has over 700 flamekeepers worldwide and welcomes everyone regardless of sex or gender. You can join as part of a nineteen-person cill or as an individual. Most of these groups have members all over the world. Because each member can practice in their own home, it allows you to be part of a group with wide-reaching membership.

You can also consider starting your own cill like Blake and I did. We're not affiliated with any outside group, just an independent flamekeeping cill. Nineteen members are best, although if you're close to nineteen, you can have a couple people double up on shifts. We found that using a social media group page was a great way to organize our members and a place to keep documents that may be downloaded by our flamekeepers with guidelines, ideas, invocations, printable candle labels, and other information we thought would be useful. We create a daily post with a GIF of a different flame with an announcement of whose shift it is every day just as a reminder. Many of our members then post a photo of their altar after the flame is lit. A photo is not necessary, but it's a beautiful way to connect with the rest of the group, and it's inspiring to see the different ways in which people create their sacred space. Some members post healing or other energy requests to the group, so it's a wonderful way to sup-

A LITTLE BIT OF MAGIC

Wells are sacred to Brigid. Taking a healing bath during a flametending shift can be beneficial to mind, body, and spirit.

port each other too. We even have a member who does divination for the group during her shift.

You don't have to join any group or organization in order to be a flamekeeper; you can also commit to the practice on your own if you prefer. You may choose a special day to begin and then just create your own schedule and commit to lighting your candles and honoring Brigid every nineteen days.

Something that I've noticed is that life events of mine seem to line up in interesting ways on my shift days. When I've needed extra healing because of medical stuff, it seems to always line up with a shift day for me, like the day before or after a doctor's appointment. There have been days when a family member really needed some extra love and compassion, and then my phone would notify me that it was time for my shift. When my husband and I had to help our cat cross over because she was so sick and we could no longer help her, the tiny footprints that the vet cast in clay for us were illuminated by Brigid's flame upon my altar. The first time I spoke on the phone with my brother, whom I had never met, I was sitting on my bed and Brigid's flame was glowing on the shelf above me, blessing our conversation.

She's seen me through good times and challenging times. She's blessed my meals and soothed my wounds. She's strengthened my resolve and inspired my work. For me, keeping her flame has been a practice that has increased my quiet times of introspection, boosted my mindfulness, and helped me grow my sense of fellowship one little candle at a time.

Further Reading

Weatherstone, Lunaea. *Tending Brigid's Flame: Awaken to the Celtic Goddess of the Hearth, Temple, and Forge.* Woodbury, MN: Llewellyn Publications, 2015.

Daimler, Morgan. *Brigid: Meeting the Celtic Goddess of Poetry, Forge, and Healing Well.* Pagan Portals. Alresford, Hants, UK: Moon Books, 2016.

Neal, Carl. *Imbolc: Rituals, Recipes & Lore for Brigid's Day.* Woodbury, MN: Llewellyn, 2016.

Tantric Kundalini
Serpent Rising Spell

Sasha Graham

The icy peaks of the Himalayas reach for the stars at the highest point on earth. The air is crisp and thin. Lack of oxygen makes your lungs work harder. It feels like falling in love. Your breath quickens. Your heart beats faster. You get dizzy. The sapphire blue sky unfolds across glacial lakes that mirror the sky. Monks wearing crimson and jewel-toned robes gather to chant, study, and maintain monasteries filled with prayer wheels, sacred art, and radiant, sparkling Buddhas. Tiny farming towns are full of indigenous women, many of whom marry two husbands (often brothers), weave long braids into their hair, and wear course black clothing with intricately carved silver embellishments. The higher the elevation, the more ornate a women's jewelry. Children work alongside their parents. Picnic lunch breaks are taken at the stupa, the sacred, holy spot of each village.

At 12,000 feet, you are the closest you'll ever be to the Sun. The landscape blows dust in your eyes and the wind sends your hair flying like Medusa's snakes. You stop at a jagged mountain passes and spy advancing storms. Snow clouds grow and growl at you like massive bodhisattvas, the fierce deities and destroyers of obstacles. You gulp thermoses full of hot, sweet tea and eat deep-fried salty, spicy potatoes out of parchment bags. The road spindles like a ribbon beneath you and snowflakes fall on your cheeks. Sleep comes easily to a tired body that's been exposed to the elements all day.

It's no coincidence that wild, mind-expanding spiritualities occur at the top of the world. Mountain cultures are renowned for intoxicating mysticism, from the Andes to the Carpathians. Religious architecture usually points up. Churches often have steeples. Temples, synagogues, and mosques have towers and spires pointing up to the sky. In Tibet, at the top of the world, most private homes and monasteries have flat roofs. You can't get any higher—you've arrived. Westerners seeking gods, spirits guides, and angels look up. Eastern practitioners seeking gods and deities look within.

The Himalayas span northern India, Nepal, the Kingdom of Bhutan, Pakistan, and Chinese-occupied Tibet. Just as some of the world's major rivers, such as the Ganges, the Tsangpo-Brahmaputra, and the Indus, rise in the Himalayas and flow downward to an expanse of over 600 million people, so does the culture of spirituality and religion move downward from the highest point on earth. The Himalayas are a melting pot of tradition and deep magic. Sages, adventurers, and seekers meet, exchange ideas, and return to their respective cultures. Magics, sutras, traditions, and rituals pass through generations from teacher to student, from guru to disciple.

Yoga's categorical rise in popularity in the West brought with it all the mysticism of the East. The words *tantric* and *kundalini* fill the imagination with ideas of wanton sexuality and esoteric yoga. The

description of a coiled serpent at the base of the spine may have some people scratching their heads, wondering if in fact there's an actual snake coiled up down there.

The Tantric Kundalini Serpent Rising Spell is intended to capture the essence of authentic personal power and infuse it into every aspect of your life and body. Kundalini is your life force and the energy lying dormant within you: the seat of personal authenticity. Wake and infuse this energy to break old habitual patterns and create an alignment with your highest good. You become "lit" from the inside.

The awakening process occurs in the subtle body. The subtle body is invisible, although some people can detect colors and auras or know when a person is nearing death or about to become pregnant. The subtle body is the place of energetic centers, chakras, thoughts, feelings, and emotions. You can compare it to the "gross anatomy," which is your measurable bones, blood, and physical self. The subtle body is the energy you exude and the "vibe" you give off.

What Is Tantra?

Tantra refers to the hidden mysteries of Buddhism and Hinduism and is derived from ancient tantric texts. Tantric practice is broad and diverse across the Himalayas and Asia, carrying many different traditions. The word *tantra* means "to weave" in Sanskrit. This understanding comes from a combination of two words: *tantoti*, which means "to stretch" or "to expand," and *trayati*, which means "liberation."

Tantra embraces all aspects of life, not just sex. While tantrics embrace sexual energy as part of the universal life force, a tantric can be completely monogamous, even celibate, while practicing. Tantra extends the idea of sexual union to all aspects of life

A LITTLE BIT OF MAGIC

Tibetan tantrics engage in the tummo practice, whereby they employ breathing exercises and visualizations to build an intense internal heat, enabling them to sit outside naked for over twenty-four hours in the coldest nights of the Himalayan winter.

so practioners continually engage in states of bliss. It doesn't mean the tantric avoids bad thoughts and feelings altogether. They are human, after all. But the tantric does not confuse or partake in the identification of thoughts or feelings. They notice thoughts and emotions like one observes a passing cloud. They practice the art of nonattachment. They bring themselves into presence by engaging the senses and partaking in the wonderment of any moment. The tantric body becomes a finely tuned instrument of the universe.

Snake symbolism can be traced back as far as ancient Mesopotamian art and is used today as a symbol of modern medicine. A symbolic coiled snake at the base of the spine is potent image. Our small intestine rests, snakelike, at the bottom of the belly near the root of the spine. If the small intestine were pulled out, it would measure an an average of twenty feet. Our snakelike guts are the place of decomposition. This is where we process food, absorb what we need, and excrete the rest. It exists near the root chakra, the center of security and grounding. It is in this very space of rootedness that the snake waits for its awakening.

Snakes inhabit dark places, caves, rock walls, and wet marshlands. They are indicative of deep, dormant energy—the very place of the shadow, darkness, and restful sleep that gives way to a new possibility. The snake emerges from the deepest, darkest place to find the warm light of day. It is the ideal metaphor for the flowering of our true power.

Serpent Rising Spell

Perform this spell to harness the generative power inside you. Indulge and enjoy every pleasure the universe has to offer you. This is a long and enjoyable enchantment. Take your time. Seclude yourself in nature. Spend an entire afternoon or evening performing it. Read through the entire spell, adapting and substituting whatever makes sense for you. Use what suits you and disregard the rest. Magic is a personal and creative act. Your instincts are the most important ingredient. Perform this where you will not be interrupted, and repeat as often as you like.

You will need:

Sage or palo santo for smudging
Bath or pool of water
Fire pit or candle
Your favorite indulgent food (dark spiced chocolate, cheese and
wine, fruit dipped in cinnamon-whipped honey, etc.)
A beautiful piece of music
Deck of tarot cards

Strip naked and stand before a mirror, observing yourself in your natural state. Gaze without judgment in a place of pure acceptance. Look with eyes of love. Move closer to the mirror and peer intensely at your own eyes. Look for your own active awareness looking back through your eyes. Smudge yourself with the smoke of the sage or palo santo.

You will now work with the five tattvas. *Tattva* is the Sanskrit word for "principle," "reality," or "truth." The tattvas are similar to the four elements in Western ceremonial magic. You will bring yourself in alignment with each tattva.

Earth: Remain naked or, if you prefer, put on comfortable clothing. Go outside and lie on the ground. Feel the earth beneath your body. Feel how the earth supports you. Imagine the entirety of the planet as your physical body makes contact with it. Breathe in the scent of the grass. Burrow your fingers into the warm dirt. Connect every inch of yourself to the ground beneath you. There is no separation. This is where you came from and where you will return. Say, "I am the earth, the earth is me." Stay here as long as you like, focusing your attention on the quality of fecund, rich earth.

Water: Slowly and mindfully step into a prepared bathtub, hot tub, swimming pool, lake, pond, or river. Feel the water engulf your toe, foot, ankle, and calf. Give yourself over to the sensation of water. Feel it move inch by inch up your skin. Lie back and allow your hair to spill around you. Let the water tickle and fill your ears. Allow just your face to break the surface while the rest of

you is submerged. Say, "I am the water. The water is me. I am the ocean and river. I am fog and mist. I am snow and ice. I am clouds and rain. There is no separation." Stay here as long as you like, focusing your attention on the quality of wet, buoyant water.

Air: Leave the water and step into the air. Allow the air to dry your body. If there is a breeze of wind, let it caress you like a gentle touch. Say, "I am air, wild and free. I am the wind." Focus on your breath. Inhale and exhale. Stay here as long as you like, focusing your attention on the quality of crystal clear air.

Ether: Sit with your legs crossed. Feel the spaciousness around you. Feel the pregnancy of the air. Feel the space inside of the space. This is the place of manifestation and the true nature of the ever-expanding universe. Say, "I am space. I am ether. I am manifestation and manifestation is me." Stay here as long as you like, focusing your attention on the quality of luminous silence and space.

Fire: Light a small fire if you have access to a fire pit or light a single candle. Focus intently on the dancing flames. Observe the nature of fire. Allow the fire to warm your palms. Let warmth saturate your skin. This is the nature of energy, heat, and combustion. Say, "I am the fire and the fire is me. I burn with the energy of a thousand stars." Stay here as long as you like, focusing your attention on the transformative quality of fire.

Now you will work on the subtle tattvas.

Either bring your food outside with you or return inside to eat by the light of a candle.

Smell: Pick up your favorite indulgent food. Breathe in the scent. Move into the heart of the scent. Close your eyes. Can you distinguish between the food and the other smells of the air, the space, the grass and flowers? Dissect everything you can smell. Inhale the odor of everything around you. Smell deeper.

Taste: Bite your favorite indulgence, slowly. Truly, deeply taste it. Can you find the unique flavor? What tastes do you taste? What does it remind you of? Move deeper into the flavors with each mindful bite. Continue to eat as if each bite were the first bite. Taste deeper.

Form: Observe the form and shape of your food. What forms existed before its present state? See the individual ingredients. Imagine what will happen to the form after you eat it. All form is transitory.

Touch: Touch your own hand. Feel your skin, flesh, and bone beneath it. Your skin is the largest organ of your body. Feel your shoulders, your face, the underside of your arm. Touch the ground beneath you. Touch your soft hair. Trace your own soft lip with your finger.

Sound: Play your beautiful piece of music. Take a sound bath inside the notes. Allow it to move through your body. Hear every note. Hear the silence in between. Allow your body to be carried away by the melody. Allow the song to end and listen to the

poignant silence surrounding you. What sounds do you hear? Listen deeper.

Spread a tarot deck into a circle on the ground. Sit inside the circle with legs crossed. Allow your spine to remain straight and rest your palms on your knees. Focus on the breath. Allow your inhales and exhales to become longer.

Focus on the base of the spine. Imagine a coiled snake resting there. Feel heat and power where the snake resides. Let your inhale move down the spine and your exhale pull the energy up. Let your breath bring the snake up the root of your spine. Allow the snake energy to rise. Imagine the snake light up your body as it moves up through your genitals, stomach, heart, throat, third eye, and ultimately the crown at the top of your head. Feel power rise and radiate through every part of your body. Imagine yourself illuminated by the essence of cleansing fire. Let it radiate out of your skin and eyes. Know this is the state of your true, perfected power. Your authentic self, apart from what you've picked up along the way, apart from what you've inherited from your family. This wild, energetic being is the true state of who you are. Live inside it. Let it illuminate you.

Pull a tarot card for a piece of advice, parting thought, or guiding inspiration as you take yourself and your beautiful energy out into the world.

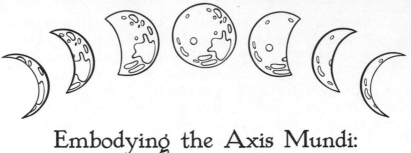

Embodying the Axis Mundi:
Orienting the Cosmological Self

Jhenah Telyndru

Throughout time and around the world, cultures have developed religious cosmologies that represent their understanding of how the universe is organized. We can often observe these cosmological maps in cultural myths and iconography, particularly those that describe the creation of the world. Cosmological and cosmogenic myths encode a culture's concept of the structure of the universe and serve to define the natural order of the world— and humanity's place within it. These can incorporate everything from the patterns of the seasons and the rules of society to the workings of the family unit and the moral expectations of the individual, and they often define where the individual stands in the context of the whole.

A common feature of these cosmologies is the inclusion of the concept of the sacred center, which can often serve as a key to understanding a culture's guiding priorities—but spiritually, it can be so much more. Whether omphalos, holy mountain, or perpetual hearth fire; whether sacred tree, ceremonial pole, or standing stone—whatever marks the sacred center can also take on the role of the *axis mundi*, the world axis that connects earth and sky, that bridges what has been with what is yet to be and is the point at which all directions meet. Although called by many names and taking many forms, the axis mundi is used in many cultures as a bridge between the worlds, particularly by those who are in service as healers and those who engage in trance journey work.

Many modern-day Pagans, polytheists, and practitioners of magic include a cosmological element in their ritual workings. Depending upon the tradition, rituals often begin with the defining of sacred space (as with the casting of a circle or the raising of a nemeton), an orientation of the ritual in space and time (as with the calling of the quarters or the honoring of the Three Realms as in some Celtic traditions), and an acknowledgment of the sacred center (as with the lighting of the hearth fire or the use of a central altar).

In many magical practices, much time and energy is spent in aligning ourselves with the outer world and the forces of nature through the use of correspondences. For example, in those traditions that call the quarters in ritual, there is more going on than acknowledging the four directions. For many, each direction also includes a corresponding element and its qualities, a guardian or watchtower who guards the door to the energies associated with that direction, spirits and divinities who are of a like energy, and other allies holding elemental energetic resonance, such as animals, stones, planets, and bioregions. Typically, the center is also honored and called upon, revealing its nature as the place of union where all energies meet and from which all energies emanate.

While how this is done varies from tradition to tradition—often as a reflection of the cultural roots that may inform the path in question—this ritual creation of a microcosmic echo of the cosmic order is a powerful act of magic. For the work done within this construct isn't happening in someone's dedicated temple space, backyard circle, or living room; rather, it is taking place

A LITTLE BIT OF MAGIC

"Every microcosm, every inhabited region, has a centre; that is to say, a place that is sacred above all."
—*Mircea Eliade*

at the very center of creation—that place between where all things meet—and its intention emanates outward in all directions, horizontally through space and vertically through time. It is said that what occurs between the worlds takes root in all the worlds, and when we use ritual as a vehicle to journey along the bridge of liminality, our ability to effect change in the world and in our lives is magnified.

To be truly whole, we must come to know ourselves as well as we can so that we may acknowledge and accept all that we are—not just the parts of us that are already sovereign and empowered, such as the gifts we've been blessed with, the achievements we are proud of, the skills we have mastered, or the experiences that bring us joy and fulfillment. Wholeness requires that we also accept the places we are broken, the wounds that we carry, the challenges that we stumble over, the things we are ashamed of, the fears we have developed, the resentments that we've nurtured, the illusions that limit our vision, and the sorrows and vulnerabilities that bring us to our knees. Seeking out and accepting our shadow aspects allows us to bring them into the light of consciousness, a necessary step for our healing and evolution.

Our Cosmic Map

I am fond of saying that we are not apart from nature, but a part of nature, and in the context of this discussion, this means that our cosmological constructs apply to more than just the universe that exists around us; they are also a model for the universe that exists within us. The four directions, the three realms, and the sacred center— all these hold personal correspondences and can be used to organize our inner landscapes and orient ourselves in relation to the greater pattern of all that is.

Let's take a closer look at our personal cosmological map in order to see what understanding we can reach about how we have ordered our universe. First, in our inner cosmology, the four directions and their four corresponding elements are present.

The Watchtowers
The east is aligned with air and represents our mental health and our abilities to communicate, to be ethical and fair, to learn new

things, and to discern what is real from what is illusion. The level of objectivity that informs our beliefs, our perspectives, and the truths that we carry with us—shaped by personal experiences and what we have been taught by our family of origin and society—are the eastern watchtowers through which we understand the world and our place within it.

The south is aligned with fire and represents our energetic health, our will, our passions, the ways in which we express ourselves, and how we use our energy in the world. The choices we make, the impulses we follow, the disciplines we develop, the work that we do in the world, and those things that motivate us to take action are the southern watchtowers through which we effect change in the world and within ourselves.

The west is aligned with water and represents our emotional health, our intuitive process, our receptivity and adaptability, and

our ability to be in balanced relationship with ourselves and others. Our ability to engage in reflection, our level of emotional discernment, how we react to the people and situations in our lives, our receptivity to innate wisdoms, and the degree of awareness of our shadow are the western watchtowers through which we connect with the world and the different aspects of the self.

The north is aligned with earth and represents our physical health, our personal environment, the resources at our disposal, and our ability to manifest the reality of our lives. The amount of personal responsibility we take, the level of commitment we invest, the choices we make around the allocation of our resources, and the boundaries we build and maintain are the northern watchtowers through which we experience the world and create our place within it.

The Three Realms

Next, we can explore the Three Realms and their temporal resonances within us.

The Realm of Sea is the dwelling place of the ancestors and the source of tradition, and it represents the energies of our past. It waters the roots of our identity, holds the keys to our healing, nurtures our sense of belonging, and holds the deep wisdom that can only be birthed from experience. It is our sacred memory.

A LITTLE BIT OF MAGIC

It is said that what occurs between the worlds takes root in all the worlds, and when we use ritual as a vehicle to journey along the bridge of liminality, our ability to effect change in the world and in our lives is magnified.

The Realm of Land is the home of the living and the sacred grove of our learning, and it represents the energies of our present. It provides the landscape for our life's journey, tests the strength of our character, gives us the tools to be cocreators of the universe, and presents opportunities for us to enter into right relationship with our sovereign self. It is our sacred duty.

The Realm of Sky is the abode of the gods, the cosmic template that sets the patterns of existence and represents the energies of our future. It illuminates the course of our spiritual evolution, reveals the eternal nature of our soul, unveils the mystery of unity with all that is, and awaits our return to Source. It is our sacred destiny.

The Sacred Center

Finally, let us consider the sacred center and its resonance at the heart of who we are.

The Sacred Center is aligned with spirit, the source that contains all other elemental energies within it. It is the axis mundi, the World Tree, and the bridge that connects what is above with what is below, what is within with what is without. It is the heart from which all aspects of our being emanate and the place that acknowledges all parts of ourselves as one. It holds the power of integration, which permits us to view ourselves, our lives, and our world from a place of wholeness

I invite you to consider the relationship between what is around us and what is within us, using the self—the whole self—as the axis mundi, the bridge of connection. In order for us to be in clear connection with the outside world, we must first work to discover, acknowledge, and come into right relationship with all aspects of the self within us. To do this great work, we must practice the art of spiritual integration. Integration assists us in embracing the truth of who and what we are, with the intention to work toward wholeness rather than endlessly striving, in vain, to achieve some illusory perfection.

The Working

Stand or sit comfortably upright and adopt a natural breathing rhythm. Take some time to focus on your exhalations, and as you exhale, release any physical discomfort, mental chatter, or emotional distress that is keeping you from being present and clear. When you feel you have discharged all that you can, bring your attention to your inhalations, and as you inhale, breathe in the pure, vibrant life-force energies that emanate from the heart of the earth below you. Direct this energy to fill in the spaces left behind by all that you've exhaled and released, and permit it to replenish the whole of your energy field with its vitalistic power. Repeat this process until you feel fully grounded, fully present, and fully open to receive.

When you are ready, envision yourself alone in the empty vastness of a universe yet unformed. You are a tiny point of light in the center of an infinite darkness that stretches out around you in all directions. Breathe this point of light larger and larger until you give off enough light to see that below you is a solid surface. Stand upon it. Root yourself in it. Know that it exists there in the center of all creation because you will it and that the first thing that ever emerges from the void is that which bridges force and form . . . that which separates light and darkness . . . that which connects all things and nothing.

Your point of light is the fire that catalyzes this universe's creation, and it begins to expand and elongate, taking on a more defined form. Imagine this light, this essence of all that you are, starting to embody the vision you've chosen of the axis mundi. Breathe this experience into being. Know that this energy is not something that is forming around you—it *is* you. Use the creative power that you possess to fully embody the form of the axis mundi . . . to fully embrace the role of the bridge . . . to know, without any shred of doubt, that everything in existence begins exactly where you are and returns here as well. And so it is. And so you are.

From this place of Sacred Center, bring your awareness downward and delve deep into the cosmic reflection of the Realm of Sea. Connect with what has come before. Acknowledge and embrace your past. Ask what the past needs most for you to know at this time. Pay attention to how this makes you feel. Ask how you can best embrace this lesson at this time. Bless the Realm of Sea within you. Bless the past and memory. And so it is. And so you are.

Bring your awareness upward through to the amorphous potentiality of the Realm of Sky high above you. Connect with the vision of what is yet to be. Acknowledge and embrace your future. Ask what the future needs most for you to know at this time. Pay attention to how this makes you feel. Ask how you can best prepare for this lesson at this time. Bless the Realm of Sky within you. Bless the future and its unknowable potential. And so it is. And so you are.

Bring your awareness to ground and center into the abundant, life-giving presence of the Realm of Land all around you. Connect

with the vision of all that is here and now. Acknowledge and embrace your present. Unwaveringly rooted here in the center of your cosmological map, visualize the four cardinal directions stretching out from where you stand like shimmering pathways of light that extend endlessly out into the distance until they disappear beyond your sight. You are the nexus of the four-strand web that they weave across the sacred landscape of the now, and just as they extend out from you, you can call their energies back to you. Considering each in turn, allow the space around you to become filled with the visions of the energies they hold as you ask your questions of them.

Turn to the east, which holds the power of air, and call its energies back to you. With a yellow cosmic gusting, the energies reflecting your engagement with the air pathway return to center . . . return to you. When your awareness is fully immersed in the energies of air, ask to see the ways in which you express the energies of air in your life, from a place of both balance and imbalance. Ask to be shown what you need most to know about your relationship with air and the east. When you receive the answers to these questions, thank the energies of air and envision a clear and healthy channel of air energy running toward you and away from you into the east.

Turn to the south, which holds the power of fire, and call its energies back to you. With a red cosmic blazing, the energies reflecting your engagement with the fire pathway return to center . . . return to you. When your awareness is fully immersed in the energies of fire, ask to see the ways in which you express the energies of fire in your life, from a place of both balance and imbalance. Ask to be shown what you need most to know about your relationship with fire and the south. When you receive the answers to these questions, thank the energies of fire and envision a clear and healthy channel of fire energy running toward you and away from you into the south.

Turn to the west, which holds the power of water, and call its energies back to you. With a blue cosmic crashing, the energies reflecting your engagement with the water pathway return to center . . . return to you. When your awareness is fully immersed in the energies of water, ask to see the ways in which you express the energies of water in your life, from a place of both balance and imbalance. Ask to be shown what you need most to know about your relationship with water and the west. When you receive the answers to these questions, thank the energies of water and envision a clear and healthy channel of water energy running toward you and away from you into the west.

Turn to the north, which holds the power of earth, and call its energies back to you. With a green cosmic quaking, the energies reflecting your engagement with the earth pathway return to center . . . return to you. When your awareness is fully immersed in the energies of earth, ask to see the ways in which you express the energies of earth in your life, from a place of both balance and imbalance. When you receive the answers to these questions, thank the energies of earth and envision a clear and healthy channel of earth energy running toward you and away from you into the north.

When you are ready, bring your awareness to the vision of your whole self, standing in the Sacred Center of your universe, a shining embodiment of the axis mundi, which connects all things. Here in the center, which holds the power of spirit, call all your energies back to you. With a cosmic illuminating, the energies reflecting your engagement with the spirit pathway return to center . . . return to you. And it comes from every possible direction, converging upon you in the form of an energetic sphere. When your awareness is fully immersed in the energies of spirit, ask to see the ways in which you express the energies of spirit in your life, from a place of both balance and imbalance. Ask to to be shown what you need most to know about your relationship with spirit and the center. When you receive the answers to these questions, thank the energies of spirit and envision a clear, healthy, and integrated pulsing sphere of spirit energy moving toward you and away from you through time and space.

Be present in this moment. Experience all the energies that compose your personal universe as they become enmeshed with each other, forming a bright and shining whole. Take three deep, anchoring breaths and allow yourself to fully settle into the centered oneness that comes with every act of integration. The more you are able to embody your vision of the axis mundi, the stronger your ability to bridge the worlds becomes.

Conclusion

Committing yourself to perform this meditative working regularly will serve to empower you as an individual, help you establish a strong internal locus of esteem, and present you with a powerful tool that will allow you stand firmly in the center of the universe, serving as the bridge that brings you to wholeness. The more you embrace the self as an axis mundi, the more you will be able to achieve healing in the inner landscape while actively creating a life in right relationship with all that is in the outer landscape.

Halos:
They're Not Just for Angels
James Kambos

It was always too early in the morning when my mother and grandmother would drag me to church. I hated church. Going to church meant having to dress up. That meant my tie would be too tight, my dress pants would be scratchy, and my dress shoes would pinch my toes. On the way inside the church my mother would always stop to light a candle and pause to say a prayer for some troubled friend or relative. Since it was a Greek Orthodox church, the walls surrounding the candle area were covered with religious icons. Some depicted Jesus, others were of the Virgin Mary or numerous saints. In the candlelight the somber expressions of the religious figures appeared soft and ethereal. But what I remember the most were the halos. Surrounding the head of each figure was a halo. The background of most of the icons were metallic gold. The halos were usually deep red or another shade of gold. Other halos appeared to emanate as light rays from the head of the subject.

Suddenly it no longer mattered that it was early or that my dress clothes were uncomfortable. Now I was mesmerized by the halos. Each head was surrounded by one. To me the halos were magic. In the soft, flickering candlelight, the halos spoke to me. As an eight-year-old boy, I thought the halos were so pretty.

I still do.

As an adult, I began to study Paganism. Though my faith began to change, my encounter with the Orthodox Christian religious art and its fascinating use of halos remained with me. In college I studied ancient history and ancient art. That's when I began to learn more about halos and their meanings in different cultures.

One of the main lessons I learned about halos is this: halos aren't just for angels. In popular belief angels are frequently seen with a radiant, glowing halo, usually floating just above their head. But as you'll see, halos have been depicted in various ways by artists since ancient times. You'll also see that halos aren't just associated with angels or Christian art.

About Halos

To begin with, a halo is usually a religious art design that depicts a person having a gold or white light glowing around the head area. This glowing light is normally round or oval in shape. The halo can be found in Pagan art, Christian art, and the art of other faiths as well.

Sometimes the halo, as I mentioned earlier, is edged in deep red to set it off from the gold backgrounds, which are popular in much of the religious art. In my collection of Greek Orthodox icons, I have one of St. James. In this icon, instead of using a red border around the head, the artist uses a deeper gold to create the halo. The gold halo in this case is a slightly different shade of gold from the background, which shows the halo off beautifully.

Other times halos may be made by using a semicircle of pointed ray shapes emanating from the subject's head. In cases like this the halo is made to resemble a star or the Sun. There are also depictions of the Virgin Mary wearing a halo of stars. As you can see, a halo can take many forms.

The halo can also be known by other terms. *Nimbus, disk, aureole,* or *crown of light* may also be used instead of the word *halo.* Halos may be depicted differently by different artists and faiths, but most agree that a halo is a radiant light surrounding the head of a holy or saintly person. Interestingly, Jesus was never mentioned in the Bible as having a halo.

Halos aren't just found in religious art. They can also occur in the natural world. Halos can be found around the Moon, beside the Sun, and even around a candle flame. When halos are seen in the natural world, they frequently have deep mystical meaning. But I'll touch on that later.

Now, let's take a look at a brief history of halos and their significance in art and magic.

Halos and Their Pagan Origins

Halos began as a Pagan art form. From the very beginning, halos were used by ancient artists to help depict the divine power possessed by a god or goddess or by a holy and powerful human. Halos began as usually round or oval. They may have appeared as a disk, a radiant light, or as rays. But halos were always positioned around, behind, or just above the head of the subject. Due to their association with Paganism, Christian artists avoided using halos until the fourth or fifth century CE.

The first people that used halos in their art were the ancient Egyptians. The ancient Egyptians used a solid coppery-red disk shape to represent a halo. To the Egyptians of the ancient world, this disk-shaped halo had deep meaning: it represented the life-giving Sun.

This halo, or solar disk, always rested directly on top of the head of an ancient Egyptian goddess or god. The best example is of their greatest god, Ra. Ra is always depicted with a human body but with a falcon head, and always resting on his head is the regal Sun disk. Then, coiled around the solar disk is a sacred serpent. To the ancient Egyptians the halo (disk) was one of their most important sacred symbols. They probably used it in their religious art more than any other ancient society.

Not far across the Mediterranean Sea, the sacred art of the ancient Greeks also began to flourish. Though not as devoted to the halo design as the ancient Egyptians, the Greeks did incorporate the halo into their holy art also.

Two notable examples are found in art depicting the ancient Greek gods Helios and Hyperion. Helios, the Sun god, is usually seen wearing a halo made of Sun rays around his head. Hyperion, the god of the heavens, or heavenly light, is frequently depicted wearing a halo of radiant white light.

From ancient Greece, the concept of using halos to represent the divine power of a god or goddess spread west and east. The ancient Romans appear to be next in using halos with some of their deities.

The Greeks' influence in halo design can also be found east of Greece in pre-Islamic Syria. While in college, I discovered there was an obscure Sun god named Malakbel worshipped in present-day Syria. He is also shown wearing a halo of Sun rays, very similar in appearance to the Greek god Helios.

As time passed, other ancient civilizations, such as the Chinese, had solar deities that appear wearing halos of gold light. Eventually, the Buddhists also showed the use of halos in their religious statues.

As I mentioned earlier, Christian artists didn't begin using

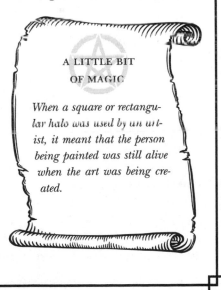

A LITTLE BIT
OF MAGIC

When a square or rectangular halo was used by an artist, it meant that the person being painted was still alive when the art was being created.

halos until about the fourth or fifth centuries CE. I never really understood the delay. At first, it seemed Christian art tried to distance itself from artistic styles that had Pagan roots. However, once Christianity began using halos in its art, the results were stunning: halos can be found in paintings, church frescoes, and mosaic tile floors. Christian artists eagerly expressed themselves by using halos on holy figures such as angels, Jesus, the Virgin Mary, and many saints. Halos were also used to express the deep reverence held toward a special person such as an emperor.

Magical Halos

Not all halos are created by the hands of talented artists. Some occur in nature. Here are some examples of other halos you may see:

Sun Dog: Sun dogs usually happen at sunrise or sunset on a winter day. They're created by light being refracted from ice crystals on either side of the Sun and may appear red. They don't form a complete halo but may form a column on each side of the Sun. Why they're called "dogs" is anybody's guess. In weather lore they're believed to precede rain or snow. In some Native American traditions, they serve as a mystical sign that a positive change is coming to the world.

Lunar Halo: A ring around the Moon, or lunar halo, can also be seen sometimes. It may happen in winter or summer. Lunar halos are caused by moonlight being reflected and refracted by ice particles at high altitudes. This halo can also indicate coming precipitation. Spiritually, when you see a lunar halo, it's a good time to perform protection magic.

Candle Magic: Those that practice candle magic may also see a halo form around a flame. When this happens, especially if the flame flickers, it is usually a sign that a spirit is near.

• • • ☽ • • •

You may encounter halos frequently in magic. For example, they are sometimes featured on figures in tarot card decks, or you may see a halo in a dream. When encountering these sacred symbols, remember—halos symbolize enlightenment.

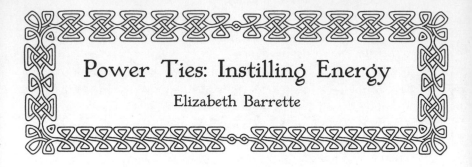

Power Ties: Instilling Energy

Elizabeth Barrette

Magic is all about energy. When we craft a magical artifact, create a spell, or perform a ritual, then we are channeling energy to achieve a desired effect. The objects and actions we use in this process serve to gather, shape, and direct energy. There are many ways to instill energy. Let's explore some of them.

Materials

Rare Materials

Rare things typically hold more value and power than common things. Sometimes this is chance, like a shell that is normally white having some purple. A three-leaf clover is common; a four-leaf clover is rare and collects more power. It takes more effort to find the rare ones among the common ones. Other times this is more concrete: the best examples of any material will be less common than the average examples. An unflawed jewel is rare, while flawed ones are common. Because rare things are improbable, they also help manipulate probability, which is one way that magic works.

Quality Materials

The better the quality, the more useful something is in magic. One reason is the energy it brings to the artifact or spell. Another is durability. Cotton will stand up better than cotton blends. A perfect stone can hold more energy and is less likely to break under the strain compared to a flawed one. If a flaw has meaning, though, it may be of use, like a swirl of glaze that seems to suggest a face on a ceremonial bowl.

Magic—like electricity—can be absolutely ruinous to materials, especially flimsy ones. I tend to fry electronics. I've known friends who bleached carnelian or broke hematite. I've seen someone go through a brand-new trench coat in two weeks, to the point that I could tear the cloth with my hands.

So when you choose a material for magic, examine it closely. How thick is it? How clear? Are there any chips? How even is the color? Is it tough or fragile? Choose the best quality you can find and afford. It will last longer, and you can do more with it.

Expensive Materials

Money is energy. When you pay for costly goods—or hire someone to do work you can't—you're trading some of your energy for them. This has significance of its own, even before you add in other aspects. As described earlier, what is rare and fine is valuable, and that raises the price. Expect to pay more for things worth using in magic.

Different traditions have different opinions on this topic. Some encourage people to buy the best offerings they can afford. Others say that money taints magic, and supplies or tools should never be bought but instead found or made. Some consider buying okay but not haggling. Which stance you take on this issue is up to you.

Choosing an Item

Finding an Item

Finding just the right thing to use in a spell or ritual takes patience, luck, and observation. This ties into many other aspects too. It takes time to search, whether you're picking it up off the ground or buying it in a store. I have a knack for finding holey stones, so I always look for them, but a long time can pass before I find one—and occasionally I'll find several close together. Other folks have a knack for locating things through online vendors. You might be looking for something with certain rare features or exceptional quality. A woodworker will walk past many saplings before choosing one to cut and make into a staff. As mentioned, finding something is acceptable in most if not all magical traditions, while buying things may not be.

Making an Item Yourself

Crafting your own tools and supplies is among the most powerful magical practices. You put a little bit of yourself into everything you make. For this reason, many Pagans learn crafts such as herbalism, candlemaking, woodworking, jewelry making, dyeing, spinning, weaving, sewing, knitting, or crochet. Woodburning, soapmaking, bookbinding, and ceramics are uncommon. Blacksmithing and glassworking are quite rare. If you can't make the whole item, buying parts to assemble and decorate will carry some of the same effect.

Think about what crafts you already know how to do. How could they apply to making magical tools and supplies? If you don't know any crafts, or your current ones don't readily apply to magic, then you may decide to learn something new. Consider what kind of things you'd like to make and what skills you would need. There are many books on crafts, a few on magical crafts in particular, and sometimes you can find workshops at a Pagan event.

Commissioning an Item

If you can't make something for yourself or can't do it well enough, then you can hire someone else to do it for you. Items made just for you are more special than mass-market ones. Many people commission altar tools or magical artifacts when they want something with specific features. In terms of raising power, it doesn't matter whether you trade favors or pay cash; it's the energy transfer that matters. Bear in mind that some traditions consider it wrong to mix money and magic.

Borrowing Power from a Source

Power can be borrowed from a source, directly or indirectly. For example, dipping something in seawater or scooping some into a container can borrow energy from the ocean. An antler handle on an athame, a buckskin shirt, and a deer-toe rattle are all ways of invoking the qualities of the deer as a spirit animal—caution, agility, swiftness, and so on. Less directly, you might use a picture of the ocean or a deer to convey a similar effect. Direct methods tend to bring considerably more power than indirect ones, but they are more difficult, sometimes risky, and not always feasible. Indirect methods are more accessible, if less powerful.

Adding Symbols

Energy can be not only added but also directed by placing symbols of power on magical artifacts or tools. Icons, offering bowls, and

other dedicated tools may have their deity's symbol put on them. Elemental tools can be consecrated to their element in this manner. Anything can be written upon with runes, ogham, or another magical alphabet to bind it to its owner or to a specific purpose. Browse magical alphabets and lists of symbols to find things that you can use.

Symbols may be added in various ways. Carving, woodburning, stamping, embossing, and painting are among the most common. Symbols may also be drawn with oil or water, usually saltwater. A craft store will have many useful tools and supplies for marking your materials. Bear in mind that some things, such as magical inks, you may have to buy from a Pagan supplier or make yourself.

Traveling a Long Way

According to some traditions, travel builds energy. If you've read about magical quests, this is one reason why. The principle can apply to items from far away—very useful if you are ordering online—or those you obtain locally and then carry or send on a trip. It also applies to traveling in person to visit a special place, collecting distant ingredients, and so on.

For this reason, meteorites are some of the most powerful artifacts, whether they are stone, metal, or peridot. The good ones are extremely expensive, but decent nuggets can be found at a somewhat more affordable price. Sending an item on a trip around the world is quite effective, and I've been party to this several times with books autographed by fans that were meant to be handed over to the author when full.

A Sacred Place

Some places gather more energy than others. They may be rare, very high or very low, unusually shaped, positioned where streams of energy cross, or special for other reasons. Power pools in these places the way water collects in a lake. Spells or rituals conducted there, items made there, or things taken from there will all share a part of that power. Be careful not to take anything that would detract from the place.

You can look up lists of sacred sites, but some are crowded and others are completely fenced off so nobody can reach them anymore. It is often better to look for places that fit the role but are less famous. Any mountaintop or cave has a good deal of energy. All the oceans are potent, and any decent beach will grant you access. A big river or lake has different energy than salt water. Forests, especially old-growth forests, are teeming with life. A desert is very serene.

Less obvious but more practical, you can also *create* a sacred space—not just a circle that you raise and release but a permanent physical place. It can be a room, a corner of a room, or a shrine outside. We have several ritual spaces in our house and several more outside, which we have used for years. A friend has a new house and is creating ritual spaces one at a time indoors and outdoors. Think about the spaces in your home, outdoors, and in nearby areas such as parks. There may be more potential close at hand than you realize.

Devoting Time

The more time you spend on a project, the more power it gains. This comes in various forms. One aspect involves continual action. An old-growth forest is powerful in part simply because it has been growing for a long time without interruption. Another aspect is repeated action. There are spells designed for casting over seven nights, nine nights, and so on—often with a candle that you burn down one knot at a time while you work each night's casting. You can add power to a complex magical artifact by working on it during each season of the year, day of the week, hour of the day, type of weather, and so on. This is ideal for things like a carved staff that naturally take many hours of work to complete.

Traditions occupy a place that spans both of these aspects. They can go back for a long time, and they involve doing the same thing over and over again. Some traditions are very old, practiced by many people, such as gathering under the Full Moon. Others are much younger, like the water-sharing ritual in the Church of All Worlds. It is natural for families, covens, and other groups to create their own traditions as a way of defining themselves, in addition to carrying on traditions from elsewhere. Think about the traditions you keep and what kind of new ones you might wish to add.

A Mass of People

The more people involved in a ritual, the more power they can raise. Many people practice alone, as solitaries, and that's fine. They can still gain an echo by doing things at the same time as others, such as the Full Moon. There have even been group rituals flung over a wide range, available to anyone who wants to partic-ipate. I've seen rituals designed to go off an hour at a time, like a string of firecrackers, wrapping around the world by time zones.

However, it's easier to raise power with people gathered to-gether. Most covens have about four to eight members. The upper end of small-group work is around thirteen. Medium groups usu-ally number in the dozens, as when several covens in a tradition gather for a sabbat. Pagan festivals and public rituals can attract a crowd of several hundred.

You need different tools and techniques for each size. What works for a small group won't work for a large one and vice versa. I have a palm-size pentacle that I wear for larger groups, because you can't see a dime-size one from across our ritual meadow. Any activity that has to be done one person at a time is only good for a small group, unless you can subdivide the circle and run several sections simultaneously. Mass waves, like people do in a stadium, or mass dances only work with a larger group. These all raise power in different ways.

Correspondences

Correspondences create connections. They can link to an outside energy source in order to empower an object or activity, or they can signify a goal where the power should go. Do both in turn and you create something like a pumping station, which draws power in and then directs it to a desired location.

Many different correspondences exist, and they overlap with each other. Colors, stones, and herbs are sacred to various deities. The elements have a whole host of symbols for each one. The season, Moon phase, and hour of day all relate to time. Astrology tells you which stars or signs are active presently and what types of magic they will strengthen or weaken.

Working with Sets

Looking at the previous sections, you can see that many signs of power come in sets. Collecting all of a set (for small sets) or a sacred number (for large sets) will raise more power than just one or two things. Any of the correspondences can be worked in one or the other of those ways. For example, you might collect symbols of all four elements or choose three green stones related to healing. I've taken part in a water-sharing ritual that included contributions from all the major oceans and several sacred springs. For travel or sources of power, consider all the oceans or all the continents. If you have favorites, make a list of the sets you like to use.

Charging

Charging spans a variety of ways to gather energy and instill it into an object. Some of these use energy from a natural source. Pretty much anything can be left in moonlight or sunlight to charge it. Leaving it in moonlight for a full cycle is especially powerful. Some things, such as magical stones, can be submerged in a natural body of water like a lake or a river. Other types of charging use personal energy instead. Chanting and dancing are two ways of gathering energy from people and pouring into a ritual or a spell.

These generate more energy the more people you have. Just be careful not to overdo it, because charging with personal energy can be exhausting.

Combining Methods

To maximize the power in a given spell, ritual, or magical artifact, simply combine as many methods as you can. Some combinations work especially well. For example, traveling a long way and devoting a lot of time to a project will connect space and time. Using rare, high-quality, expensive ingredients will create a potent magical artifact. Stacking together many correspondences will allow them to reinforce each other. When planning a magical activity, always watch for opportunities to increase its power.

The Only Love Spell
You'll Ever Need

Divina Cornick

Love is the most treasured and pure form of magic there is. It gives life, purpose, and drive and can propel even the simplest moment into a thing of legend.

Unfortunately, so many people go day by day finding love to be elusive. Perhaps they feel cursed or forgotten, forever doomed to be without it. Some might believe it's a myth, giving up on beholding it forever.

I grew up hating the word. I'd seen people throw it about so often, to people they didn't even like, manipulating people with its power. They said it to get something they wanted and change their circumstances. Of course, that "love" was faked. I'd watch the situation disband, dismantled by an ugly foundation and unable to take root. It scarred me. I was young and didn't understand. I sadly then believed love didn't exist, that it was a thing of dreams and story, like unicorns and mermaids.

Years went by and I was still living day by day in a haze, shocked by the brutal adult world but still clinging to magic and the Lady I had met on my path. The Goddess, whom I know to be both the darkness of death and the light of birth, had opened my eyes to a lot of things I'd never known as a child.

It was the Goddess who finally showed me love . . . and it wasn't where I thought it would be.

Love Spells and Self-Love

I don't think I know a Witch who hasn't cast a love spell in one form or another. Whether they lit a red candle or two or held a full ritual under the Moon, they tried something to bring someone into their life.

Anyone who believes in the power of manifestation has made a list written in the present tense about the things they wish to have. Things. A new job. Healthier habits. The perfect partner, someone who listens, likes long walks on the beach . . .

The only problem with all that is that we're looking for our dreams outside of ourselves. We're looking for what we want in the physical world when magic—when love—is actually rooted in our souls. So it's only natural that we can only find true love inside ourselves.

It's both simple and complicated, isn't it? It sounds simple, like something we should already know. Of course we need to love ourselves. We've been hearing it over and over, in every metaphysical bookstore or blog we've come across. But self-love is tricky.

Please understand that self-love is unconditional. Self-love is not dependent on anything. It doesn't matter if you yelled at your dog when they knocked your favorite mug off the table, shattering the porcelain and sending coffee everywhere. It doesn't matter if you've lied or stolen or cheated someone in the past.

Self-love is loving yourself because underneath our skin and human mind, we are all divine beings.

Self-love is your birthright.

Unconditional Love Ritual

Now it is time for the only love spell you'll ever need. It might not be what you think it would be or even think it should be, but it will help guide you to finding the unconditional love already inside yourself. This spell will help you obtain the truest form of love that you absolutely deserve.

You will need:

Candle placed in each quarter (most common are yellow for east, fire for south, blue for west, green for north, and white for center)

Mirror

Wand or athame (optional)

Cast the Circle

The Witch's circle is a divine reminder that we are part of the cosmic flow. It shows us that there is no beginning and no end to life. It is a constant movement, one wrought with change, ebb, and flow. We use the circle in ritual to also cut a line through this physical, mundane, human dimension and cross through time and space to the magical realm. It is a place away from the distractions of everyday life and problems. It is where we are most at home with our power.

To begin, stand at the most northern part of your intended circle ritual space. Hold out your hand, or you can also use a ritual wand or athame. You will walk the circle around your altar three times. With every passing of north, raise your hand upward. Starting at north, with your hand pointing to the ground, begin:

> *May light enter my circle and dance all around,*
> *So nothing unwelcome can enter, not even a sound.*
> *May light make the air clean and the fires alive;*
> *May the water be fresh and the earth simply thrive.*

At north again, for the second turn, move your hand so it's pointing straight out from your shoulder and continue:

> *May the light wrap around me, gentle like a blanket and fierce like a*
>   *shield;*
> *Tall walls of flames, alive with power so they'll never yield.*
> *May the light blind my enemies, protecting my workings from sight.*
> *May the light lend to my ritual all power and might.*

At north again, for the third and final circuit, move your hand so it's pointing up at the sky. Say,

May the light rise, flourish, and blossom like a brilliant and beautiful flower.
May it be wild and graceful, forming an unstoppable cone of power.
For I am a Witch and the light is my friend.
Like a token of love, may this ring blaze strong without beginning or end.

Stand at north again and strongly clap your hands together, saying,

By their power and by their love, this circle is sealed.

Call the Quarters

The quarters are part of not just the natural world but also the cosmic flow and divine truth. They are part of our circle of life, often bringing us life itself with the air we breathe and water we need to survive. Like the circle, they are a bridge between worlds, and now we shall call them to protect us and also bring us tools we'll need for the ritual to work.

Stand facing east with your arms open and your face tilted slightly up so you are gazing into the air. Light the yellow candle and say,

Oh Great Dawn and first light of a new day,
I humbly ask that you bring hope and blow all doubts away.
Come into my circle with thought and love.
Help me open my mind and heart with the wisdom of the earth below and comsos above.
Hail and welcome!

Stand in the presence of east for a moment and close your eyes. Feel the gentleness of the fresh start you're being offered. Feel the fierce surge of power and open yourself to any other messages that might be waiting for you.

Stand facing south with your arms open and your face tilted slightly down as if looking down at a fire. Light the red candle and say,

Oh Mighty Noon and bright light of midday,
I passionately ask that you bring heat and burn all my fears away.
Come into my circle with action and love.
Help me grab on to new possibilities with the courage of the earth
below and the cosmos above.
Hail and welcome!

Give yourself a moment to bask in the presence of south. Close your eyes and feel the intensity of the courage you're being blessed with. Know that you are just as alive as the great fires and you have no limits.

Stand facing west with your arms open and your face tilting slightly up to look up at the sky. Light the blue candle and say,

Oh Gentle Sunset and last light of this beautiful day,
I softly ask that you bring joy and wash all my old pain away.
Come into my circle with experience and love.
Help me learn from my past with the compassion of the earth below
and the cosmos above.
Hail and welcome!

Do not be afraid of the west and her secrets. Stand before her with an open heart and allow the loving waters to wash away all that no longer serves you. Also, be sure to listen carefully. Sometimes, the messages of the west are as loud as crashing ocean waves, but other times they come to you like gentle trickling waters of a stream. This is where you let go. This is where your tears can cleanse your soul and heart. Take all the time you need.

When you are ready, stand facing north. Open your arms and tilt your face slightly down so you are gazing at the earth.

Light the green candle and say,

Oh Powerful Midnight and the sensuous darkness of the night,
I strongly ask that you bring all my desires into the light.
Come into my circle with mystery and love.
Help me embrace myself as the god(dess) I am with all the divine
   wisdom of the earth below and cosmos above.
Hail and welcome!

Take a moment to take in the knowledge that north wants to share. Stand tall and confident, open and ready for whatever the gods deem you ready to learn. I will remind you that most lessons we learn, our souls already know. It is simply our human mind that needs to remember and often be reminded.

Go stand at the center of your circle with your arms open. Light the white candle, tilt your face up, and say,

Oh Cosmic Light and universal love,
You are the center, the everything, the truth of above.

Tilt your face down and say,

Oh Endless Dark and cosmic flow,
You are the center, the mystery, the divine secrets of below.

Level out your chin, making it parallel to the floor so you are centered, and say,

Arise from below,
Descend from above.
You are my form, my spirit, the meaning of love.
Meet in my circle, the Sun and the Moon.
Let us all dance and chant and swoon.
Hail and welcome!

Take a moment to acknowledge all the beautiful elements, gods, goddesses, forms, spirits, and blessings you have called into your circle.

Your mind, heart, body, and spirit are now ready for the main working. Understand that you have always been deserving of the greatest and truest form of love. Sometimes we just need to shed the mundane cords attached to us in order to meet it.

Cast the Spell

Standing at your altar, place the mirror before you, face down.

Wave your hand over the mirror three times and say,

May the powers that be bless this glass and frame.
Melt away the past, the pain, and the duling game.
Give me the strength to bear witness to the truth and light.
Let me see my true love; grant me this sight.

Now lift the mirror so you may gaze upon your true love. Close your eyes and take a deep breath. Let any and every motion rise through you. Sit here as long as you need. Look upon this mirror whenever you need to as you go back to your everyday life. Remember, you are the essence of love and magic.

Closing

The circle is open but never broken. This circle was drawn for the intention of creating a sacred and safe space for this specific working, but we are always part of the circle just as we are always part of the magical world. As you end the ritual, walk the circle counterclockwise once with your hand or tool extended out to draw up your circle. You may let the candles burn out or snuff them out; it's your preference.

Once you are done, touch your hand or tool to the earth (or a plant if you don't want to go outside) and allow any excess energy to return to the Great Mother. Keep the intention that all love stays with you.

Ground and center after the ritual. Take a few moments to meditate on what you experienced and to sit in your vibration, to hold on to those feelings and experiences.

May you love. May you be loved.

Blessed be.

Water Magic

Herbal Tea Magic

Autumn Damiana

Everyone loves tea, right? Well, I didn't for many years. I couldn't understand what was so special about hot plant water. And then I gave up caffeine, which made drinking tea seem out of the question. But then I discovered a delicious herbal mix called Blue Eyes, and my experiments with herbal tea began. What I discovered is that herbal tea is not just for drinking: weaker tea solutions can be used for other purposes as well, like as a magical wash or an addition to a ritual bath.

Tea magic involves many types of witchery, including Kitchen/ Cottage Witchcraft, Green Witchcraft, herbalism, elemental magic, and potion making. Here I will only be discussing herbal tea, not tea made from actual tea plant leaves. Herbal tea for drinking is technically called a *tisane* and any other herb and water preparation is an *infusion*, but for simplicity's sake I'm going to use the generic word *tea* for both.

I give instructions throughout the article for which herbs to use (based on my own experience), but realistically there are way too many to list here, so I suggest you find a good list of magical herb correspondences to refer to (see the resources list at the end of the article).

Caution: Make sure that you only use edible herbs for anything that you will consume or absorb through your skin! If you have doubts or questions about any herb, please consult your health care provider.

Basic Equipment and Instructions

Brewing herbal tea is a simple process: boil water in a teakettle or pot, add the water to the herbs, and ta-da! You have made tea. Unlike tea made from actual tea leaves, you can let most herbal teas steep indefinitely without any adverse effects (such as bitterness). This means that for brewing, you have a lot of options. You can use a tea ball or tea infuser spoon, or add the loose herbs to your cup or even to a pot of boiling water and strain them out later. A French press coffee maker is a really efficient tool if you make tea often. In addition, you may want a mortar and pestle to break up some herbs and spices before brewing.

Herbal tea can be made using either fresh or dried herbs. For magical teas, there are two schools of thought: one is that fresh herbs have purer energies; the other is that dried herbs make a better tea, and because they are easier to find, you have more choices. Whether you prefer fresh or dried, the recipe for one eight-ounce cup of tea typically calls for three teaspoons fresh herbs to one teaspoon dried. All this information applies to iced teas as well. The recipes I share are for dried herbs (except where noted), so adjust accordingly for fresh.

A quick word about water: obviously stick with tap or well water or any store-bought kind for drinking! For everything else, you can boil naturally collected water if you wish, but it must be clean, clear, and free from debris. You can make any kind of tea using bottled spring water.

Simple Tea-Drinking Magic

- Stir your tea clockwise to generate positive energy.
- Draw symbols, sigils, or words over your tea's surface with your athame, wand, or index finger to program it with intent.
- Drink a cup of tea as an elemental meditation: you have fire, water, herbs (earth), and steam and scent (air) present.
- For added power, choose flavorings with magical correspondences that match your tea. Pick from a variety of dried fruits, fruit juice, flavored extracts, sweeteners, dairy or milk alternatives, and spices.
- Make a dream pillow with edible herbs. To align your body's energy with the pillow, drink tea made from one or more of the same herbs before going to bed.
- To begin your morning, charge your tea with this affirmation:

    Strong in body, pure of heart, with clear mind, this day I start. In truth and love and light I go—as above, so below.

- To end your day in the evening/night, charge your tea with this affirmation:

    I close this day with lessons learned, experienced gained, and wisdom earned. From these may good be brought about—as within, so without.

- Dedicate a teacup or mug to be used strictly for magical workings.

Candle and Cup of Tea Spell

This spell is designed to draw something toward you. Pick an herb that corresponds with your goal—try mint for prosperity, dandelion for health, chamomile for peace and tranquility, or hibiscus for love.

White tea light or votive candle
Plate

Single-herb loose-leaf tea
Teacup or mug

Place the candle in the middle of the plate. Make a circle around the candle with the loose-leaf tea. Light the candle and spend a few minutes visualizing your spell coming true. Then, stare into the flame and recite this charm three times:

As I gaze into the light, I can see my future bright.
Herb and water, wax and flame, the gift of _____ is mine to claim.
Therefore, _____ will come to me—this is my will, so mote it be.

Let the candle burn down completely. (If you have to extinguish and relight it later, that is okay.) In the meantime, gather up the loose-leaf tea and brew it either alone or added to another tea blend. Hold your cup or mug of tea, and as it cools, look at it from an angle where you can see light reflecting off the surface. Repeat the charm again three times. Then, slowly sip your tea, and you will internalize the magic, drawing your goal toward you.

Ritual Bath Teas

As stated earlier, you should only use edible herbs in your ritual bath, since you will absorb small quantities of the herbs through your skin. That being said, this is a great opportunity to enjoy the properties of any herbs that you would not necessarily want to drink as tea.

Making a magical tea for your bath has several advantages. For one, you don't need to use a large quantity of herbs to extract their magical essence. Also, using an herbal tea is a lot less messy than adding the herbs directly to your bath. And last, you can make your tea ahead of time and store it for future use.

The strength of your bath tea is up to you. Any weak tea will contain the magical properties of the herbs used, but stronger tea may be more to your liking. In general, use between ½ cup and 1 cup herbs for a weak tea and 1½ cups or more for a stronger tea.

Add the herbs to 1 quart of boiling water. Let steep for at least 15 minutes. Strain out the herbs and then add the tea directly to your bath by itself or with Epsom salts, baking soda, oatmeal, milk, and so on. Or you can pour it into a glass container to keep in the refrigerator. Here are a few recipes to try:

All-Purpose Floral Bath Tea
Use this recipe monthly or as needed to ensure love, money, protection, and general good fortune.

½ cup rose
½ cup jasmine
½ cup calendula

Mental Health Vacation

Fresh ingredients have water in them, so this tea uses more plant matter than the others. Each one has healing properties, and together they will help you destress and lift your spirits.

¼ cup fresh ginger, chopped
½ cup fresh mint
1 cucumber, sliced
1 large lime, sliced

Elemental Salt Blend

This is my personal remedy for grounding and centering. The elemental correspondences were taken from *Cunningham's Encyclopedia of Magical Herbs*.

¼ cup lavender (air)
½ cup rosemary (fire)
¼ cup lemon zest (water)

Add tea to bath with ½ cup or more of coarse sea salt crystals (earth). I also use this blend for magical washes by reducing the salt to just a pinch or two dissolved directly in the tea.

All Other Preparations

This section is for herbal tea uses that are not for consumption, but because I'm a Kitchen Witch, I've included mostly edible herbs. The sky is the limit for these preparations—use one herb alone or combine any number to achieve the magical correspondences you desire. The quantities are also up to you. I've added recipes (which you can double or triple), but you can adapt the single cup or bath tea instructions or simply use your own judgment.

Sun Tea and Moon Tea

Many people brew Sun tea to drink, but this is not recommended since the water in a Sun tea does not get hot enough to kill bacteria that might be present. However, you can still make Sun tea to use in a nonedible preparation. Put your herbs in a sealed glass container and place it in the Sun for 3 or more hours. The Sun's rays will imbue the tea with masculine, expansive, joyful, and energizing vibes. Sun tea is best used during the daytime, on a solar holiday (sabbat), or during the waxing half of the year.

Moon tea is made just like Sun tea, except you will leave it out overnight for at least 9 hours in an area where the Moon's rays will fall on it sometime during that period. Your Moon tea will absorb feminine, introspective, intuitive, and relaxing qualities. Moon tea works best during the nighttime, on a lunar holiday (esbat), or during the waning half of the year.

Both Sun tea and Moon tea have a lot of applications, depending on how you magically charge them. They are perfect for baths or spells and rituals with a solar or lunar focus. I like to use them as magical washes—add them to your mundane cleaning supplies for a magical boost, or use them to energetically cleanse your altar, ritual tools, crystals, and so on.

Purifying or Holy Water

Not everyone can or wants to burn incense or sage to purify an area. Instead, you can spritz this tea around to dispel negativity. It has a slightly medicinal scent that mellows over time, but you can dilute it further or add essential oil if this bothers you.

For this blend, I save and dry evergreen needles from my Yule trees. *Caution*: Some evergreens are poisonous. Do not use this on your skin!

⅓ cup water
¼ teaspoon tarragon or dill
½ teaspoon lemon zest
½ teaspoon fragrant evergreen needles
1 bay leaf
3 whole cloves, broken up
Pinch of sea salt

Strain the tea though a coffee filter and then transfer it to a fine mist spray bottle, or use an herb sprig like an aspergillum to sprinkle it.

Scrying Herbal Potion

"Exotic" herbs like star anise and wormwood work well in this tea, so I've devised this simple shortcut.

1 cup water
¼ teaspoon thyme
2 tablespoons fresh apple peel, minced
1 cinnamon stick, broken into pieces
1 tablespoon of absinthe liqueur (This is available in mini bottles if you don't want to buy a whole one.)

Strain the tea thoroughly and then add the absinthe. The scent of it will fade as the tea cools. Use this tea to wash your magical mirror or fill your scrying bowl. You can also use it to spritz your tarot cards, pendulum, or other divination tools.

Tea-Leaf Reading

Although readings are usually performed with actual tea leaves, you can try your hand at it with loose-leaf herbal tea. This form of divination, called *tasseography*, is one of the easiest fortune-telling methods practiced today. The modern form most often used in Western culture dates back to seventeenth-century Europe (which is when tea first became available there), but the practice likely started thousands of years ago in China, where tea comes from. There are dozens of books and other resources available if you are interested in this subject. See the resources below, and maybe check them out over a cup of your favorite tea!

Recommended Resources for Herbal Tea Magic

AzureGreen (www.azuregreen.net): Magical tea blends, bulk herbs, tons of witchy supplies.

Cunningham's Encyclopedia of Magical Herbs by Scott Cunningham: Probably the most popular book on magical correspondences for herbs, trees, and other plants.

Cunningham's Encyclopedia of Wicca in the Kitchen by Scott Cunningham: Magical correspondences for everything you might flavor your tea with.

The Cup of Destiny by Jane Lyle: Comes with a tasseography cup!

English Tea Store (www.englishteastore.com): Everything you need for tea.

The Magickal Cat (www.themagickalcat.com): Witchier supplies and a good herbal grimoire.

Mountain Rose Herbs (www.mountainroseherbs.com): Teas, tea blends, tea accessories, and bulk herbs and spices.

Tea Leaf Reading for Beginners by Caroline Dow: A great starter book.

Limpias:
Cleansing the Soul
Daniel Moler

About a decade ago I was diagnosed with PTSD from undergoing a violent attack. A consequence of the assault resulted in a life of perpetual panic and turmoil. My body's resources were taxed; my immune system failed, and I was in and out of the hospital for years, living almost continuously on antibiotics. The doctors had no idea what to do to help me. I was lost. I felt alone and broken, like there would be no medical solution. But then one day I was introduced to a *curandero*.

A curandero (curer) is an adept of the branch of alternative medicine called *curanderismo*. Curanderismo traditionally represents folk healing practices that originate in Latin American cultures. I have met curanderos and curanderas from Mexico, Ecuador, Bolivia, and most specifically—in this case—Peru. Curanderismo generally leans heavily on herbal and folk remedies to treat illness, with a strong spiritual component intertwined. This spiritual interface relies on local, family-oriented traditions that are passed down from generation to generation, often through long, interpersonal, and rigorous apprenticeships.

Like all family traditions, these practices evolve over time and will often merge with other traditions. For instance, my curandero originated from a lineage in Peru. Like many folk traditions, Peruvian curanderismo is based upon an indigenous ancestry that relies heavily on animistic paradigms (the idea that all of the natural world is conscious). At the same time, Peru has a colonial culture. When the Spanish invaded, the shamanic priests of the time were keen and eventually learned to adopt Catholic practices and iconography, uniting the two traditions into an amalgamation that could adapt to the chaotic circumstances of the time. You can observe a similar blending of traditions in Voodoo, Hoodoo, or Santería.

Beyond its history, curanderismo is based on a very practical relationship with wellness and the human body. With a strong spiritual framework, its animistic approach (that all things are conscious) treats the physical body so that the human can evolve free of obstruction. There are many ways of treating illness as a curandero, but one of the first that I was introduced to was a process called the *limpia*.

Like all curanderismo practices, defining limpias can vary depending upon the lineage, region, or curandera herself. According to author and curandera Erika Buenaflor, limpias can be explained as the "cleansing rites that can clear, heal, and revitalize the mind, body, spirit, spaces, and situations, as well as facilitate soul retrieval—recovering sacred essence energy that left the body as a result of trauma." In other words, limpias are ritual practices that cleanse the soul of the heaviness weighing it down so that the soul has room to breathe and grow.

The Energy Body

As stated before, animism is the idea that all life is conscious, but another way of perceiving that concept is that all life is energy. Therefore, *we* are energy. Our physical body not only holds the electromagnetic frequency of our physiological framework, but it also contains the mental, emotional, and spiritual constructs of our being. The activity of consciousness does not just reside in the brain. All the systems of the body (nervous, endocrine, respiratory, etc.) have parts to play in the way we interact with the world around

us. From the way we receive information to how we respond to it, our entire being acts in a cohesive harmony that we are rarely aware of.

The combined chassis of the four bodies (physical, emotional, spiritual, and mental) results in a homogenous schema often referred to as the energy body or aura. In Peruvian curanderismo, we call this the *poq'po* (pok-poh), the bubble of awareness that makes up our full, collective consciousness in all four bodies. The poq'po is not only our individual container of identity but the matrix of interconnection with the outer world. Indeed, it is everything we are—body, heart, mind, and spirit—and it is our duty to take good care of it so that our relationship with the world is clean and clear.

Because the poq'po is an integrated system, one body within that system will affect all others (not just one . . . *all*). Therefore, in

Peruvian curanderismo, one of the primary causes of illness can be due to trauma. Let me explain.

When I was attacked, the violence implemented upon my physical form naturally punctured the essence that makes up my poq'po on the physical plane. This attack—being implemented by a person I had once trusted—affected my mental body as well, plaguing my thoughts with betrayal. The consequence of these violations upon the poq'po cascaded into a domino effect that impacted the other bodies of my being: my heart was broken due to the betrayal (emotional) and eventually my faith in others and indeed the wider universe diminished (spiritual). With the mental, emotional, and spiritual bodies out of commission, my physical body could no longer heal. My immune system failed and I went through years of cyclic illness that just fed on itself, spiraling into an ever-worsening scenario where I failed to live in the moment—terrified of the future, based upon the trauma of the past.

Despite that, the medicine of curanderismo paved a pathway toward a brighter future. A limpia is based on the concept that when the poq'po is violated (which can be physical or verbal, emotional manipulation, trying circumstances, etc.), a construct of density that pervades one or many of the four bodies is created. That construct—called *hucha*—is a blight upon the poq'po, hindering the free flow of energy required for the soul to operate clearly in life, like a clog in a pipe. How many times have you said the words "I feel heavy today"? The feeling of being heavy in the world is a result of an accumulation of hucha within the poq'po. Density attracts more density. The less we cleanse ourselves the more likely our current hucha will attract more. Notice how when you are already feeling down, everything else seems to be falling apart? Like bad luck? This is because the hucha from your body has not been cleared. Like too much dirt on a window, hucha

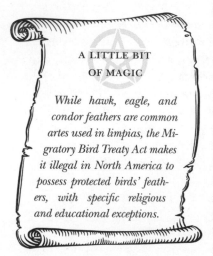

A LITTLE BIT
OF MAGIC

While hawk, eagle, and condor feathers are common artes used in limpias, the Migratory Bird Treaty Act makes it illegal in North America to possess protected birds' feathers, with specific religious and educational exceptions.

will often prevent us from seeing and accepting opportunities to improve our current situation. A regular limpia practice can keep our palate clean, providing a healthier state of mind, body, heart, and spirit to create the conditions of life we need to pursue our own well-being.

Limpia Basics

Again, everything is energy and conscious. If we are unable to at first heal ourselves, we should open ourselves to receive assistance from other aspects of the universe. The tools and implements of curanderismo are essential to the limpia process. Understanding that the tools one uses have their own consciousness is helpful in two primary ways:

- Knowing we are a part of a participatory universe, surrounded by allies facilitating our collective success
- Tapping into the intrinsic quality, power, and personality of the tool to benefit the limpia effort

The tools for energy clearing are generally called *medicine pieces* in most shamanic cultures, but in Peruvian curanderismo they are referred to as *artes*. An arte can be most anything you want it to be. However, the primary artes used for limpias often include a feather (specifically from a hawk, eagle, or condor), a stone or crystal (gathered from a natural setting or space that is sacred), or a staff or wand (normally crafted from a holy tree). There are other items that can be used, such as ritual swords, seashells, crucifixes, and even a bouquet of flowers. The choices are limitless. Be creative. The most important thing is that whatever arte you decide to use, its power and qualities resonate with you. You must understand the personality of the tool you are using.

For instance, a feather is light, and it comes from our winged relatives, so its power is about reaching the heights of the heavens, thus directing us toward our spiritual nature. A stone comes from the earth, so its power is inherently grounding and connects us to our physical presence in the material world. A wooden staff comes from a tree, an organism that both reaches to the heavens and connects to the earth, thus acting as a bridge between the spiritual and physical realms, a conductor of balance. There are a variety of meanings of each arte, and the only true interpretation of their usage can come from the practitioner, for it is your will and imagination that will guide the arte toward its healing potential.

The Limpia Process

After discovering which arte you would like to use, the following process can be executed to perform a basic limpia. For this example, we will use a stone, one of the simplest tools a prospective curandera can easily find just by going on a walk outside.

Commune in Sacred Relationship with the Arte

Sit with the stone and ask its permission to be used. Everything is conscious, so the stone will have a role to decide whether or not it wants to be used. Listen quietly with the stone in your hands and listen to your heart. If your intuition feels right about utilizing the stone for the intended purpose, then move forward with the process. If not, return the stone and move to finding another arte to use.

Bring Awareness to the Area of the Poq'po in Need

With the stone in hand, quiet your thoughts and begin to scan your body with your intuitive awareness. Pay special attention to areas of pain and discomfort: maybe sections of the body are unusually warmer or colder than others. Don't notice just the physical qualities but also the mental, emotional, and spiritual places that seem out of balance. All these imbalances are housed somewhere within the physical form . . . remember, the poq'po is a comprehensive and integrated system. All four bodies work in conjunction.

Use the Arte to Remove Hucha

Bring the stone to the area of the body that garnered your attention. Imagine the stone magnetically attracting the hucha into it, extracting it from your body. You can also imagine the hucha as a dark blot or mass, being sucked away by the arte. Sometimes it is helpful to scrape the area of the body with the stone several times, almost like you are sweeping dust away. The power of your imagination is useful here. Whatever imagery you can bring to direct your will toward removing the area of imbalance, the better. There is no

right or wrong. A good arte will be glad to assist you in removing any hucha to clear up your field of energy.

Return the Hucha to the Earth

"What? Why would I do that?" you might ask. Well, many shamanic cultures believe the reason why humanity is out of balance is because we do not utilize Mother Earth properly. We must love and care for her, but at the same time she feeds on the hucha of humanity in order to create life. Imagine it like composting in order to create fertile soil for growth. This has been the natural mode of relationship between humans and the earth for centuries—it is just something we have forgotten in the modern world. An arte acts as a medium between you and the earth in this way. You can use your breath to blow on the stone, pointed toward the earth, with your intention directing the hucha out of the stone into the soil of the planet in order to regrow as new and better things. Another way to permanently ensure the hucha is returned to the earth is to ritually bury the stone. If you want to reuse it, sometimes cleansing it with sage or with *agua de florida* (floral water) is a good method as well.

Regardless, the hucha should be returned to Mother Earth, who knows best how to transform our imbalances into new and better things.

Reciprocity with Gratitude

The primary currency of the natural world is the sacred reciprocal exchange of thanksgiving for any sort of relationship. Thanking the stone for its assistance is vital to establishing a rapport with the unseen powers of the universe. This can be done via silent prayer, kiss, song, or dance—whatever way best expresses your heart's gratitude. Not only the arte itself should be thanked, but the earth and the wider universe as well, all integrated parts of the vast cosmic play in which we all have a role.

$$\bullet \ \bullet \ \bullet \ ) \ \bullet \ \bullet \ \bullet$$

This method is about as simple as one can get, but as with any shamanic practice, limpias are an artform. Find out what works best for you. Understanding how the four bodies work together to make a harmonious system (the poq'po), anyone can set out on the path of clearing out space within their own essence, returning their soul to its rightful path of evolution and wellness. Adopting a regular practice of limpias for myself has been integral to my own healing path, supporting a life of balance and well-being.

Resource

Buenaflor, Erika. *Cleansing Rites of Curanderismo: Limpias Espirituales of Ancient Mesoamerican Shamans.* Rochester, VT: Bear & Company, 2018. Page 2.

Weather Magick:
Ethics and Application

Charlynn Walls

Witches attempt to bring balance to the world around them for the greater good. We seek to correct imbalances and right the wrongs we see. So what happens when we introduce weather and climate into the equation? Do we still attempt to do no harm, or do we try to do what is best for ourselves?

As we continue to move forward, we encounter a lot of questions about how we respond as a community. Is recycling enough, or do we need to reduce our carbon footprints? With any question, we must weigh the pros and cons. Will we be upsetting the natural order of the world? Are we working just for our own personal gain? Will the impact we have be positive and benefit not only ourselves, but also the world, plants, and creatures around us?

Ethics

With the weather there is never a 100 percent certainty about what is going to happen. This also translates to what we as Witches can do with our knowledge of the weather. We certainly cannot take the easy route. Being a Witch is not an easy path to walk, and this is no different. We have to do what is in the best interest of all. We have to be willing to take the route that is of the most benefit to the world around us. We cannot only look to take advantage of an immediate gain for ourselves.

We are currently being faced with increasing temperatures in our oceans, which are affecting the current. Iceland most recently recorded the death of a glacier, the impact of which will be a rise in sea levels. The further-reaching impact will be the flooding of coastal regions around the world. Weather across the globe is changing and making us take note. We have to decide if we are active or passive participants. I, for one, would like my actions to

have a positive impact on the world around me. There are many situations in which I can impact the world surrounding me and my family.

There are two types of weather magick that are most often used by practitioners. The first is used to counteract weather in a given area that might be invasive or harmful. This often happens when a natural disaster is imminent or when we are trying to keep it from having a widespread impact. Two instances that come to mind are altering the course of a hurricane so that it will avoid populated areas and bringing rain to alleviate a forest fire.

I have also seen people do work to ensure good weather for festivals. This particular utilization of weather magick is less for the good of all and more for the good of some. While there can be quite an impact on the human component, it does not typically have a positive impact on any other component of the ecosystem. The only instance when this would be ethical to do at a festival is when there could be a loss of life due to a natural disaster.

One of the most conscientious and appropriate ways to approach magick used to counteract weather is to first ensure that there is no loss of life. This adheres to one of the most basic tenets of Wiccan teaching: do no harm. Making sure that these actions are responsible also shows that the individual wielding the spells has the best intentions at heart for all involved.

One way to do so would be to attempt to maneuver the weather out of your immediate area. A technique that I was taught that does this responsibly is the canoe method. This is a method I learned from a coven member many years ago, which I will outline later. With this technique, you minimize the chance of significantly altering the weather patterns in your area. It also provides minimal impact on the flora and fauna of the area. For those who follow the rede, we need to ensure that our actions are not harmful to any of those around us. Altering weather has ethical implications that have to be considered: Should we be trying to alter weather patterns or natural disasters to accommodate human needs? If we do, what impact do we have on the environment further down the road?

The second type of weather magick is enhancing magickal practice with the weather that is currently at your disposal. This method utilizes the weather that is happening in your area to aid your magickal workings. This works alongside the weather and weather patterns to produce desired changes. It enhances or boosts your magickal workings.

Let's take a look at how we can incorporate both into effecting magickal change. When possible, work with any known weather patterns in your area. When you move with the natural progress of currents or jet stream patterns, you will have more success. This will aid you in your work to hurry weather out of your area.

Canoe Technique

When a weather system is threatening to directly impact the area you are living in, try the canoe technique. It is one that you can utilize quickly to keep your area safe. The canoe technique can be employed when a warning such as flood, thunderstorm, or tornado has been issued for your area. An important safety tip is to only use this technique if you feel the areas beyond your own will be minimally impacted.

If you have time, look at the radar for your area. This will let you examine the patterns currently impacting your region. Is the system pushing north or south? Is it pushing west or east? Take these current system predictors into account when you are focusing your intent on moving the system around you.

When the warning has been issued for your area, you will need to pull up the map of your area, if you are able to. There may be times when you cannot, such as in the instance of a power outage. If you cannot pull up the most current weather map predictions, then use the information you have based on historical data for the area. Identify the area the warning is coming from, what area it is likely to impact, and where it is like to move to based on all current information that you have.

Visualize the area and how the system will impact you. In your mind's eye, see yourself and the area you are in within a canoe. See the system move into you and the canoe, and move yourself and the canoe to a position to directly impale the incoming weather. See the system split around your canoe. This canoe can continue to move and spin as the system impacts you. As it connects, see it spinning and then splitting around you. As it does, it moves around you and continues off into the most likely direction based on all information you have. The system not only splits around you, but it also slows down. It continues to bring rain and wind but in a diminished capacity from what it brought previously.

Enhancing Your Magickal Practice

When the weather patterns are a part of your daily routine and not escalating into something serious, you can harness the effects to enhance your magick. Here are a few simple spells that will allow you to do just that.

Cleansing

Water has long been a staple of symbolic change. Water seeks to move and flow, rarely stagnating. It seeks the path of least resistance. If you, or the item you are trying to cleanse, are able to be outside in a rain shower, you should do so. If you are in an area where that is not possible, you can utilize the moving water of a shower.

You will want to feel the water moving around you or the item. You will start feeling it at the top of your head, and it will progress down your body and into the ground. If it is an item, the water will flow around it and into the container holding it or into the ground. The goal is to remove the negative and replace it with a clean slate. While the water is moving around you, say,

Water moving swiftly, carry away all negativity.

This will help prepare you or any item you are cleansing for the magickal working that is about to occur.

Charging Items

Spells that charge items for a magickal purpose can be very effective. This can be accomplished during a Full Moon or during a lightning storm. Here we will focus on charging an item with electrical charges. The electrical charge is very effective for storing energy in a stone, jewelry, or any other item that you want to be able to use as a conduit for magickal energy.

When working to store energy in the item, you will want to place it in a vessel either outside or on a windowsill. Then, focus on directing the energy into the vessel. You will want to be able to see the electricity flashing between the clouds or from the clouds to the ground. Make sure you are safely inside a building but can see the flashing of the lightning.

When you can see the lightning flashing in the distance, you will want to take a deep breath, and as you are exhaling, focus on the item in the vessel that is to be charged. Say,

Lightning flashes, and this item seizes the opportunity to become more.

Repeat until you feel that the item has filled its reservoir. It is now ready to be utilized in your desired magickal capacity.

Banishing (Moving On)

When you want to banish or remove something from your life, you may want to consider utilizing the power of wind. Wind can provide a slow and steady change over time, like when windblown sand blasts against solid stone, or it can also provide sudden change, like when wind removes a branch from a tree.

Decide if you need a gradual change or a something more immediate. Then decide on an appropriate weather event to help facilitate your magickal needs. If it is a more gradual need for moving a person or thing out of your life, you can wait for a fairly windy day. Use that energy to provide the movement for the change in your life.

If the need is more serious, you may opt for a wind storm or time when tornado watches are in effect for your area. Always make sure you are safe prior to doing any magickal working, and then you can move to make a sweeping change in your live. Regardless of severity, you can invoke this change by stating,

Winds of change, banish _____ from my sight.

Conclusion

There are many ways that you can interact with your environment to effect change. It is up to you to decide if your impact is acceptable or not. Your own ethical guidelines will provide a roadmap. As practitioners of magick, we have to work with what we have at our disposal. We have to exhaust our natural means of influence over friends and family prior to working magick to effect the changes in our weather and climate change.

I encourage you to provide influence over our weather patterns and press dangerous weather out of our immediate areas only when loss of life is imminent. We can also harness the weather in our local areas to assist us in providing a magickal boost to our work. Through these and other magickal means that are at our disposal, we will be able to impact our world and become the champions and stewards that are necessary for today.

Cauldron Magick:
Potions, Brews, and Fires

Walter J. Carey II

Next to the black conical hat, the cauldron is perhaps one of the most iconic symbols of the Witch and the magickal arts. While there is a universal connotation of magick and mystery that follows the cauldron, its full potential is not as frequently harnessed. When we craft magick, much like when we perform mundane tasks, we look for tools that will aid our effort. We use our wands to direct energy, cut energetic doorways with the athame, and ring bells to welcome spirits. Like the other tools we have, the cauldron is a powerful artifact in its own right; however, it often gets relegated for use only as decoration or burning loose incense. Artwork frequently depicts Witches and sorcerers working magick in a circle with a large metal cooking pot directly in the center. The symbolism of the cauldron in this setting could be attributed to the ideas that the crucible was representative of deep and hidden knowledge. Magick crafters are seekers of wisdom and truth; this is at the core of our practice. We go out into the world to learn as much as we can so that we can discover our individual truth and bring clarity to our spirits. I challenge you to dust off your cauldron or move it from the corner of your altar and bring it front and center as we journey down this path of enlightening and transformative magick.

Irish lore tells of a magickal race who came to this world and brought with them the four treasures of the Tuatha Dé Danann, one being the Dagda's cauldron, to Ireland. This magickal vessel is said to never empty and no one is left unsatisfied. Here the cauldron is a nurturing source that sustains life. There is also the Gundestrup cauldron, found in Denmark and believed to have been made in the Roman Iron Age, dating it to be around 2,000 years old. While it was found in Denmark, the style appears to be Celtic in nature. This vessel is quite large and suggests the possibility it was intended for the hospitality of many. These are just a few examples of the life-giving and transformative power of a simple cauldron.

Cauldron Materials and Safety

Before delving into working with our cauldrons, there are some things that are worth considering. Not all vessels are created equal, and for most, it will not be suitable to use the same one for potions and for magickal fires. One of my favorites is cast iron. Cast iron cauldrons are durable and heat evenly, and I cannot ignore that old-world aesthetic that stirs something ancient deep in my bones. While these are some fantastic reasons to choose cast iron, be aware that they do take some additional maintenance over aluminum

pots, such as the need to season and protect from rust. Cast iron is usually the more expensive option; however, its easy to unearth a cast iron cauldron in fair condition at an antique or flea market for much less. I use one for cauldron fire spells and one for mixing and brewing my potions.

Aluminum pots are great for potion making in that they are inexpensive and lighter to move around than cast iron. However, they are not ideal for magickal fires due to the risk of leaving behind scorch marks. Because aluminum pots are much thinner than cast iron, you can easily overheat and burn the surface they sit on, such as an altar cloth. If you do decide to use an aluminum pot for potions, I encourage you to use one that does not have a nonstick coating unless you are using utensils that are not metal. The scraping of metal can cause the coating to particulate into your brew, and sometimes these particulates are toxic. Further, never cast a magickal fire in a pot with a coating, ceramic or otherwise, as this can releases fumes that you do not want or need in your home.

Potion Making

One of the first images of a cauldron that many will mentally conjure is that of a large three-legged pot over a fire with a mystical brew simmering within it. Potion making holds a special place in my heart. Because crafting a potion requires a hands-on, physical approach, there are more opportunities to infuse intention and energy into the individual components. This creates a multifaceted magickal artifact. Here is a short list of tips to add additional magick into any potion that you make:

- Charge herbs one by one before adding them into a mix or mortar and pestle.
- While grinding herbs, use the pestle like a wand and direct intent through it into your ingredients and focus on their energies blending as your grind.
- Mindfully choose a direction for stirring your cauldron and when blending herbs: clockwise for drawing toward you and counterclockwise to banish and push things away.
- Slice or peel fresh roots to expose the flesh and roll them into a dry ingredient to coat the root, merging the two ingredients together before they go into the pot.

Vision Quest Potion

This is a fantastic recipe to use when you want to dig a little deeper during meditation, dreaming, or spirit work. While it will help you see and journey beyond the veil of reality to see things more clearly, I have found that this potion also gives one a slight euphoric experience, making you feel a little lighter. Perhaps this aids the mind and spirit in shifting gears. When you are seeking specific answers or just want to get to understand yourself better, mix up a pot of this magickal tealike potion and prepare to have light shed onto your situation. You could pair this with tarot or other divinatory work. You can either make this potion in a tea ball and add hot water to the ingredients, or you could brew this up in your cauldron. You'll need the following:

40 ounces water
1 tablespoon chamomile
1 teaspoon mint
1 teaspoon catnip
2 teaspoons lavender
2 teaspoons mugwort
2 cups milk
½ teaspoon nutmeg, ground
2 tablespoons honey
Small mesh strainer

You will want a large pot to brew your potion base and then a smaller pot to use to prepare the milk. In your large pot or cauldron, bring the water to a high simmer.

While the water is heating, in a mortar and pestle, add and grind the chamomile, mint, catnip, lavender, and mugwort. Don't crush the herbs too soon, as the oils will escape into the air. As you are grinding the herbs, build your cone of power with the intent to be given vision and guidance. (To bring up my cone of power, I plant my feet firmly onto the ground and through my body pull in energy from the earth and my surroundings, allowing it to build and spiral up my body to the top of my head. I visually direct and project the built-up energy into my ingredients, or if doing a spell, out into the ether. In short, I turn my body into the magick wand.) Channel this energy through your arms into the mortar and pestle.

In your small pot, warm the milk over low heat to not scald it. Add in the nutmeg and the honey. Stir occasionally.

When the water has come to a high simmer, add in the herbs and increase the heat. Stir your cauldron with a clockwise motion until you have a bubbling cauldron.

As soon as the water reaches a double bubble, remove the cauldron from the heat and cover to allow your potion to steep for 7 minutes. Remove your milk mixture from heat at this point as well.

Drain your brew through a strainer to remove all the herbal bits. Your potion is ready to take you on a journey now.

Simply pour a cup of the potion in your favorite cup or mug and stir in some of the infused milk. Sip and ease yourself into a relaxed state for an insightful meditation, vision-filled dreams, or any form of divination. Keep a journal nearby. Leftover potions can be saved, sealed, and chilled for 2 to 3 days.

Caution: Some herbs, such as mugwort, may not be safe for those who are pregnant. Check with a health care professional about safe herbal consumption.

Ill-Be-Gone Potion

Here is a great little concoction for when you feel a cold coming on and you want to nip it in the bud. Even when I am feeling worn down, drinking this helps me perk up and keep going. You will need:

1 tablespoon dried elderberries
40 ounces water
1 tablespoon dried hibiscus
2 teaspoons dried mint
2 teaspoons dried rosemary
⅛ teaspoon ground clove
⅛ teaspoon ground cinnamon
1 teaspoon freshly grated ginger
Honey (optional)

Pour the elderberries into the mortar and crush with the pestle so that all of them are cracked open. Place these into the cauldron and add the water. Turn on your heat and bring to a high simmer.

As your cauldron comes to temperature, blend together the hibiscus, mint, rosemary, clove, and cinnamon, infusing your intention

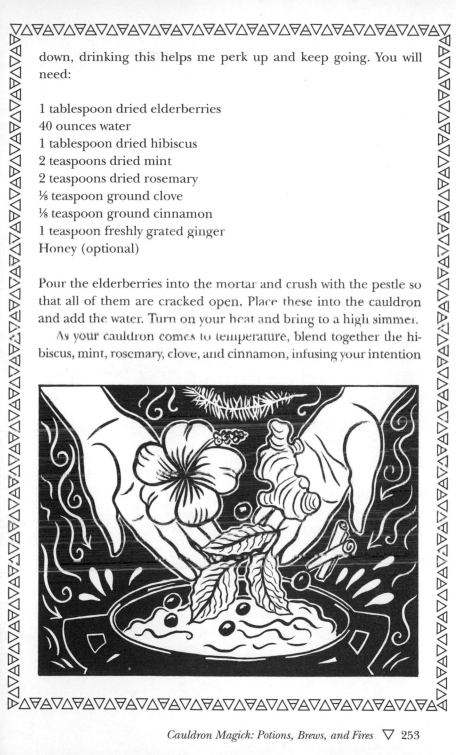

of good health. Empower the ingredients to banish illness while you blend counterclockwise.

As the pot comes to a boil, add in the grated ginger. Allow for it to boil for about 1 to 2 minutes. Add the remaining herbs and remove the cauldron from the heat.

Let the potion steep covered for 5 to 6 minutes. Strain out the ingredients. It should have a reddish color to it.

Pour a cup; add honey if you wish. Breathe in the sweet and spicy aroma of the potion. As you drink it, feel the warmth chase out the cold.

This brew can be stored and chilled for 2 to 3 days. A little orange zest can be added after cooking if you would like; however, it is not advisable to add citrus to a cast iron cauldron. When storing potions, it is always wise to label them so that someone does not unintentionally drink them or, if you are like me and make potions frequently, forget which bottle is filled with what.

Cauldron Fires and Spells

When I am not simmering a broth or brew, it is just as satisfying to ignite some transformative magick inside a cauldron with a magickal fire. These cauldron fires can be used for anything from drawing things into your life to sending them away. While it's easy to get an herbal blend to smolder on a charcoal, I find that my intentions manifest more quickly when I use a more energetic means to put my request into the universe. For those who want a cauldron fire with a little more tenacity, add in a splash of dragon's breath. This liquid accelerant is my go-to for my cauldron fire spells. You only need a few ingredients to make this potion, and a little goes a long way when using a smaller cauldron. I usually add herbs to my cauldron when casting fire spells, though you could use this on its own with just a piece of paper. It is a simple way to cast a wishing spell or even to banish something that no longer serves you.

Please be mindful of your surroundings and yourself as you work with fire. Take care to keep all surfaces protected from excessive heat; be aware of and prepared for the best way to extinguish the type of fire and learn the applicable local ordinances or laws.

When indoors, keep the space well ventilated. Let's not manifest any accidents or harm while working our magick.

Dragon's Breath

2 cups isopropyl alcohol
1 teaspoon dragon's blood resin, ground
3–5 drops dragon's blood oil (optional)

In your mortar and pestle, grind your dragon's blood resin into a fine powder. This should be easy to do as it is not an extremely hard resin.

To an airtight container that is also easy to pour from, add in the 2 cups of rubbing alcohol.

Add the ground resin and oil, seal, and shake. If you have ground the powder enough, it should easily mix, and the liquid should become a deep red color.

Pour into a bottle for storage. Stopper the bottle and keep in a safe place. When using the mix for a magickal fire, you should only need to use 1 to 2 tablespoons to get a nice sustainable fire. I advise using matches or a long-necked lighter for safety.

• • •) • • •

While these are some easy ways to incorporate your cauldron more into your practice, the possibilities are limitless. Experiment and see what you can come up with. There are a number of ways that you can use the cauldron; play around and soon it will become your favorite and most used magickal tool. Allow yourself to get inspired and test potions of your own conception—create a special potion grimoire. As mentioned before, the cauldron is a symbol of deep, hidden knowledge. What will you let it reveal to you?

The Magic Touch

Suzanne Ress

Have you ever stopped to consider how essential our hands are to expressing ourselves and to communicating with one another? Without speaking or understanding a word of a local language in a foreign country, anyone with good command of their hands can still manage to make herself understood.

Gesturing, waving, shaking hands, and back patting are all simple and somewhat superficial ways we communicate with our hands, but we can use these "digital members" for transcendent and profound self-expression and for connecting to a greater energy. The human touch can convey more—at times far more—than human words can aspire to.

Because our hand movements are so precise and quick, creativity and emotions can easily travel through them from the brain

and heart. We use our hands to express ourselves in otherwise inexpressible ways, through painting, creative writing, and sculpting, as well as in creative cooking, construction, and other handcrafts. Artists, writers, and all creative people, you know what I mean when I write that your hands can say much more than your tongue through your chosen discipline.

Our hands can convey all manner of emotions. Negative emotions are shown by a slap, a punch, a rude gesture, a pinch, hair pulling, and brushing or pushing away. Neutral but closed emotional states are often shown by hiding your hands in your pockets, behind your back, or under your arms or by balling them into fists.

The Need for Touch

The range of positive emotions we can express through our hands and primarily through touch is the biggest group, and, I dare say, it would be nearly impossible to convey our deepest feelings of kindness and affection without touch.

Perhaps our first magic touch in life is our mother's touch. Human babies not only crave human touch, but, without it, they cannot thrive, as demonstrated by studies done in the 1940s by Rene Spitz on hospitalism: babies raised in isolation speak later and less, have delayed physical development, and are unable to respond normally to their environment and to other people.

But what happens after babyhood? Is there a certain age at which we outgrow our need for touch? Toddlers and young children usually love holding someone's hand, being carried now and then, having their hair stroked, or hugging others. Even school-age children, in relaxed moments, usually enjoy receiving a gentle back rub from a parent. As young teenagers, just the brush of the hand from a special person can be so thrilling that they may replay and fantasize the event for days afterward. And often, that thrill has more in it than mere skin-to-skin contact.

Think of how many love songs there are about that special touch from a loved one:

- Elton John's "Healing Hands"
- Kiss's "Magic Touch"

- Conrad Sewell's "Healing Hands"
- Taylor Swift's "Gorgeous"
- Shelby Lynne's "Just for the Touch of Your Hand"
- The old Platters' song "The Magic Touch"

It isn't just a teenager's overactive hormonal imagination. It has been recognized throughout history and in all cultures that there is a high concentration of spiritual energy in the touch of our hands.

Energy Healing

In premedieval times and all the way into the eighteenth century in some countries, it was believed that kings, queens, and other sovereign rulers had a special touch called the royal touch, which had powerful healing energy. This was much sought after by lesser individuals with grave afflictions.

Reiki is a time-honored Japanese holistic therapy method, and reiki masters use their hands for passing spiritual healing power, or life energy, to a patient during treatment, for healing, stress reduction, alleviation of illness symptoms, and general well-being. In reiki treatment the master's hands move above the patient's body with little or no physical contact, directing energy. Or else the master's hands are used for contact and massage on the patient's body.

Indian Ayurvedic medicine and the more recent American therapeutic touch, as well as the Tellington TTouch, also make use of the healing power of touch. Holistic massage techniques such as shiatsu, Rolfing, and reflexology also use the human hands to try to balance life force energy during the massage. Universal life force, orgone energy, God, the Great Spirit—call it what you will, but no one is able to explain its origin. It is all around us, in all living (and some say nonliving) things, inside us, outside us. There must be a way to harness and use it for good.

Religions like Judaism and Christianity have traditionally practiced the custom of the laying on of hands to invoke God's presence or to confer a blessing (as in christening a baby). The rabbi, priest, or pastor's hands are the instruments through which God's energy or blessing passes. Using oils, sometimes scented, in anointment is thought to be a way to strengthen the blessing or conference of energy.

In comparison to other parts of the body, the hands have a much stronger magnetic field, according to various studies done over the years, starting in 1971. In a more recent one, done by the Indiana University School of Medicine and reported in the *Journal of Scientific Exploration*, healers' hands measurably influenced the flow of energy over and around mouse subjects.

Handshakes

Those readers who have attended a traditional Catholic mass will know that usually after the liturgy, members of the congregation are invited to rise, shake hands, and utter "peace" with other people near them. Shaking is always done with the right hand, which in this case is considered a way to pass peace and togetherness throughout the entire congregation.

Hand shaking or palm pressing has long been practiced in many cultures throughout the world and is used for meeting, greeting, parting, congratulating, expressing thanks, and demonstrating good sportsmanship, agreement, trust, respect, and equality. We always shake with bare hands, and if one is wearing gloves, the right one must be removed or the significance of the hand shake is nullified. Touching another person's hand palm with your own is thought to be the human equivalent of what dogs and other animals do when they meet each other—need I explain?—sniffing the other's anal sacs, which contain pheromones and other chemical scent information about each individual's gender, health, diet, and mood. It's called chemical communication, and it gives dogs a socially acceptable quick overview of who they are dealing with.

A study done by the Weizmann Institute showed that humans frequently unconsciously raise their right hand to their nose after shaking, for a quick sniff. In May 2015, the Weizmann Institute's Department of Neurobiology reported that the amount of time a person spent sniffing his or her hand more than doubled after shaking hands with the experimenter. The study found that, even when the experimenter wore gloves while shaking the subject's hand, chemical signals in the form of scent from the bare-handed subject remained in measurable amounts on the glove.

A Comforting Touch

I personally believe that the palms and fingers of the human hand exude energy all the time and that, between people attuned to one another, the energy can be very strong, to the point of profound nonverbal communication.

Have you ever been listening to an upset friend spout off at you about his problem and tried placing your own hand gently on his shoulder or taking his hand in both of yours? He will immediately calm down. I call this magic.

Hand-holding is often the very first meaningful touch between lovers and can illicit thrilling paroxysms of pleasure, not just because it may be a precursor of what lies ahead, but because for two spirits really tuned in to each other, the energy exchanged via the hands is enormous.

Holding someone's hand can be very comforting, whether that someone is a lost child, a grieving adult, a worried friend, or a confused stranger. I love to see elderly couples, perhaps together for many decades, holding hands, and, likewise, childhood playmates.

And, in some places in Europe, grown female friends hold hands publically (male friends, instead, generally choose to link arms, one of them laying his arm on the other's forearm).

The hamsa, a North African and Middle Eastern hand symbol, also called the Hand of Fatima, is used as a protective talisman, and is believed to bestow happiness, luck, and health on its carrier.

Touch in Spellcasting

In magic spellcasting, the energy reaching our hands can be more finely focused by using a wand or athame, or merely an index finger. Hand-holding, palm pressing, laying on of hands, and massage can all be used to great effect in Wiccan and Pagan ceremonies and for magic.

To increase the power and the magic energy in your hands, there are a few exercises you can do regularly with good results. The following one can be done alone.

Absorbing Magical Energy

When you have a good chunk of time, around an hour, and you are certain not to be bothered, turn off your phone, double-check to make sure you will not be disturbed, and lie down in a comfortable place. This can be a bed, a sofa, the floor, outdoors on the grass or in the woods, or on a bench—anywhere, as long as you are comfortable and will not be disturbed. Close your eyes, open the palms of your hands at your sides, breathe deeply, and get completely relaxed.

When you feel relaxed, focus your attention on an inner visualization of golden light beams streaming into the palms of your hands from an invisible source over your body. The light streams freely in with each deep breath you inhale. When you exhale, the light flows back up into the source. As you continue to breathe deeply, visualize the light above you getting higher and wider. The light is really pouring, flowing through you as the light's source becomes so big that it is everything around you. Really try to feel the magnetic energy flow through your palms as you do this. Continue for a while and then, gradually, let your mind go, but continue the deep breathing.

After several more minutes of this, allow your breathing to return to its usual flow. After a few more minutes, slowly open your eyes. The more often you do this exercise, the more easily magic energy will flow through your hands.

When you feel the effects of the greater energy flow through your hands, use it! You can start in subtle ways: when you shake someone's hand, transfer some of your energy to them and feel it happening. Try focusing your energy into your hand, placed at the right moment on someone's shoulder or upper arm. Consciously pass energy to them in this way.

When you hold an old person's, a friend's, or a child's hand or when you touch or stroke a pet or other animal, give them some of the energy. You will be amazed at the immediate positive response you receive.

Resources

Moga, Margaret, and William F. Bengston. "Anomalous Magnetic Field Activity during a Bioenergy Healing Experiment." *Journal of Scientific Exploration* 24, no. 3 (September 2010): 397–410. https://journalof scientificexploration.org/index.php/jse/article/view/22/166.

Spitz, René A. "Hospitalism: An Inquiry into the Genesis of Psychiatric Conditions in Early Childhood." *The Psychoanalytic Study of the Child* 1, no. 1 (1945): 53–74. https://doi.org/10.1080/00797308.1945 .11823126.

Weizmann Institute of Science. "Nice to Sniff You: Handshakes May Engage Our Sense of Smell." Weizmann Compass. May 13, 2015. http:// www.weizmann.ac.il/WeizmannCompass/sections/briefs/nice -to-sniff-you.

Vision Boards as Magickal Spells

Raven Digitalis

Vision boards are focal items that carry a particular set of intentions, with the goal of bringing about certain qualities, traits, experiences, and manifestations into one's life. For some people, these boards are more like affirmation boards, with positive written messages. For others, they're more like image collage art pieces. Some prefer to simply focus on symbols, while others prefer to create a piece that combines these approaches. When used with daily focus, vision boards are believed to help the mind and spirit align to the energies and intentions at hand, thereby shaping one's own life experience.

Choosing to Begin Crafting

On a visit to India a couple of years ago, I had the pleasure of hand-delivering a copy of my latest book, *The Everyday Empath*, to my beloved friend Vishnu. As a fellow empath, he was thrilled to receive a copy of the book and also asked if the book contained information about creating vision boards.

"Indeed it does!" I proclaimed.

My dear friend explained that he had become familiarized with vision boards due in part to the new age work of Louise Hay, whose teachings promoted affirmations, visualization, and metaphysical healing techniques related to the law of attraction.

"So, what does *your* vision board look like?" he asked.

"Ummm . . . I haven't really made one yet."

"But Raven! Here we are, you and I, discussing our life's goals, and you haven't made a vision board to focus on daily? Let's work on this!"

What can I say? He was right! Shortly after returning to the States, I went to a local dollar store for a big piece of cardstock. With art supplies handy and a dedicated sacred space in which to work, I started crafting the first pieces of a magickal vision board.

I know all too well how easy it is, in the midst of life's hectic flow, to put off "little" things like this, but the fact of the matter is that intentional art is an act of magick, and magick itself is art. The vision board need not be restricted to any kind of fluffy feel-better practice but can become an empowering spell that can be as deep as the heart of a Witch.

Choosing Proper Colors and Symbols

To begin, decide whether you'd like to create the board on paper, on a tack board, or even virtually. Plan the size of your board accordingly. Beware that sometimes the board will have a mind of its own, and new things are likely to enter your mind once you start working on it more diligently. When putting thought into the construction of your vision board, consider how many photos, phrases, symbols, and other items you wish to include.

You may wish to draw common symbols on your vision board—as long as they are aligned to your intentions—such as pentagrams, hexagrams, dollar signs, hearts, flowers, smiley faces, and anything meaningful to you personally. You may also wish to include sigils on your vision board. These are self-crafted symbols using a particular method that represent specific manifestations in an abstract form. The early-twentieth-century occultist Austin Osman Spare originally popularized the use of personal sigils in magickal work. Magickal folk of all varieties utilize sigils in modern times, either standalone or in conjunction with other forms of spellcraft or ceremonial workings. For those readers who are more Witchcraft inclined, I can't recommend the book *Sigil Witchery* by Laura Tempest Zakroff highly enough (see the resources and further reading list at the end of this article for other recommendations).

Maybe your board will focus on various manifestations, which is common, or maybe it will be focused on one goal in particular,

thereby becoming a spell for a particular solitary purpose. While vision boards are often created to be "life general," consider creating individual spells as vision boards or using a board as part of a spell's creation.

When choosing the colors for the vision board, including its base paper material and the color of markers and decorations used, it's wise to bring to mind some of the common metaphysical color associations: red for love, blue for insight, green for healing, black and white for any purpose . . . you know the drill! If you study or practice Western mysticism, you may also wish to consider the colors of esoteric alignments related to the seven chakra centers on the human body, as imparted in ancient Vedic and yogic texts.

Choosing the Right Words

I'm a big fan of a beautiful and simple book called *The Golden Key to Happiness* by Japanese Shinto author Masami Saionji. Something that especially stood out to me in this book was her emphasis on the power of words. In one part of the text, she discusses that the words we say or think over and over actually create a sort of self-hypnosis. This self-induced hypnotic state can be challenging to break when we become accustomed to thinking in certain patterns and expecting certain results in our lives. Saionji also emphasizes that the thoughts of the past create the thoughts of the present, and the thoughts of the present create our future experience. Although it's easier said than done, we do have the power to control our thoughts and realize when the mind is playing tricks or is conditioned to a particular modus operandi.

When choosing words for your vision board, you may be inspired to simply incorporate a scattering of words of power. Little affirmations such as *loved, abundant,* and *happy* can really go a long way. If you speak various languages, try incorporating a bit of each. Unleash those creative juices!

Be certain that your board doesn't make use of negative statements. Don't begin things with "I am not," "I do not," or "I will not," for example. Regardless of positive intentions, a negative statement tunes our psyche to a negative energy, which is associated with loss, have-nots, and ideas of imperfection. Instead, we are focusing on bringing out that which we desire to access and amplify in our lives. The words "not sad and not poor" have a totally different energy, psychologically and magickally, than "happy and abundant."

We are each the center of our own universes by default, so remember to make the board about yourself. Use yourself as the subject. (Trust me, it's not selfish; it's necessary!) While it would be wise to say something like "I am a positive influence on friends and family," it would not be wise to place that power on others with statements like "My friends and family respect me." Can you feel the difference between the two statements?

It's also essential to limit statements to present-moment action or being. Instead of "I will achieve my goals," you'll want to write "I am achieving my goals." This is still a true statement because you

A LITTLE BIT OF MAGIC

Vision boards are powerful metaphysical tools that can help folks of any spiritual path. When we utilize our unique occult knowledge, vision boards demonstrably become life-crafting pieces of magickal art.

are intentionally choosing to activate this statement, and it becomes truer every day.

The concept of vision boards is becoming widespread due to its creative power and stories of success. My brilliant cousin Tracy Olson King is a businesswoman who works within numerous professional spheres yet keeps spiritually connected and mindful despite a hefty workload. One of the companies she operates is LyfeSpark, which allows users to create virtual vision boards, meet realistic life goals, and receive direct personal support.

When I consulted Tracy about my vision board, she gave a memorable tip about affirmations. She advised me not to use phrases like "I am working my hardest to be better" or "I am striving to do my best." Instead, replace words of struggle or toil with more optimistic terms that imply an ease of natural order. In this case, something like "I am evolving toward self-actualization" would be more fitting. This sort of terminological optimism is also good advice for how we communicate every day!

Equally important to writing "affirmative affirmations" is that your words must be believable. What I mean is if you write "My life is happy and joyful" on your vision board, part of your unconscious mind might give a negative internal response, such as "That's a lie and you know it."

Words carry incredible power. The knowledge of the mind's interplay with a magickal affirmation can allow you to more carefully select the words you utilize. Following this example, it may be better to write something like "I create happiness and joy in my life every day." So write things that you know are true, and identify qualities you are intending to strengthen.

Writing "I am safe" could be a good idea because you *know* it's true even if your anxiety or stress tries to convince you otherwise. (However, if you're genuinely *not* safe physically or emotionally, then it's time to make serious life changes, possibly with the help of legal or psychotherapeutic professionals.)

Here are some ideas for phrases that you might feel drawn to write, with examples of alternate affirmations that carry a more positive tone:

Example Affirmations		Better Phrasing
I will always be happy.	→	I am creating happiness.
I release the past.	→	I create a positive future.
I work diligently against stress.	→	I choose peace.
I'm not depressed or anxious.	→	I have control over my emotions.
I am going to travel soon.	→	I look forward to seeing the world.
Everyone respects me.	→	I have self-respect.
I am wealthy and rich.	→	I am actively creating financial stability.
I refuse to be single anymore.	→	I am openly attracting my soul mate.
I am powerful and influential.	→	I am becoming more self-confident every day.
I have strong magickal powers.	→	I am a child of the gods.
There's nothing I can't do.	→	I am achieving my goals.
I free myself of disease.	→	I create health and healing.
I banish fake friends and toxic people.	→	I choose to surround myself with good people.
My life is free from struggle.	→	My life is abundant and joyful.
I wish for health, happiness, wisdom, and love.	→	I attract health, happiness, wisdom, and love.
I am not sad.	→	Happiness is my natural state.
The universe will meet all my needs.	→	All my needs are becoming met.

Choosing Imagery and Visuals

Here's where things become a bit tricky and where we must use our intuitive powers—and our knowledge of both magick and psychology—to determine which kinds of imagery to use on our boards, if any.

It's standard in new age thought to create vision boards that are heavily image-based collages, kind of like a real-life Pinterest. The idea is to cut and paste inspirational images from magazines or print photos from online and affix them to our board as items of focus. Commonly, you'll see people using photos of happy people, scenic landscapes, ideal body types, fancy cars, and whatnot. But, like I said, this is where things get tricky in a magickal sense.

If we are cutting and pasting photos of other people's happiness, is that really inspiring our own . . . or could it create jealousy instead? On a metaphysical level, is having the image of two smiling people in love inspiring *us* to manifest the same, or is it sending energy to the people in the photo? This is what I tend to believe, which is why my own vision board displays a very limited amount of actual images (all of which are drawings) and no magazine cutouts.

For this reason, I feel that sketching and drawing images on a vision board is miles more effective. This way, the image of people, places, fat stacks of cash, or whatnot actually comes from the mind and hand of the practitioner themselves. This seems far more magickal than latching onto external images of the goals we are achieving.

Additionally, for people like us who are more esoterically minded, photos or clippings of representations of gods or deities and symbols could be much more relevant and magically connecting. Gods and angels, for example, do not exist in the human dimension. This is why connecting to their images on a vision board can be safe

and encouraging due to their divine energetic embodiments. This can also strengthen a person's devotion to their patron god(s). Like everything, it's up to the practitioner's intuition and creative spark!

Choosing Herbs, Stones, and Spell Components

If you have a little collection of "small powerful stuff" you've found in nature or that has been gifted to you, this could be an ideal opportunity to utilize these items. It's easy to accumulate little stones, charms, berries, and other special items because Witches and mystics know a powerful item when they see it. Rather than letting these things accumulate in a pouch, drawer, or box, or even scattered about your altar, consider affixing some of them to your magickal vision board.

A few items that I may suggest affixing to your board, if you get the calling to do so, include feathers, leaves, incense sticks, found objects, small gemstones, metal charms, incense resins (dragon's blood, copal, frankincense, etc.), and raw herbs. Be sure to consider the metaphysical property of any item you affix to your spell.

An easy way to seal items to your board is to use a hot glue gun, although any reliable "fixing" method will do. When you affix the object, incorporate your own affirmation or spoken spell. Make it an intentional act. Magick follows intention. Most importantly, *know* that you are performing important esoteric work to help improve your life. Improving your life, by extension, helps improve the lives of everyone you touch.

Timing and Procedure

It's essential to be in a positive, encouraging state of mind when creating or ritually empowering a vision board—or *any* creative act of manifestation magick, for that matter. We get out what we put in. While it's advisable to mystically surrender to the gods during times of high stress, positive manifestation work needs to be performed when we can lend that vibrational boost to the working at hand.

You may wish to consider the Sun or Moon's current astrological position (and to be mindful of any retrogrades) when crafting your board. Daily planetary rulerships may also be taken into consideration:

Sunday: Sun
Monday: Moon
Tuesday: Mars
Wednesday: Mercury
Thursday: Jupiter
Friday: Venus
Saturday: Saturn

As far as timing goes, I *finally* began creating my vision board on July 4, 2019. It wasn't until I had nearly completed the project that I realized that I was crafting my board on America's Independence Day! This was fun to realize, because the timing was unconscious (intuitive?) and was most definitely in alignment with many of the "freedom" themes I was manifesting with the board!

After you have finalized your board precisely as you'd like it, and after you have performed your own personal magick to enchant the piece as a living spell, consider where to place the board. Personally, I do not like to show the board to other people, in order to "keep it secret, keep it safe," by not dispersing the energy to others. I chose to staple my big board on the ceiling right above my bed so that it is the very first thing I focus on upon rising for the day. I have found this method to be profoundly effective.

However you choose to craft the board and wherever you choose to place it for daily reflection, follow your intuition and believe in yourself. You are the magick; you are the power. Happy crafting!

Resources and Further Reading

Bennett-Goleman, Tara. *Emotional Alchemy: How the Mind Can Heal the Heart.* New York, NY: Harmony Books, 2001.

Byrne, Rhonda. *The Secret.* Hillsboro, OR: Atria Books/Beyond Words, 2006.

Ellwood, Taylor. *Inner Alchemy: Energy Work & the Magic of the Body.* 2nd ed. Magical Experiments Publications, 2018.

Gawain, Shakti. *Creative Visualization: Use the Power of Your Imagination to Create What You Want in Your Life.* Novato, CA: New World Library, 1995.

Saionji, Masami. *The Golden Key to Happiness.* Utsono, Japan: Gratitude Books, 2003.

Zakroff, Laura Tempest. *Sigil Witchery: A Witch's Guide to Crafting Magick Symbols.* Woodbury, MN: Llewellyn Publications, 2018.

Color Correspondences

Color magic uses various hues to influence energy. It can attract or repel, strengthen or weaken. It expresses thoughts and feelings that don't fit easily into words. People choose colors of clothes, jewelry, walls, and carpet to create desired effects. In magic, we use altar cloths, candles, gemstones, bowls, and other altar tools to channel this energy. Coloring pages help people relax.

Different cultures may use different correspondences. Western cultures associate white with life and black with death; Eastern cultures tend to reverse those. It comes from interpretations. Red is the color of blood, which can suggest vitality or danger, depending on how you look at it. So there is no "right" or "wrong" meaning. Use the color associations that resonate with you.

Maroon: Crone, drama, respect, sensuality

Crimson: Determination, righteous anger, survival

Scarlet: Action, female sexuality, vitality

Red: Fire, strength, danger

Orange: Creativity, addiction, opportunity

Gold: God, Sun, justice

Topaz: Male sexuality, memory, fast effects

Yellow: Air, joy, charm

Lime Green: Growth, speed, end frustration

Green: Envy, money, health

Teal: Acceptance, abundance, happy home

Turquoise: Work-life balance, guilt, receiving

Blue: Water, truth, family

Indigo: Will, spirit, psychic

Purple: Wisdom, emotions, power

Lavender: Knowledge, intuition, divination

Violet: Calm, gratitude, tension

Coral: Mother, nurturing, emotional energy

Pink: Love, compassion, partnership

Fuchsia: Fight depression, self-direction, self-worth

Rose: Maiden, romance, friendship

Brown: Earth, stability, memory

Tan: Construction, food, past life

Black: Dark Moon, defense, grounding

Gray: Balance, loneliness, rest

Silver: Goddess, Moon, dreams

White: Crescent Moon, purity, peace

Ivory: Full Moon, luxury, animal magic

Shadow Self Spell

The shadow self contains the instinct and impulses you've hidden away. It is the unacknowledged psyche where thoughts, desires, and weakness exist and the holding area for all things you'd rather not acknowledge about yourself. While the shadow self is a catchall for murderous tendencies, nefarious behavior, and subversive sexual desires, the shadow also contains glittering treasures. Belief systems and passions you talked yourself out of reside in the shadow. Talents, ability, and strengths dwell in your shadow, especially if someone told you not to embrace them.

Powerful shadow magic is unleashed by seeing and feeling what is there. We don't always have to act upon our hidden and dark impulses, but we must allow them to be present, especially when rich, wonderful things are tucked away inside us. Then we are free to authentically align with universal life flow. Enter the forest. Walk your path.

You will need:
Moon tarot card
Black candle

Gaze into the Moon tarot card. Feel the magnetic pull of the Moon in the root of your spine. What wants to emerge? What did you once desire that someone talked you out of?

Light the candle on a table. Color the candle in the illustration. Continue coloring, moving out with from the candle's glow while mentally sifting through what you've hidden away from yourself. Feel what has been repressed for all these years. Open yourself. Pull it out. Look at it. Journal it. Embrace it.

—*Sasha Graham*

Revealing Our Inner Mysteries

Do you remember that teacher who made you nervous because you knew that *they* knew that you hadn't finished your assignment before you even spoke to them? That's the tarot's High Priestess. She *knows* you. Her job is to show you yourself and make you understand what your next step is, whether it has to do with a relationship, your career, your family, or your purpose in life. It's hard to see the pattern when you're in it, and we can always use a new perspective to help us adjust our behaviors to align with our most authentic selves. One of the most difficult things that we can do is analyze our own behavior as earnestly as we analyze others, and she is just the woman to help you do it.

Unlike the Empress, the High Priestess is not interested in being your friend. She has a job to do, and it's not to help you figure out your life. Her job is to discover the deeper mysteries in life, and she takes a moment out of her day to help you figure out yours. She's kind of like your mother's younger friend who knows your entire history and won't rat you out to your mom but will still be straight with you when you're acting like an idiot.

The High Priestess invokes the memories of oracles past. A person you would honor, make an offering to, and ask for guidance. She stands between a pillar of white and one of black, showing balance. She wears the triple Moon and the crescent Moon, symbolizing her connection with intuition and the gifts and struggles that that brings with it.

With this spell, we're going to let the High Priestess look into us and answer our questions. We might not like it, but we don't go in front of and petition the High Priestess without a good reason, do we?

What is it that sits in the back of your mind, squatting there like a malevolent toad? What is keeping you up at night? What is that one thought that keeps going through your mind?

Got it? Now we're going to fix it.

Self-Divination with the High Priestess

You will need:
Blue candle
Crayons, markers, or paint
Paper
Pencil

Take a deep breath.

Light your candle, blue to show respect for the High Priestess in her traditional robes.

Look into her eyes and think about your problem.

On the open scroll, write down your problem. Name it.

Allow yourself to truly see who you are. Where your flaws are. Where your strengths are. Examine yourself and then write a list. Conversations that you could have. Boundaries that you can draw. Habits you can shift. This isn't just about other people—this is about us and how we interact with other people.

Write down keywords for three small steps you can take to begin shifting this problem in the right direction. We're not looking to solve this in one step. We want to course-correct so that we can get a little closer to our goal.

Write your steps down on your calendar on your phone. Set reminders.

Fold the paper and place it under the candle. Let the candle burn until it's finished.

Practice viewing yourself with the same objective, unblinking eyes as the High Priestess. It's a hard but necessary thing to take a few steps back from ourselves and figure out that, sometimes, we're the problem in our own life. Luckily, we're the only things in this world that we can truly control.

—*Melissa Cynova*

Contributors

ELIZABETH BARRETTE has been involved with the Pagan community for more than twenty-seven years. She has served as managing editor of PanGaia and dean of studies at the Grey School of Wizardry. Her book *Composing Magic* explains how to combine writing and spirituality. She lives in central Illinois. Visit her blog *The Wordsmith's Forge* (ysabetwordsmith. livejournal.com) or website PenUltimate Productions (penultimatepro-ductions.weebly.com).

DANIELLE BLACKWOOD is the author of *The Twelve Faces of the Goddess*. She is a certified archetypal astrologer and a registered counseling therapist (RTC). As a priestess, she has been facilitating workshops, classes, ceremony, and retreats on astrology and women's mysteries since 1994. Visit Danielle online at danielleblackwood.com.

BLAKE OCTAVIAN BLAIR is a shamanic and Druidic practitioner, ordained minister, writer, Usui Reiki Master-Teacher, and musical artist. Blake blends mystical traditions from both the East and the West along with a reverence for the natural world into his own brand of spirituality. He is an avid reader, knitter, and pescatarian. Blake lives in New England with his beloved husband. Visit him on the web at blakeoctavianblair.com or write to him at blake@blakeoctavianblair.com.

WALTER J. CAREY II has been a practicing Witch for over fifteen years and High Priest of the Coven of the Phoenix for five years. He lives in Bloomington, Indiana, with his husband. He completed his undergraduate degree at Ball State and has an MBA. Connect with him on Facebook or visit his coven's page at facebook.com/TheCovenofthePhoenix.

CHIC AND S. TABATHA CICERO are Chief Adepts of the Hermetic Order of the Golden Dawn as re-established by their mentor, Israel Regardie. The Ciceros have written numerous books, including *The Essential Golden Dawn*, *Self-Initiation into the Golden Dawn Tradition*, *The Golden Dawn Magical Tarot*, and *Tarot Talismans*. Both are prominent Rosicrucians: Chic is currently Chief Adept of the Florida College of the SRICF, and Tabatha is Imperatrix of the SRIA in America.

KERRI CONNOR has been practicing her Craft for thirty years and runs an eclectic family group called the Gathering Grove. She is a frequent contributor to Llewellyn annuals and the author of *Spells for Tough Times*, *Wake Bake and Meditate: Take Your Spiritual Practice to a Higher Level with Cannabis*, and *Wake Bake and Meditate: 420 Daily Meditations*. Kerri resides in northern Illinois.

DIVINA CORNICK is a writer, yoga instructor, and Gray Witch living in South Carolina with her dog. She holds a BA in international studies and loves to skydive, read, hike, and garden. She specializes in weaving magic on the yoga mat, bringing movement to the Craft and using the body to focus the mind and ignite the soul. You can follow her adventures on divinacornick.blogspot.com, instagram.com/divinacornick, and instagram.com/yogascopes.

MONICA CROSSON is the author of *Wild Magical Soul, The Magickal Family,* and *Summer Sage.* She is a Master Gardener who lives in the beautiful Pacific Northwest, happily digging in the dirt and tending her raspberries with her family and their small menagerie of farm animals. She has been a practicing Witch for thirty years and is a member of Evergreen Coven.

MELISSA CYNOVA is the author of *Kitchen Table Tarot, Tarot Elements,* and *Kitchen Table Magic.* When she was fourteen, a kid in her class gave her a deck of tarot cards for unknown reasons. She's been reading ever since. In addition to being a prolific tarot reader, she teaches classes at her kitchen table and at tarot conferences. She lives in St. Louis, Missouri.

AUTUMN DAMIANA is an author, artist, crafter, amateur photographer, and regular contributor to Llewellyn's annuals. Along with writing and making art, Autumn has a degree in early childhood education. She lives with her husband and doggy familiar in the beautiful San Francisco Bay Area. Visit her online at autumndamiana.com.

RAVEN DIGITALIS (Missoula, Montana) is the author of *The Everyday Empath, Esoteric Empathy, Shadow Magick Compendium, Planetary Spells & Rituals,* and *Goth Craft.* He is the cofounder of a nonprofit multicultural temple called Opus Aima Obscuræ (OAO). Raven has been an earth-based practitioner since 1999, a Priest since 2003, a Freemason since 2012, and an empath all his life. Visit him at ravendigitalis.com and opusaimaobscurae.org.

ASH W. EVERELL is a practicing Green Witch of four years, currently located somewhere deep in the woods of Vermont. They run the popular Witching blog *Theory of Magick* (theoryofmagick.tumblr.com), and, when they're not casting or doing magical research, they enjoy collecting vinyl records, drag culture, and spending time with their partner and cat (both mischievous!).

KATE FREULER lives in Ontario, Canada, and is the author of *Of Blood and Bones: Working with Shadow Magick & the Dark Moon.* She has owned and operated the Witchcraft shop whitemoonwitchcraft.com for ten years. When she's not writing or crafting items for clients, she is busy being creative with art or reading a huge stack of books.

SASHA GRAHAM is the author of *Tarot Diva, 365 Tarot Spreads, 365 Tarot Spells,* and *Llewellyn's Complete Book of the Rider-Waite-Smith Tarot.* She is the editor of and contributor to *Tarot Fundamentals, Tarot Experience,* and *Tarot Compendium.* Her tarot decks include the *Haunted House Tarot* and *Dark Wood Tarot.* Sasha hosts *The Enchanted Kitchen,* a short-form magical cooking series for YouTube and Heyou Media's *Mobile. Mini. Movies.*

RAECHEL HENDERSON (Chicago, IL) is a dual-class seamstress/shield-maiden and a Pagan. She has been sewing professionally since 2008 and has traveled around the Midwest selling her handmade bags, skirts, coats, and accessories at various events and conventions. She maintains a blog at idio rhythmic.com and is on Instagram and Facebook. She writes about magick, creativity, living by one's own life patterns, her family, and books.

JAMES KAMBOS is a writer and artist from Ohio. He is a regular contributor to Llewellyn's annuals and writes about the folk magic of the Near East and Appalachia. He graduated from Ohio University.

TIFFANY LAZIC is a registered psychotherapist and spiritual director, the owner of the Hive and Grove Centre for Holistic Wellness (Kitchener, ON), and a teacher at Transformational Arts College of Spiritual and Holistic Training (Toronto). An international presenter, she has conducted workshops and retreats in Canada, the US, Mexico, the UK, and India. Tiffany is the author of *The Great Work.* Visit Tiffany at www.hiveandgrove.ca.

DANIEL MOLER is a writer, artist, educator, and shamanic practitioner. He has published fiction and nonfiction works around the world in magazines, in journals, in gaming modules, and online, including *Positive Health Magazine, Cannabis Culture, The Tattooed Buddha, Sacred Hoop, Elephant Journal,* and *A Journal of Contemporary Shamanism.* He is the author of *Shamanic Qabalah, RED Mass,* and *Machine Elves 101.* Visit Daniel online at danielmolerweb.com.

THORN MOONEY is a Gardnerian priestess operating in Charlotte, North Carolina. She holds a graduate degree in religious studies, practices Historical European Martial Arts (HEMA), and works as an academic journal manager. Visit her online at thornthewitch.com.

MICKIE MUELLER explores magic and spirituality through art and the written word at her home studio and workshop in Missouri. She is the author and illustrator of *The Voice of the Trees,* the illustrator of *Mystical Cats Tarot* and *Magical Dogs Tarot,* and the author of *The Witch's Mirror* and *Llewellyn's Little Book of Halloween.* Since 2007, Mickie has been a regular article and illustration contributor to Llewellyn's annuals and many Llewellyn books.

DIANA RAJCHEL has written book reviews, articles, and books on Witchcraft for far longer than she cares to admit. She has a passion for dance, herbalism, tarot, and obscure folklore that she happily turns into spells. She serves as the city priestess of San Francisco, where she runs the Emperor Norton Pagan meetup. She also enjoys good burritos and a good hard laugh.

SUZANNE RESS runs a small farm in the Alpine foothills of Italy, where she lives with her husband. She has been a practicing Pagan for as long as she can remember and was recently featured in the exhibit "Worldwide Witches" at the Hexenmuseum of Switzerland. She is the author of *The Trial of Goody Gilbert.*

JHENAH TELYNDRU has an MA in Celtic studies and is an author and educator. She is the founder of the Sisterhood of Avalon and the academic dean of the Avalonian Thealogical Seminary. A priestess in the Avalonian Tradition for over thirty years, Jhenah has been following a Pagan path since 1986. Visit her at ynysafallon.com.

MELISSA TIPTON is a structural integrator, reiki master, and tarot reader who helps people live their most magical life through her healing practice, Life Alchemy Massage Therapy. She's the author of *Living Reiki: Heal Yourself and Transform Your Life* and *Llewellyn's Complete Book of Reiki.* Take online classes and learn more at getmomassage.com and yogiwitch.com.

CHARLYNN WALLS is an active member of her local community and a member of a local area coven. A practitioner of the Craft for over twenty years, she currently resides in Central Missouri with her family. She continues to expand upon her Craft knowledge and practices daily. Charlynn shares her knowledge by teaching at local festivals and continuing to produce articles with Llewellyn Publications.

CHARLIE RAINBOW WOLF is happiest when she is creating something, especially if it can be made from items that others have cast aside. Pottery, writing, knitting, astrology, and tarot are her deepest interests. A recorded singer-songwriter and a published author, she is an advocate of organic gardening and cooking and lives in the Midwest with her husband and special-needs Great Danes. Visit www.charlierainbow.com.